For Grandma and Grandad

Post-Fordism, Gender and Work

ANDREA WIGFIELD
Sheffield Hallam University

Ashgate

Aldershot • Burlington USA • Singapore • Sydney

Published by
Ashgate Publishing Limited
Gower House
Croft Road
Aldershot
Hampshire GU11 3HR
England

Ashgate Publishing Company
131 Main Street
Burlington, VT 05401-5600 USA

Ashgate website: http://www.ashgate.com

British Library Cataloguing in Publication Data
Wigfield, Andrea
    Post-Fordism, gender and work
    1.Women - Employment 2.Women - Employment - Case studies
    3.Feminist economics - Case studies 4.Feminist economics
    5.Labor economics 6. Labor economics - Case studies
    I.Title
    331

Library of Congress Control Number: 2001088796

ISBN 0 7546 1087 X

Printed and bound by Athenaeum Press, Ltd.,
Gateshead, Tyne & Wear.

Contents

List of Figures   *vi*
List of Tables   *vii*
Acknowledgments   *viii*

PART 1   THE THEORY

1   Introduction   3

2   Flexible Specialisation or Post-Fordism?   6

3   The Implications of Post-Fordism for
         Gender Relations at Work   50

PART 2   EVIDENCE FROM THE CLOTHING INDUSTRY

4   The Nottinghamshire Clothing Sector   91

5   Team Working and Numerical Flexibility   104

6   Team Working, Functional Flexibility and
         Technological Change   133

7   Post-Fordism, Gender and Work -
         Some Conclusions   187

Bibliography   *198*
Index   *228*

List of Figures

Figure 2.1   Post-Fordism   37

Figure 4.1   Typical Team Layout -
              Toyota Sewing System (TSS)   98

Figure 4.2   Typical Team Layout - Kanban   100

List of Tables

Table 2.1   Historical Periodisation of Economic Activity   13

Table 2.2   The Contrasts in Production Flexibility
             between Fordism and Flexible Specialisation   19

Table 2.3   The Strengths and Weaknesses of Flexible
             Specialisation and Post-Fordism   47

Table 4.1   Characteristics of the Team Working
             Systems in the Sample of Companies   101

Acknowledgements

I am indebted to many people, without whom this book could not have been completed. I am particularly grateful to all the managers and employees who spared time to complete questionnaires and participate in interviews. I would also like to thank Juliet for her assistance in the preparation of the final version, and all those who have read and commented upon various drafts of chapters.

PART 1
THE THEORY

1 Introduction

Since the 1980s there has been extensive debate concerning the extent to which advanced industrialised nations have experienced economic restructuring. Much of this discussion focuses upon the pattern of economic development, in the western world, during the last two centuries. Particular attention is paid to the shift away from craft production towards the end of the nineteenth century, the dominance of Fordism during the twentieth century and the emergence of a more flexible mode of production from the 1970s onwards.

The classification of this restructuring, following the Fordist era, has provoked most academic discussion, drawing in commentators from various political and ideological backgrounds, incorporating Monetarists, Neo-Classicists, Keynesians, Regulationists and Neo-Marxists. These commentators can be divided into two principal schools of restructuring: the French Regulationist School, as exemplified by scholars such as Aglietta (1979), Boyer (1988a) and Leborgne and Lipietz (1988, 1990) who refer to the replacement of Fordism as Neo or Post-Fordism; and the Institutionalist School, advanced by commentators such as Piore and Sabel (1984), who refer to the Fordist successor as Flexible Specialisation.

Extensive differences exist between the underlying assumptions of these two theories, but there are also some similarities. Both indicate that in recent years there has been a search for a new form of economic development based on production and labour flexibility. Further, and perhaps more importantly in the context of this book, both largely fail to incorporate a gender dimension into their analysis. Neither adequately address changing gender relations as part of their account of the search for flexibility. A factor which is surprising given that women's participation in the labour force has continued to increase (McDougall, 1998; Central Statistical Office, 1999b). It is therefore crucial that these inadequacies are redressed and that the restructuring debate is 'genderised'.

This book attempts to do just that. It incorporates a gender dimension into the economic restructuring debate, thus challenging and developing existing knowledge in this field. Part one links Post-Fordist and feminist theoretical perspectives in order to explore the implications of economic restructuring in the workplace for gender relations. This raises a number of questions relating to issues around numerical flexibility, functional flexibility and technological change. Part two attempts to answer these questions by drawing upon an empirical study of 33 clothing companies, half of which have adopted Post-Fordist production techniques based on team working.

The book is divided into six main chapters. Chapters two and three form part one of the book and chapters four, five, six and seven constitute part two. The principal aim of chapter two is to examine the Institutionalist and Regulationist theories of economic restructuring. It explores the stages of economic development which preceded the new mode of production, paying particular attention to the Fordist phase and explanations for its rise and decline. The conflicts, contradictions and similarities between the two accounts of the Fordist successor are then explored and attempts are made to outline a preliminary model of economic restructuring within which a gender informed analysis can be inserted.

Chapter three draws upon existing feminist theoretical knowledge, particularly that concerned with gender relations and the labour market, to develop a series of theoretical arguments concerning the implications of economic restructuring for gender relations. The discussion centres around three main issues: numerical flexibility; functional flexibility; and technological change. Examples are drawn from the implementation of team working in the manufacturing sector.

In order to test accurately the theoretical arguments arising out of part one of the book, part two examines the empirical investigation of the introduction of team working in the Nottinghamshire clothing industry. Chapter four provides an introduction to this part of the book, explaining the nature of and rationale for the empirical investigation. It outlines the key characteristics of the clothing sector in Nottinghamshire, and explains the choice of the sector and locality. The research methods utilised are also briefly outlined.

The empirical investigation explores a number of questions which fall into two categories: 1. numerical flexibility - does team working lead to an expansion of numerical flexibility which has damaging effects for female labour? How does this affect women who have caring responsibilities? Does team working facilitate flexible working arrangements and the provision of childcare facilities, thereby mediating the constraints faced by working women?; 2. functional flexibility and technological change - are models of team working which lead to job enlargement and which utilise technology in a way which deskills more likely to be implemented than those which lead to job enrichment and which utilise technology in a way which upskills when the workforce is predominantly female?

Chapter five focuses upon the former. The extent to which team working encourages an expansion of numerical flexibility is examined, particular attention being paid to the level of redundancies and part-time work. The implications of these findings for female team members, especially those who have caring responsibilities, are then analysed and the extent to which team working can mediate the constraints faced by working women is explored.

Chapter six explores the latter. The extent to which team working leads to functional flexibility, in terms of job enlargement and job enrichment is examined, and the role that technological change plays in this process is explored, particularly the way in which new technology can upskill or deskill. The resulting implications for the female workforce are analysed and the validity of the various dichotomies (job enlargement versus job enrichment and upskilling versus deskilling) are assessed. The way in which the method of work reorganisation and gender relations play a part in this process are then examined.

Chapter seven pulls together the various strands of the book. It revisits the conclusions of each of the preceding chapters and discusses the theoretical and policy implications.

2 Flexible Specialisation or Post-Fordism?

Introduction to the Economic Restructuring Debate

Two principal theories of economic restructuring have recently emerged. On the one hand, there is the French Regulationist School, exemplified by Neo-Marxists such as Aglietta (1979), Boyer (1988a), Leborgne and Lipietz (1988, 1990) and Lipietz (1997). Piore and Sabel (1984), on the other hand, pursue a different political and ideological perspective, forming the Institutionalist School. Other theorisations of the transition also exist but are peripheral to the debate and therefore shall not be elaborated upon here (see Amin, 1994 for an overview of other literature in the field).

Regulationists and Institutionalists agree that Fordism (having been the dominant mode of production during the twentieth century) is now in decline and is being replaced by more flexible modes of production. However, there are major discrepancies between the two theories, which encompass explanations for the decline of Fordism, the classification of its replacement, and the implications for labour relations. These disparities can be explained by the contrasting ideological underpinnings of the two theories. The Institutionalists (Piore and Sabel, 1984) take an indeterminacy view, arguing that a new technological paradigm of Flexible Specialisation 'just happened' to develop, whilst those grounded in Regulationist theory offer a deterministic explanation, suggesting that economic development is determined by the capitalist mode of production and the mode of regulation.

However, there are variations within the Regulationist framework. For example, Aglietta (1979) suggests that the new mode of development can be classed as Neo-Fordism, based on a simple expansion of the fundamentals of Fordism. Other Regulationists argue that a single solution to the crisis of Fordism has yet to emerge, and that a number of replacements for Fordism are possible. This is particularly true of Leborgne and Lipietz (1988, 1990) and Lipietz (1997) who argue that Post-

Fordism (which encompasses a range of alternative regimes of accumulation) can be viewed as the Fordist successor.

Both schools analyse the implications of economic restructuring in terms of production and labour organisation. The way in which they explore the latter, in particular, has consequences for the extent to which gender relations can be incorporated into the debate. The principal aim of this chapter is therefore to critically examine these two schools, exploring the conflicts, contradictions and similarities between them in terms of production and labour flexibility.

The chapter is split into three main sections. The first section explores Fordism, drawing upon the Regulationist and Institutionalist explanations for its rise and decline. The second and main part of the chapter concentrates upon the replacement of Fordism, exploring the two contrasting theoretical viewpoints of this phase of 'flexible' production. Attempts are then made in the third section to outline a preliminary model of economic restructuring within which a gender informed analysis can be inserted.

The Fordist Phase of Economic Development

During the evolution of industrial society four distinct phases of economic development have been encountered, the first three of which have previously been identified elsewhere (Blackburn, 1985): phase one - 1750s to 1850s - craft production; phase two - late nineteenth century to the end world war I - Taylorism; phase three - the inter war period to 1973 - Fordism; and phase four - 1970s to date - Post-Fordism or Flexible Specialisation. Each of these phases are characterised by the methods of production and work organisation dominant in that period. However, this does not indicate the exclusive existence of any particular prototype in any one time period. We are interested here only in the third phase - Fordism.

Characteristics of Fordism

During the Fordist era, multinational corporations became dominant and the region became the secondary location for economic activity. Large numbers of workers were employed in organisations, working on the Taylorist principles of scientific management (Gartman, 1979). The crucial date surrounding the development of Fordism was 1914, which was when Ford introduced the $5, eight hour day, working week on the first car assembly line at Michigan, in the USA. Ford combined the assembly line with Taylor's principles of the division of labour. The coordination of these two concepts allowed work to be conveyed to the workers, enabling the speed of work to be determined by the movement of the assembly line (*ibid.*). Consequently, Fordism facilitated a rise in labour intensification and therefore productivity (see table 2.2 for a more detailed definition of the production techniques utilised under Fordism), the latter occurring to such an extent that commodities could be mass produced (Harvey, 1989; Aglietta, 1979).

These two concepts, labour intensification and mass production, are central to the notion of Fordism. Firstly, to examine labour intensification. As Fordism involved the utilisation of Taylorist principles based on the division of labour it led to the emergence of an unskilled workforce, performing highly fragmented tasks. Wherever possible Ford attempted to reduce the number of jobs requiring skill, knowledge and judgement, replacing these by simple, repetitive, unskilled tasks. A good example of this deskilling process is provided by Gartman:

> There applied for work at this factory one day a man who represented himself to be a skilled erector of automobiles. The plant needed such a man and so hired the applicant and assigned him to the assembly of an automobile. It soon became apparent that the employee did not even know where or how to commence the assembly.
> The superintendent said to him:
> We thought that you were a skilled erector of automobiles
> I thought I was
> Where did you work?
> At Ford Motor Company
> What did you do?
> I screwed in nut number 58
> (Gartman, 1979, p.203).

Attempts to break down work tasks into the most repetitive, least skilled form possible continued to prevail throughout the post-war years as Fordism spread, not only throughout the USA but to other advanced industrialised sectors (Brecher, 1979). This deskilling process, together with the mechanisation of the pace of work, led to labour intensification. At the same time the piecerate payment system, whereby workers are paid in relation to the volume of the commodities produced, became widespread. This exacerbated the degree of labour intensification, with workers being forced to produce at substantially higher rates than previously, in order to achieve equivalent or higher levels of income (Gartman, 1979; Lamphere, 1979).

It was not, however, solely the labour process which was affected by the emergence of Fordism, it had implications too for the production process. This is where the second concept of Fordism becomes apparent - mass production. Production was structured around the semi-automatic assembly line, which together with fixed purpose, product specific equipment facilitated the mass production of standardised commodities. Mass production realised the benefits of economies of scale, whereby unit costs fall continuously with output. Large multinational corporations therefore became widespread, enabling the large batch production necessary to maximise these economies of scale (Schoenberger, 1988; Harvey, 1988).

However the success of mass production was not just dependent upon the presence of multinational corporations but also on the transportation and sale of large batches of commodities to the consumer. This link between the producer and consumer was facilitated by technological advances in transportation systems which facilitated the distribution of mass produced commodities (Piore and Sabel, 1984) and mass retailing which enabled the storage and the sale of mass produced commodities (*ibid.*).

However, neither the multinational corporation alone, nor advances in transportation and retail systems could solve the basic dilemma of mass production, i.e. that the success of mass production is dependent upon the existence of its counterpart, mass consumption (Schoenberger, 1988). Ford recognised this, and it is widely agreed that this is what distinguished him from Taylor. He acknowledged that mass production required mass consumption and that this necessitated not just changes in production techniques, but changes in the mode of life too (Harvey, 1988; Lipietz, 1988; Schoenberger, 1988).

Ford initially advocated that a mass consumption society could be achieved via a $5, eight hour day, working week, thereby ensuring worker discipline and providing them with sufficient disposable income and leisure time to consume mass produced commodities (Harvey, 1988). Ford believed that corporate power could be utilised to regulate the economy, by increasing wages to increase effective demand. However, corporate power proved an insufficient tool and so the state intervened in order to reinforce the trend of mass consumption. Hence the welfare state emerged, enabling those who were either not employed on the Fordist production line or were unemployed to enjoy mass consumption. This was achieved by a comprehensive system of social security benefits and in some instances the introduction of a minimum wage. Simultaneously, Keynesian demand management policies were adopted which helped to insulate the Fordist system against cyclical fluctuations in demand and maintain stable levels of mass consumption. At times of depressed demand, government spending was raised in order to stimulate effective demand and stabilise the economic system (Piore and Sabel, 1984; Harvey, 1988; Jessop, 1993).

The development of Fordism, with the aid of multinational corporations, technological advances in transportation systems, the growth of mass retailing systems, the development of the welfare state and Keynesian demand management policies stimulated a period of unprecedented economic growth in the USA. This success was recognised throughout the western world and consequently by the end of the second world war, countries such as France, Germany and the UK had followed suit. Hence Fordism became the dominant mode of production in advanced industrialised countries during the post war period and remained dominant until the early 1970s.

Explanations for the Rise and Decline of Fordism

Although the Institutionalists and Regulationists agree on the broad definitions of Fordism, their explanations for its rise and decline tend to diverge somewhat. The Institutionalists take an indeterminacy view of economic restructuring, arguing that society is not a totality and that relationships are not governed by a single principle (Piore and Sabel, 1984). They recognise a range of possibilities in terms of economic development and that a number of distinct choices can be made between two dominant technological paradigms - Fordism (mass production) and Flexible Specialisation (craft production).

They argue that throughout industrial society these two types of production coexist, but periodically 'branching points' are encountered where choices between the two are required. At the first branching point, what Piore and Sabel (1984) refer to as the first industrial divide, mass production and therefore Fordism was chosen in preference to craft production. Although the latter continued to exist.

The Institutionalists argue that there was nothing inevitable about the development of Fordism and that a number of occurrences just happened to prevail simultaneously, allowing it to expand. Thus Piore and Sabel (1984) argue that Ford's $5, eight hour day, working week and later the development of both Keynesian economic policies and the welfare state ensured that the mass production of Fordism was sustained by the development of mass consumption. Had these policies not been adopted, Fordism would not have expanded. They therefore advocate that nothing is inevitable in terms of economic development and that the rise and eventual success of Fordism is attributable to pure chance and blind decision making (*ibid.*).

The Institutionalists take a similar view of the decline of Fordism, arguing that a number of situations just happened to occur simultaneously leading to a breakdown of the system. Piore and Sabel (1984) attribute the deterioration of economic performance and the collapse of the Fordist system to three principal factors, which they believe coincidentally prevailed.

Firstly, they argue that mistakes in economic policy were made, such as the adoption of floating exchange rates, restrictive economic policies based on high interest rates and the Russian wheat deal. These, together with a number of unforeseen accidents, such as an expansion of social unrest as a result of a deepening economic recession and the prevalence of two oil crises, led to economic difficulties during the late 1960s, early 1970s, undermining the viability of Fordism. They argue that these accidents and mistakes led to an expansion of inflation and unemployment and subsequently the rate of economic growth slowed down and demand fell. As a result mass markets for standardised products disintegrated, acting as a disincentive to entrepreneurs to invest in the long term, product specific machinery required for mass production (for a more detailed explanation see Piore and Sabel, 1984; Sabel, 1982, 1989; Bowles and Gintis, 1982).

The second explanation indicates that the crisis was due to a limitation of the system. By the 1960s mass domestic consumption began to reach its limits and started to fall as the majority of the population had already purchased the full range of existing consumer durables. Markets became saturated and there was a shortfall in demand. The mass consumption required to maintain the mass production of Fordism was therefore no longer apparent (Piore and Sabel, 1984; Sabel, 1989). Piore and Sabel (1984) additionally point out that technological innovation and the presence of a low waged economy in newly industrialised countries such as Argentina, Brazil, Mexico, Taiwan and Hong Kong exacerbated the situation, enabling these countries to produce more competitively priced, standardised goods, therefore accelerating the saturation of industrial markets.

Thirdly, Piore and Sabel argue that at the same time there was a change in consumer demand. Consumer sovereignty meant that customers no longer demanded mass produced, standardised, commodities but sought more diversified, specialised commodities which had a higher degree of design content. They argue that this change in consumer behaviour was marked by the re-emergence of craft production and the development of small, design led, retail outlets selling semi-customised products (Piore and Sabel, 1984).

The Regulationist explanation for the rise and decline of Fordism is somewhat different. They view economic restructuring as a total package of relations and arrangements which regulate and stabilise production and output (Aglietta, 1979; Boyer, 1988a; Leborgne and Lipietz, 1988, 1990; Lipietz, 1987). They have a much more socially deterministic view of economic development, advocating that society is governed by the Marxist concept of the capitalist mode of production. Regulationists argue that within the capitalist mode of production the fundamental goals of economic activity are both the valorisation and the accumulation of capital (Lipietz, 1987). They suggest that in attempts to achieve these fundamental goals, various models of economic development will prevail. Regulationists believe that each model of economic development can be analysed from two different perspectives, as a regime of accumulation and as a mode of regulation.

The regime of accumulation is a phase of relatively stable capitalist development and is defined by Leborgne and Lipietz (1988) as, 'the macro-economic principle which describes the compatibility over a prolonged period between the transformations in production conditions and in uses of social output' (p.264). The mode of regulation, on the other hand, mediates crises tendencies which are inherent in the capitalist accumulation process and is described as:

> The combination of forms of adjustment and contradictory behaviour of individual agents, with the collective principles of the regime of accumulation. These forms of adjustment may include cultural habits, as well as institutional elements, such as laws and agreements
> (Leborgne and Lipietz, 1988, p.264).

Hence, the mode of regulation ensures that the regime of accumulation operates correctly, stimulating economic growth. However, Regulationists believe that each cycle has limits due to inherent problems in the capitalist mode of production and when these limits are met over-accumulation occurs (i.e. the coexistence of idle capital and idle labour). In these circumstances the mode of regulation will no longer be able to create the regime of accumulation positively. Consequently a restructuring process is triggered off, whereby a new regime of accumulation is formed, accompanied by a new mode of regulation. Thus the process of economic development is viewed as being determined by the crises tendencies of the capitalist mode of production.

Regulationists have provided a historical periodisation of economic activity covering the nineteenth and twentieth centuries (table 2.1). They agree with the Institutionalists that although one regime of accumulation is dominant in each era, others coexist. An age of intensive accumulation is therefore one in which intensive methods predominate (Dunford, 1990).

Table 2.1   Historical Periodisation of Economic Activity

1. Industrial Revolution to early twentieth century	2. Early twentieth century to 1930s	3. Post war period to 1973	4. 1973 onwards
Extensive accumulation	Intensive accumulation - without mass production (Taylorism)	Intensive accumulation - with mass production (Fordism)	Post-Fordist accumulation
Old mode of regulation	Competitive regulation	Monopolistic regulation	Semi-flexible mode of regulation

Source: Dunford (1990)

Regulationists suggest that up until the 1930s the development of Fordism was well under way, however the mode of regulation remained competitive and so wages and effective demand were determined by market conditions. As a consequence, there was a lack of high, stable, purchasing power and more importantly a lack of mass consumption (Dunford, 1990). The regime of accumulation was moving towards Fordism but could no longer be mediated by the existing mode of regulation. During the post war period substantial economic restructuring occurred and the mode of monopolistic regulation formed, thus stimulating mass consumption and enabling the intensive regime to reach its climax in the development of a fully fledged Fordist system. The Regulationists argue that this new mode of regulation was triggered by two policies: the emergence of the welfare state (Ashford, 1986; Bruce, 1972; Jessop, 1993); and Keynesian demand management (Harvey, 1988; Lipietz, 1987), both of which helped to stimulate mass consumption. Thus Fordism was the outcome of a new mode of monopolistic regulation designed to mediate a new regime of intensive accumulation.

Regulationists similarly explain the decline of Fordism as the result of crises tendencies present within the capitalist mode of production. They argue that its decline was attributable to the exhaustion of the system of accumulation, given the available mode of regulation. Lipietz (1987) suggests that an increase in the capital/output ratio (i.e. an increase in the amount of investment in capital required to increase the volume of production) in the late 1960s triggered an economic downturn in the Fordist mode of production. As a result, more complex capital equipment geared to increasing productive capacity per person could no longer be introduced at a cost which made it worthwhile and the general level of investment decreased (Lipietz, 1987). Lipietz (1992a) argues that simultaneously working class militancy increased, as workers eventually reacted against the constant increases in labour intensification under Fordism and were no longer willing to accept the denial of human responsibility involved in Taylorist management techniques. These factors together had the cumulative effect of a fall in productive growth and employment, leading to an increase in unemployment and therefore a reduction in effective demand, undermining mass consumption and leading to a crisis of over-accumulation (Leborgne and Lipietz, 1988; Lipietz, 1987, 1992a).

Lipietz (1987) then points out that in an attempt to revive the mass markets of consumption, western countries turned to newly industrialised countries such as Brazil, South Korea and Mexico for a new source of demand, and consequently Fordism spread to these regions. This led to an international division of labour, whereby advanced industrialised countries took advantage of cheap, unskilled, primarily female labour in developing countries. However, Lipietz argues that this process tended to exacerbate rather than solve the crisis, so instead of providing a source of new demand, it proved a source of competition to the developed world. This further reduced western employment and therefore both effective demand and mass consumption fell even more. Hence the Regulationists view the presence of under-consumption as a result of the crisis of Fordism and not as a principal cause of it, as the Institutionalists suggest.

Aglietta (1979) states that the crisis of Fordism was further worsened by a number of external shocks to the system, the principal one being the sudden oil price increases experienced as a result of the Arab/Israeli war of 1973. He points out that this speeded up the already declining capitalist economies and resulted in turmoil in the economies of advanced industrialised countries.

It is therefore clear that the Regulationists provide a socially deterministic explanation for the decline of Fordism, arguing that the principal aims of the capitalist mode of production are contradictory and render each regime of accumulation, including Fordism, crisis prone.

From this brief analysis, it appears that the Regulationists' view of the economic development process and specifically the rise and decline of Fordism is more convincing than that of the Institutionalists. The benefits of the Regulationist account of the rise and eventual decline of Fordism are threefold.

The first and underlying advantage of the Regulationist theory relates to consistency. Throughout their work they adopt a determinacy argument, advocating that the economic development process can be explained by crisis tendencies within the capitalist mode of production which periodically involve a restructuring process. The Institutionalists, on the other hand, take an indeterminacy approach to economic development, advocating that it is the outcome of chance decisions which just happen to simultaneously occur at a number of societal branching points. Consequently their theory lacks a convincing, reasoned explanation for both the rise and decline of Fordism. Moreover, at times their arguments appear both confused and contradictory. When analysing the rise of Fordism, Piore and Sabel (1984) argue that it was due to a chance decision, but they contradict themselves arguing that the development of Fordism was inevitable after all, due to the powers of its competitive strength. Such contradictions are also prevalent in their discussion of the decline of Fordism. On the one hand they argue that its decline was due to a number of accidents and mistakes and on the other hand they state that it was inevitable due to its inherent limitations, which eventually resulted in the emergence of under-consumption.

Market saturation as an explanation for the decline of Fordism is a second source of controversy between the theories. The Regulationist explanation of the decline of mass consumption and in turn market saturation appears much more convincing than that advocated by the Institutionalists. They argue that mass consumption eventually declined, as a result of inevitable reductions in both productive growth and profitability, which in turn led to a reduction in employment and effective demand. Piore and Sabel (1984), on the other hand, provide a much less satisfactory argument, advocating that markets eventually became saturated as the majority of the population possessed the commodities produced under Fordism. They overlook the fact that technological change permits the constant innovation of existing commodities and the creation of new items such as video cassette recorders, camcorders, compact disc players, microwave ovens, digital versatile disc players - the list is endless. These innovative procedures together with the fact that having obtained one commodity such as a television, households then purchase an additional one, lead to a maintenance of a high level of demand for mass produced commodities (see Williams, 1987 for a more detailed explanation).

The final advantage of the Regulationist theory concerns the way in which it acknowledges that the economic development process is determined by wider societal relations. While the Institutionalists argue that a change in consumer tastes have triggered the emergence of flexible, specialised production and ultimately the decline of Fordism, the Regulationists acknowledge that this is unlikely in a capitalist society where consumer sovereignty is limited and where the advertising industry, together with institutions such as the media and schools, have influential implications for customer demands and tastes. As Dicken (1986) explains, 'fashion is supply rather than demand led'.

Post-Fordism or Flexible Specialisation

Although the Regulationists and Institutionalists disagree fundamentally about the explanations for the rise and decline of Fordism, they agree that a more flexible form of production is emerging which is characterised by a search for production and labour flexibility. However, this is as far as the similarities between the two theories prevail, with the classification of this recent restructuring process, even with respect to its title, proving a cause of conflict. The Regulationists refer to the Fordist successor as Neo or Post-Fordism, while the Institutionalists label it Flexible Specialisation.

Institutionalists and Flexible Specialisation

Piore and Sabel (1984) argue that due to changing consumer demands there has recently been a breakdown in mass production. This, together with the introduction of new, flexible technologies i.e. Computer Aided Design (CAD) and Computer Aided Manufacturing (CAM), has enabled the low cost production of small batch, semi-customised commodities, allowing producers to re-adopt craft production. Piore and Sabel refer to this as a shift towards a new technological paradigm of Flexible Specialisation.

Piore and Sabel's indeterminacy towards economic development is again prevalent here. They argue that the crisis of mass production cannot only be solved by Flexible Specialisation but by an equally viable alternative of Multinational Keynesianism.... 'there is no hidden dynamic of historic evolution. No law of motion of capitalist development makes the spread of Flexible Specialisation the inevitable outcome of the crisis of the past decade' (Piore and Sabel, 1984, p.281). Thus, they suggest that the coexistence of Multinational Keynesianism and Flexible Specialisation is a real possibility.

Multinational Keynesianism is an expansion of the principles of Fordism, involving an extension of the institutional organisation that gave rise to both the corporation and to macro-regulation. It rests on the fact that the crisis of Fordism is one of under-consumption, with a possible solution being to increase both the aggregate purchasing power and demand of nations that previously lacked mass consumption. However, Piore and Sabel argue that three related institutional mechanisms are required for this to be a viable option: an amalgamation of markets to ensure that international demand expands at the same rate as production, for example trading blocs; a stable business environment, which could be achieved by managed and controlled exchange and inflation rates; and a mechanism to apportion the expansion of the productive capacity amongst advanced industrialised countries and between them as a group.

Piore and Sabel (1984) believe that Multinational Keynesianism, with the above institutional mechanisms, is a possibility. However, the development of Flexible Specialisation, based on a return to craft production, is the alternative that they believe is emerging and which they favour.

Amin (1989b) suggests that Flexible Specialisation is 'a new organisational principle that best responds to the growth of flexible markets' (p.15). Piore and Sabel (1984) reinforce this, stating that it is a way in which firms can respond to the crisis of mass production by directly confronting the rigidities of Fordism and replacing them with more flexible methods of organisation in terms of both production and labour. These two key organisational principles of flexible production and flexible labour are central to the Flexible Specialisation supposition and are examined in turn below.

The contrasts between Fordism and Flexible Specialisation, in terms of production flexibility, are summarised in table 2.2. It must, however, be noted at this juncture that the terms Fordism and Flexible Specialisation referred to in this table are not meant to serve as ideal types. The table lists the main characteristics of each concept, but this does not infer that either Fordism or Flexible Specialisation must have all these characteristics and nor does it infer that they cannot have additional characteristics.

Flexible Specialisation advocates argue that the emergence of new technology which facilitates the flexible, small batch production of customised commodities at a greater speed and lower cost is crucial to flexible production. This technological innovation, they suggest, has been under way since the 1950s but has become prominent recently. This, together with the fact that CAM stimulates a high degree of precision and quality, as well as facilitating frequent changes in product style or design, allows firms to compete in terms of quality and design as opposed to price (Lane, 1989). Furthermore, Sabel (1989) points out that as firms adopting Flexible Specialisation tend to undergo continuous, incremental innovation procedures in terms of both products and processes they are able to constantly adapt and adjust to changing consumer demands. Thus, Wood (1989) suggests that firms adopting these new technologies no longer receive the advantages of economies of scale but instead obtain the benefits of economies of scope.

However, the adoption of new flexible technologies does not itself necessitate the emergence of Flexible Specialisation, a factor not always accounted for by the Institutionalists (although Sabel (1989) does begin to incorporate this into his analysis). Indeed, Flexible Manufacturing Systems (FMS) may be pursued and operated with Fordist criteria in mind and, although flexible technologies can play a large part in the search for Flexible Specialisation, the two are not necessarily synonymous.

Now to turn to flexible labour. The Institutionalists tend to focus substantially less on this, viewing Flexible Specialisation in a reductionist way, as necessarily beneficial to labour. They argue that it stimulates functional flexibility, where workers have polyvalent skills to facilitate the production of constantly changing products in response to changing consumer demand. Piore and Sabel (1984) argue that a breakdown in hierarchical management/labour relations are simultaneously encouraged. The workforce benefit from enhanced skills, polyvalency, more holistic work tasks and job enrichment, whilst enjoying a greater degree of autonomy and responsibility. Based on this supposition, a recurring theme throughout Piore and Sabel's work is that Flexible Specialisation is superior to Fordism, promoting a humanisation of labour.

An underlying criticism of Piore and Sabel's analysis of this is that they make a series of abstract assumptions suggesting that labour will necessarily benefit from this process, but fail to investigate the possibility that Flexible Specialisation may also have detrimental implications for workers. Moreover throughout their work they treat the workforce as a single entity, failing to acknowledge that labour is heterogeneous, particularly in terms of gender and ethnicity, and may therefore be affected by the pursuit of flexibility in different ways. These criticisms shall not be dwelt upon here, as they will be explored in detail later.

Table 2.2   The Contrasts in Production Flexibility between Fordism and Flexible Specialisation

Fordism	Flexible Specialisation
Mass production	Small batch production
Standardised products	Specialised, semi-customised products
Low value, low quality, high volume commodities	High value, high quality, low volume commodities
Infrequent changes in product design &/or production methods	Frequent changes in product design &/or production methods
Economies of scale	Economies of scope
Competition based on price	Competition based on design & quality
Product specific capital equipment	General purpose capital equipment based on the use of flexible technologies, i.e. Computer Aided Design (CAD), Computer Aided Manufacturing (CAM), Flexible Manufacturing Systems (FMS), Computer Numerically Controlled machine tools (CNC)
Periodic innovation of both products and processes	Continuous incremental innovation of both products and processes

Source: A combination of the work of Amin (1989a, 1989b); Hirst and Zeitlin (1989a, 1989b, 1991); Jones (1989); Lane (1989); Piore and Sabel (1984); Sabel (1989)

Institutionalists argue that Flexible Specialisation has taken two principal forms: the re-emergence of industrial districts; and the reorganisation of multinationals.

Industrial Districts Piore and Sabel (1984) suggest that these have been the most dramatic response to the crisis of Fordism. They were first referred to by Alfred Marshall when looking at the nineteenth century industrial structure of Sheffield and Lancashire. Marshall defined industrial districts as:

> An agglomeration of specialised small and medium sized firms in the same area, which could be an alternative mode of organising to the large firm, in

certain manufacturing industries, without relinquishing the advantages
generally attributed to the division of labour
(Quoted in Dei Ottati, 1986, p.95).

It is widely agreed (Amin, 1989a; Piore and Sabel, 1984; Hirst and
Zeitlin, 1989b) that the most advanced forms of these 'born again'
industrial districts are prevalent in the Third Italy in the areas of Emilia,
Veneto, Tuscana, Umbria and Marche. However, Sabel (1989) argues that
there are also similar industrial structures at: Baden Wurttenberg in
Germany; Silicon Valley in California; Route 128 in Boston; and Sakaki in
Japan. Brusco defines these more recent industrial districts as:

A set of companies located in a relatively small geographical area:- That
the said companies work, either directly or indirectly for the same end of
the market; that they share a series of values and knowledges so important
that they define a cultural environment and they are linked to one another
by very specific relations in a complex mix of cooperation and
competition
(Brusco, 1992b, p.1).

Italian industrial districts vary in size, ranging from 5,000 to
50,000 workers (Brusco, 1992b). Although the size of firms within the
districts are often small they can vary enormously, ranging from mini firms
(less than 20 employees) to larger companies. Firm size is dependent on
the district, for example, in Carpi, 60 per cent of the workforce is
employed by mini firms (*ibid.*).

The firms operate in a small geographical area and external
vertical integration often takes place. For example, an industrial district
which manufactures shoes consists of shoe producers, but also firms
producing shoe boxes, glue, elastic bands, buttons, buckles, leathers, and
even machines for producing shoes.

Thus, industrial districts consist of a complex web of interlinked
firms which the Institutionalists (Piore and Sabel, 1984; Sabel, 1989; Hirst
and Zeitlin, 1989a, 1989b) argue enables a high degree of production
flexibility. Indeed, as a number of authors point out (Amin, 1989a; Best,
1990; Brusco, 1992b; Dei Ottati, 1986; Goodman, 1989), industrial
districts have various common characteristics which ensure the flexible
production of high quality, design led, semi-customised commodities
required under the Flexible Specialisation paradigm.

Firstly, industrial districts consist of a network of interlinked but
independent companies without a hierarchical structure (Best, 1990). All
companies have a place in the system but no one particular position.

Brusco (1992b) identifies three categories of industrial district companies which are interlinked: companies that manufacture the finished product and deliver it to the retailer or manufacturer; 'stage firms' which carry out one or more of the production phases; and companies that operate outside the sector to which the finished product belongs, but which work for the vertically integrated sector, i.e. a sub-contracting company which produces buttons for the clothing industry should statistically belong to the chemical sector, but actually belongs to the same vertically integrated clothing sector.

The second characteristic is that firms are productively integrated with each other on a subcontracting basis. Amin (1989a) suggests that a large proportion of the industrial district firms are 'stage firms'. They perform just one stage of the production process, i.e. in the clothing sector some companies just weave, some just cut, some embroider and some simply iron etc. Bigarelli (1993) points out that just five per cent of all the firms in the industrial district of Carpi carry out the whole of the manufacturing process from design, to manufacture, to sale. This is exemplified in Becanttini's definition of the industrial districts as...'a territorial system of small and medium sized firms producing a group of commodities whose products are processes which can be split into different phases...' (quoted in Goodman, 1989, p.21).

These subcontracting firms then often subcontract again to even smaller family firms or to domestic outworkers. This complex system of subcontracting allows a high degree of productive flexibility; costs and risks can be spread between a number of firms and short term contracts can be adjusted to meet changes in market conditions. This is achieved by switching subcontractors when a particular product is required or by raising or lowering the level of subcontracting when demand fluctuates (Amin, 1989a).

Thirdly, industrial districts achieve productive flexibility through supporting systems which coordinate cooperation and competition. This stimulates a high degree of innovation, enabling a constant and continuous updating of products to match changes in consumer demand. A market for each stage of the production process exists and in each of these markets companies which perform similar processes or which produce similar products engage in fierce competition. Each company competes for a section of the market, thus triggering off innovatory procedures. However, this system of competition is combined with a system of mutual cooperation, whereby companies work closely together, basing their relationships on local customs and historical ties. Within this system a set of rules exist which are informal but nevertheless remain unviolated. So, 'swindles and frauds' are reported to be very rare (Best, 1990). Therefore, if companies are not in direct competition and an urgent order needs to be completed, they may cooperate, thereby enhancing flexibility. This can result in a formal agreement, where both companies jointly receive the order.

Other forms of cooperative procedures, based on a high degree of consultancy between the final firms and sub-contractors, also ensure productive flexibility. Individual firms often order items without a precise design specification. In these cases the customer explains to the sub-contractor the job that the item is intended to perform. If the job cannot be fulfilled by a standard component already on the market, the sub-contractor then works on a new design for the item (Brusco, 1992b). In this way flexibility of supply ensures that changes in consumer demand are met.

Dei Ottati (1986) argues that this coordination of competition and cooperation is governed by a mechanism referred to as community market. She believes that an informal code of behaviour exists within industrial districts and that this is learnt by living and working there, advocating that the cooperative mechanism is largely a communal, socially acquired one, rather than a bureaucratic, enforced law.

A final characteristic is that central to the effective operation of industrial districts and their ability to achieve flexibility, is the notion of external economies of scale (Goodman, 1989). Industrial district firms tend to be too small to achieve internal economies of scale and therefore external economies of scale are prevalent. It is more efficient for an external firm or agency to carry out specialised work for all the firms within the industry. Economies of scale are therefore internal to the industrial district but external to the firm.

Goodman (1989) argues that these external economies of scale are achieved in the Italian industrial districts in two ways: by specialist firms, as occurs in Tuscana; or by collective service provision. The latter is most common in the Emilian industrial districts and often involves the creation of regional institutions which provide a range of services in order to allow the companies to operate at a minimum size and hence achieve optimum productive flexibility, whilst taking advantages of economies of scale. A good illustration of this is CITER (Centro Informazione Tessile dell' Emilia Romagna) which operates in Emilia Romagna. This is a textile and clothing information centre and has around 500 company members. CITER is governed by elected member companies and provides three types of information related support: fashion, marketing, and technology (Ligabue, 1992b). Local trade associations also provide this collective service provision. In the Emilian industrial district, for example, the CNA

(Confederazione Nationale dell'Artigianato) provides collective services such as administration, bookkeeping and financial support to its artisan member firms (Bellelli, 1994).

From this Institutionalist analysis it is clear that industrial districts consist of a complex network of interlinked firms which enable high quality, semi-customised commodities to be rapidly produced in small batches in order to match changes in consumer demand. However, as stated previously, the Institutionalists fail to assess the implications that this form of production has on labour, simply advocating in passing that industrial districts are necessarily beneficial to the workforce, who are highly skilled and experience the benefits of functional flexibility (Piore and Sabel, 1984; Hirst and Zeitlin, 1989a, 1991).

This is a fundamental drawback in the Institutionalist examination of industrial districts. Indeed, a detailed analysis of both the concept and practice of industrial districts reveals that the system of subcontracting, which enables a high degree of productive flexibility, has a dual effect on the labour force benefiting some workers whilst proving detrimental to others. As Solinas (1994) points out, the jobs of the workers within the final firms and the 'stage' firms have different degrees of skill content and security.

He argues that the final firms are central to the production process, determining the commodities to be produced and making prototypes and samples. The workers within these firms produce the complete product and are highly skilled. However, the final saleable commodities are collectively produced by a series of peripheral 'stage' firms, each of which performs a specific stage of the production process, and are hired and fired by the final firm according to the amount and type of the product required. The workforce of these 'stage' firms perform just one, unskilled task, and are often subject to numerically flexible work practices. One 'stage' firm visited in the Carpi industrial district, for example, consisted of six women trimming the edges of knitted fabric. These women complained of performing work which required very little skill and of having insecure employment contracts, being employed when the company had custom and being 'laid off' in times of low demand (Wigfield, 1994a).

A number of observers (Harvey, 1988; Jenson, 1989b; Walby, 1989; Wood, 1989) argue that this form of dualism can be likened to the Flexible Firm Model (Atkinson, 1984), whereby the labour market is divided into a core and periphery. They argue that functional flexibility characterises the core (which is depicted by multi-skilling, polyvalency, highly skilled tasks, full-time work, job security, promotion prospects, reskilling and retraining, the availability of pension and insurance schemes etc.) and numerical flexibility characterises the periphery (which is depicted by semi and unskilled tasks, part-time work, temporary contracts, low job security, few employment rights, little chance of training and disposable labour). Although the core/periphery model is not a new concept, the search for flexibility appears to have reinforced its position on the agenda.

As the Institutionalists fail to take account of this dual effect on the labour force they inevitably also fail to recognise that this segmentation may be determined by gender. It is often argued that the emergence of both functional and numerical flexibility may have a segmented effect on the workforce in terms of gender, with male employees enjoying the benefits of functional flexibility, while their female counterparts suffer the drawbacks of numerical flexibility (Christopherson, 1989; Jenson, 1989b; Walby, 1989). Valentini (1994) reaffirms these suspicions suggesting that within the Italian industrial districts employees performing one unskilled operation and experiencing numerical flexibility within 'stage' firms are frequently female. Solinas (1994) similarly concludes that these 'stage' firms often subcontract again, to female domestic outworkers who perform one, unskilled operation and are often placed at the end of the subcontracting chain, bearing the brunt of numerical flexibility.

The Reorganisation of Multinationals Sabel (1989) develops the Flexible Specialisation thesis further, arguing that contrary to his earlier work with Piore (1984), it does not just concern industrial districts, but also incorporates the reorganisation of large corporations. He suggests that this reorganisation has taken two principal forms: some corporations have substantially reorganised production and labour and can be likened to industrial districts; others have retained the basic Fordist structure, but have adopted flexible production methods and work patterns. Sabel argues that the latter cannot be classed as Flexible Specialisation but signify a continuation of mass production. He suggests that they may have faced barriers constraining their entry into a fully fledged Flexible Specialisation mode of production or may be pursuing a long term strategy intent on modifying as opposed to repudiating Fordist principles.

Firstly, companies that have substantially changed their production and labour organisation will be examined. These corporations have experienced internal decentralisation, fragmenting into a series of operating units, each of which becomes an autonomous smaller enterprise. Ideally most of the decision making authority is decentralised to these operating units and they become treated as subsidiaries. Thus the hierarchical structure and the traditional divisions between conception and execution become blurred. Each operating unit forms the corporation's unique representative in a distinctive market and operates on a subcontracting basis (similar to the small firms within industrial districts). Sabel suggests that this flexibility is enhanced further by reorganising production on a system of modular manufacturing, based on small groups (or team working).

Sabel (1989) advocates that this process has occurred in varying degrees of intensity throughout the western world, but argues that Montedison at Ferrara in Italy is perhaps the closest manifestation of this ideal model. Montedison was a large, single, chemical plant which sub-divided into a complex of five interlinked, but independent companies. Four of the companies continued to carry out the manufacturing processes, whilst the fifth undertook service provision to the other four, carrying out activities such as technical maintenance of equipment and administrative duties. Production became organised on a modular, team working basis and as a result the workforce benefited from multi-skilling and a dissolution of the rigid management hierarchy. Sabel (1989) argues that the system at Ferrara can be likened to the interlinked firms in industrial districts, the main difference being that the service company rather than the municipality or employers' associations provides the production units with whatever they cannot provide themselves.

Central to Sabel's decentralisation model is the notion that production is reorganised around a system of modular manufacturing based on team working (Sabel, 1989). This has profound implications for the workforce and therefore requires more detailed discussion. Team working is not an homogenous term, in fact it has two main origins: from experiments in Sweden in the 1970s at the Volvo plant in Kalmar, which were based on the Quality of Working Life movement (QWL) (Miller and Rice, 1967); and from the Japanese experiments during the Toyota revolution of the 1950s and 1960s, which were centred on Total Quality Management (TQM) (Buchanan, 1994). Sabel (1989) suggests that the type of team working that is adopted by the firms mentioned here is a variant of the Swedish prototype.

He believes that team working is adopted by these decentralised operating units as a quick response manufacturing system. The traditional production line is replaced by a series of modules which are typically, but not necessarily, 'U' shaped (NEDO, 1991b). A series of teams are established, each of which works on one of these modules and contains a group of operatives who work collectively to complete the final product. As the final product is produced by a small team, rather than the whole factory, production flexibility increases. Small batches are necessarily produced by each team, and changes in consumer demand can be rapidly met by changing a team's production requirements.

Each module contains a number of workstations. There are usually more workstations in a module than there are operatives in the team working on it. Consequently operatives can move from one workstation to another as the work builds up and falls at different points. This leads to the requirement of team members who are skilled in more than one operation and who can make some decisions for themselves about how best to utilise the skills of the team (*ibid.*). Cannell (1991a) points out that in an ideal team, optimum flexibility is achieved by every member being able to complete every job within the group, enabling absence to be covered by team members. Sabel (1989) therefore agues that under team working workers become multi-skilled.

In order to encourage optimum team flexibility and motivation, changes to the payment systems are often incorporated. Piecework, which is based on individual pay incentives, is usually replaced by fixed wages, with group bonuses for either productivity or skill levels. These both act as incentives for team members to become multi-skilled, facilitating flexibility. Bonuses paid in relation to productivity require operatives to gain as many skills as possible, thus speeding up the performance of the team. Similarly bonuses paid in relation to skill levels mean that individual team members are encouraged to learn a greater number of tasks.

Sabel (1989) additionally points out that, in order to become as flexible as possible, not only are the decentralised operating units autonomous but the small teams within each operating unit are autonomous too. This affects the job descriptions of personnel at all levels and ultimately flattens existing hierarchical structures. This is reaffirmed by Tyler's study of the introduction of team working in the clothing industry (1994). He outlines four levels of company employees affected by the introduction of team working: operatives; senior management; middle management; and supervisors.

Firstly, to look at operatives. As the teams are autonomous and self functioning, Tyler (1994) argues that operatives are not only expected to be multi-skilled, but are also required to develop higher level skills such as problem solving and decision making. Sabel (1989) suggests that this is beneficial to operatives. As Buchanan (1994) points out, it reduces the division between conception and execution, enables workers to avoid the tyranny of fixed work tasks experienced under mass production, provides extended choice and freedom in the daily working routine, and offers an opportunity for mental and physical relaxation through job variety.

Secondly to look at senior managers. Tyler (1994) also suggests that instead of management dictating to the workforce, a two way communication between management and workers is promoted. As a consequence team members benefit from being able to contribute significantly to the decision making process.

Middle managers are also affected by the introduction of team working. Tyler (1994) suggests that as operatives within teams become problem solvers this responsibility is withdrawn from middle managers who instead provide support to individual teams.

Finally, supervisors are also affected when team working is introduced. Sabel (1989) argues that as the separation of conception from execution are reconfigured, the role of the supervisor changes. NEDO (1991b) point out that activities which were previously the responsibility of supervisors such as line balancing and work-flow management are transferred to operatives within the teams. Thus the ratio of supervisors to team workers often falls. Sabel (1989) argues that the supervisor's role changes, they can no longer be seen as policing but as facilitating, working with the operatives to solve common problems. As Carrere and Little (1989) point out, under team working the title of supervisors is more accurately represented by 'coach' or 'consultant'.

According to Sabel (1989), as this work reorganisation substantially changes the employment tasks of both employees and employers, extensive training is required at all levels. This is widely recognised in the team working literature (NEDO, 1991a, 1991b; Grayson, 1990; Institute of Development Studies, 1992; Stewart, 1999). As Tyler's examination of the introduction of team working in the clothing industry reveals, operatives require training at both a technical level (for wider machining skills) and at a social level (for decision-making tasks), whilst both management and supervisors require training in order to enable them to adapt to the cultural changes involved in devolving power and responsibility.

Although Sabel (1989) recognises the importance of training in order for the workforce to benefit from multi-skilling and greater autonomy, in typical Institutionalist fashion he fails to explore the drawbacks experienced by the workforce when it is not provided. The absence of such a discussion is a major weakness in Sabel's analysis.

Technical training enabling operatives to become multi-skilled is usually provided. Even if formal training is not provided, operatives will cross train each other (NEDO, 1991b), mainly out of necessity. If they are unable to perform a range of operations, team performance will suffer and earnings will be adversely affected. However, wider social training giving operatives the ability to perform more autonomous tasks (i.e. decision making, problem solving etc.), and managerial and supervisory training which encourages the devolution of power and autonomy necessary to enable operatives to perform these tasks is not always available (Buchanan, 1994). Management are understandably reluctant to initiate training which inevitably culminates in a cultural change, whereby power is transferred away from themselves to their workforce. In these circumstances Wood (1986) argues that team working does not benefit the workforce but is, on the contrary, problematic. Although team members are expected to perform a wider range of operative tasks (i.e. of a similar level) they are not encouraged or allowed to perform higher status tasks such as decision making and problem solving. Hence rather than experience job enrichment, Wood argues that operatives experience job enlargement, suffering the drawbacks of labour intensification.

Wood (1986) takes this analysis one stage further, arguing that both job enrichment and job enlargement may be experienced at the same time in the same factory, thus having a dual effect on the labour force. As some workers are trained and allowed to perform higher order tasks involving a greater degree of responsibility, others merely perform a wider range of similar status tasks. Wood argues that this dual effect may be determined by gender, with male workers experiencing job enrichment, whilst females experience job enlargement. This is confirmed by the more recent research of Elsass *et al.* (1997), which indicates that women and ethnic minorities working in 'mixed' teams tend to be assigned lower status tasks. Again this highlights a major drawback in Sabel's analysis: not only does he fail to discuss the possibility of the prevalence of job enlargement as well as job enrichment but he fails to discuss the gender implications of such a scenario.

The second group of companies which fall into the reorganisation of multinationals category are those which attempt to achieve flexibility whilst retaining elements of Fordist production. Sabel (1989) suggests that these companies adopt a Japanese variant of the reorganisation of multinational corporations strategy and represent a continuation of mass production rather than a move to Flexible Specialisation.

These corporations aim to increase flexibility without completely abandoning the distinction between conception and execution. Like the decentralised model previously discussed, a large corporation fragments into a series of operating units which are consolidated according to their product line. However, these operating units are not awarded a greater degree of autonomy, and are still regarded as divisions of the parent company. Flexibility is achieved by Just In Time (JIT) delivery systems which originally developed in the Japanese Toyota plants, JIT being defined as a...'philosophy directed towards the elimination of waste, where waste is anything which adds cost, but not value to a product' (Turnbull, 1988, p.8).

Within JIT, raw materials and parts are both produced and delivered just in time for the next stage of the production process. Ideally defect-free parts will flow through the manufacturing process, thus encompassing Total Quality Control (TQC). JIT is a highly technical system adopting multi-purpose, easily programmable machinery in order to facilitate small batch production. A Kanban system monitors the rate of production to ensure that only the quantity of parts necessary for the completion of the next stage of production are produced. Within Sabel's Japanese variant of the reorganisation of multinational corporations strategy, the decentralised operating units synchronise their production sequence to deliver their products to each other on a JIT basis. These inter firm activities then extend backwards to an intra firm level. Within each of the fragmented operating units, the factory layout is reorganised on the basis of team working (Turnbull, 1987). Sabel (1989) suggests that within this model, the type of team working that is adopted is a variant of the Japanese rather than the previously discussed Swedish prototype.

The Japanese system of team work was first developed by the Toyota car factory during the 1950s and 1960s and, like the Swedish model of team working, is based on multi-skilled operatives working in teams on a range of workstations, often within 'U' shaped modules. Workers are expected to perform the full range of tasks on the module so that they can shift jobs easily, hence achieving optimum flexibility (Sabel, 1989). However, the emphasis of the Japanese model is not on increasing skill levels in order to achieve flexibility but on introducing new technology to achieve greater flexibility. Machines and workstations are introduced which reduce the skill content of individual operations thereby making it easier for operatives to perform a wider range of tasks at a faster rate. Sabel (1989) therefore stresses that operatives under this model experience multi-tasking and not multi-skilling. He further points out that increasing worker knowledge and autonomy is not a characteristic of the Japanese model of team working, with supervisors and managers retaining overall power. Thus, just as the operating units are not autonomous, neither are the teams operating within them. Buchanan therefore rightly points out that the Japanese model of team working means something quite different from what it does in Sweden:

> The team concept is not intended to increase workers' autonomy but to
> help them to find out the problems in the production line so that no

defective goods will be produced. In the US, workers tend to take participation as having a voice in all kinds of things that in Japan are determined by management and engineers
(Buchanan, 1994, p.220).

So whilst the Swedish variant of team working is concerned with increasing worker control, the Japanese model is concerned with increasing management control (Wood, 1989). Sabel (1989) therefore argues that the Japanese model of the reorganisation of multinational corporations is detrimental to the workforce. It leads to job enlargement, intensifies work pressures, increases surveillance of shop floor workers, and reduces individual discretion with respect to working methods.

The main criticism of this aspect of Sabel's work concerns his reluctance to incorporate this form of reorganisation into the Flexible Specialisation thesis. This relates back to earlier criticisms of Sabel's work and is connected to the underlying weakness in the wider Institutionalist theory, namely that Flexible Specialisation is viewed as an ideal type which necessarily benefits labour, and that the possibility that Flexible Specialisation can have both beneficial and detrimental implications for labour is not investigated. Institutionalists believe that any system of production, even if it involves a search for greater production and labour flexibility, cannot be classed as Flexible Specialisation, unless it is deemed advantageous to labour.

The Institutionalists therefore argue that two predominant forms of Flexible Specialisation have developed recently: industrial districts; and the reorganisation of multinational corporations. As we have seen, the dominance of each of these tends to vary with the locality, indeed it is widely argued that the extent to which Flexible Specialisation is adopted and the form which it takes is dependant upon the degree to which mass production has previously been dominant. Flexible Specialisation has been more likely to develop in areas where mass production has been less prevalent (for example, Germany and Italy) and where it has continued to coexist alongside craft production (Piore and Sabel, 1984; Sabel, 1989).

However, the growth of Flexible Specialisation cannot just be attributed to the absence of mass production, but can be linked to the cultural and historical identity of the region. The emergence of industrial districts in the Third Italy has been explained by a range of historical factors. The tradition of share cropping (metayage) and the importance of the extended family has provided the region with a culture of high mutual trust relations, which has the effect of facilitating a balance between competition and cooperation and producing a population which is experienced in the day to day management of small artisan workshops, both of which are essential factors in the development of successful industrial districts (Brusco, 1986; Sabel, 1989). Added to this is the willingness of communist-controlled local and regional authorities to intervene and provide a range of infrastructure including common services, technical support, research and development and specific technical training and education (Piore and Sabel, 1984; Brusco, 1986). Thus the Third Italy is viewed as possessing the essential prerequisites for the development of industrial districts.

Similarly, specific cultural and historical factors in Germany have enacted to support strategies of fragmentation and the adoption of flexible production methods. Lane (1988) points out that the German industry during the 1950s to 1970s was less influenced by both Fordist and Taylorist techniques than were other countries. The deskilling process had substantially less impact and therefore the workforce retained their polyvalent skills. This provided the foundations for the fragmentation of large corporations into autonomous operating units and the development of more flexible methods of production such as team working, based on both a devolution of responsibility and multi-skilling (Lane, 1988).

Likewise Sabel (1989) argues that Japan has experienced substantially different historical and political developments, whereby mass Taylorist techniques have been taken to their extreme and management culture has been based on maintaining tight control over the workforce. Hence the search for flexibility has been centred on a modification rather than repudiation of mass production principles. However, Sabel suggests that the Japanese corporations which first adopted this model are slowly beginning to change towards the decentralised model, which is evident in Germany, with some large corporations in Japan laying off their own managers and encouraging them to form legally autonomous firms with the capacity for innovative production.

Regulationists and Post-Fordism

During recent years the focus of attention in Marxist discussion has shifted away from the issue of capitalism in crisis to the question of capital restructuring. The argument that Fordism has suffered a crisis and that we are now experiencing a more flexible regime of accumulation, together with a corresponding mode of regulation, has gained widespread acceptance amongst the Regulationist School (Aglietta, 1979; Boyer, 1988a; Leborgne and Lipietz, 1988, 1990; Lipietz, 1987, 1997).

Regulationists refer to the replacement of Fordism as a new regime of accumulation rather than using the Institutionalist term of a new technological paradigm, primarily because the former allows for an analysis of not only technological changes in production organisation but of wider social relations, including the implications for labour relations.

Regulationist theory maintains a determinacy view of economic development, arguing that the choice of a new regime of accumulation is constrained by the principles of both the capitalist mode of production and the mode of regulation. However, within this framework various commentators have emerged highlighting a range of new regimes of accumulation. Aglietta (1979) advocates that the replacement for Fordism is inevitably Neo-Fordism, based on an extension of the basic Fordist principles. He states that....'capitalism can escape from its contemporary organic crisis only by generating a new cohesion, a Neo-Fordism' (Aglietta, 1979, p.385).

Other Regulationists, while maintaining a determinacy view of economic restructuring, have argued that a number of replacements for Fordism are possible. This is particularly true of Lipietz (1987, 1997) and Leborgne and Lipietz (1988, 1990), who argue that Post-Fordism (which encompasses a range of alternative regimes of accumulation) can be viewed as the Fordist successor.

In order to explore the Regulationist view of the Fordist successor in detail, it is important to analyse both the new flexible regime of accumulation and the corresponding mode of regulation.

A Flexible Regime of Accumulation Regulationists, whether they be Neo or Post-Fordists, agree that a more flexible regime of accumulation has recently emerged, which is characterised by a search for both production and labour flexibility. This is therefore similar to the Institutionalist model of Flexible Specialisation.

Firstly, to look at flexible production. The Regulationists concentrate on the relationship between flexible production and labour relations, incorporating wider social relations into their analysis. Their analysis of production flexibility, as a result, tends not to be as comprehensive as that provided by Institutionalists such as Piore and Sabel (1984) and Hirst and Zeitlin (1989a).

Leborgne and Lipietz (1988) and Lipietz (1997) provide perhaps the most developed Regulationist argument in this context, advocating that new forms of organisational methods are being explored. They agree with the Institutionalists that a technical revolution is at the centre of this restructuring and that the main feature of it is the development of micro-processes and electronic interfaces such as FMS, CNC, CAM, CAD and so on.

Lipietz (1987, 1992a) explains that these flexible technologies facilitate the small batch production of constantly changing commodities, allowing firms to receive the benefits of economies of scope as opposed to economies of scale. Other Regulationists, such as Harvey (1988), Tickell and Peck (1992), Moulaert and Swyngedouw (1989), highlight additional elements involved in the flexible production process, such as the production of semi-customised goods, based on a high degree of quality and design, alongside the constant adaptation and innovation of products and processes. These characteristics are similar to those advocated by the Institutionalists (see table 2.2), but tend to appear in a less developed and less advanced form, thus highlighting a weakness in the Regulationist theory and a requirement for more analysis in this area.

Secondly, to explore flexible labour. The search for labour flexibility is central to Regulationist analysis of restructuring but different strands of the School approach this in contrasting ways. Aglietta (1979), for example, advocates that a flexible regime of accumulation will necessarily be detrimental to labour, while Lipietz (1987, 1997) and Leborgne and Lipietz (1988, 1990) envisage a range of possible effects on the labour force.

Aglietta (1979) takes the opposite view to the Institutionalists, arguing that any flexible regime of accumulation is necessarily detrimental to labour. He views Neo-Fordism as a simple extension of the basic principles of Fordism, utilising new flexible technologies as a way of further exploiting labour via both labour intensification and an extension of the deskilling process. Unlike Piore and Sabel (1984), Aglietta does not accept that labour flexibility can derive benefits for the workforce. He does concede that the technological innovation which accompanies Neo-Fordism may benefit the workforce through a reduction of the number of monotonous, operative tasks, but argues that this will not occur unless capitalism is eradicated (Aglietta, 1979).

The disparities between the work of Aglietta (1979) and the Institutionalists (Piore and Sabel, 1984; Sabel, 1989) are perhaps most clear when examining their respective analysis of the development of team working. Whilst Sabel (1989) argues that the Swedish model of team working is necessarily beneficial to labour, Aglietta believes that all forms of team working are detrimental to labour. His justification is that multi-skilling which underpins team working is damaging, promoting job enlargement rather than job enrichment. He suggests that multi-skilling is....'widened work which is just as empty as before and as completely reduced to pure duration as was earlier fragmented work' (Aglietta, 1979, p.129). Aglietta therefore views the recent euphoria about the decomposition of tasks as merely a 'lot of shameless propaganda about the liberation of man in work' (Aglietta, 1979, p.122).

Harvey's (1988) model of 'Flexible Accumulation' is similarly viewed as damaging, stimulating enhanced labour control. He suggests it utilises labour in areas which have not previously been industrialised, such as Silicon Glen in Scotland. These regions tend to have non-union traditions and consequently employers are able to recruit and exploit 'green' workers, the majority of whom are female.

The work of these Regulationists is valuable as it provides an alternative to Piore and Sabel's theory that labour flexibility necessarily benefits the workforce. However, like the Institutionalists, these commentators fail to investigate the possibility that the flexible regime of accumulation can have both positive and negative implications for labour. Leborgne and Lipietz (1988, 1990) and Lipietz (1997) have addressed these inadequacies, arguing that alternative types of labour organisation can emerge, which are both beneficial and detrimental. In general they refer to these new regimes of accumulation as Post-Fordist but on occasions use the term 'After-Fordism'. Peck and Tickell (1994) and Tickell and Peck (1995) also use this term and justify its utilisation because a single solution to the crisis of Fordism has yet to emerge. True, a single solution to Fordism has not emerged, as Gough (1996) and Taylor-Gooby (1997) point out, and probably never will. However, this does not mean that the term Post-Fordism, which encompasses a range of different scenarios, cannot be used. Indeed, the introduction of a different title creates confusion, particularly if it is used inconsistently. Therefore, throughout this book the work of these authors shall be referred to as Post-Fordist. In any case too much attention should not be paid to the title, it is the content of the discussion which is important.

The first alternative outlined by Leborgne and Lipietz (1988, 1990) and Lipietz (1997) involves a polarisation of tasks and is an extension of the Fordist principles, with a separation of conception and execution. Workers in a central planning bureau perform complex mental activities, whilst those on the shop floor carry out simple, unskilled, operative tasks. The labour force is organised by direct control, a concept derived from Friedman (1977), whereby the scope of labour power is limited through coercive threats, close supervision and by a reduction in individual responsibility.

The second alternative involves mobilising in real time the involvement of direct operators, with the aim of 'reconnecting what Taylorism had disconnected, the manual and intellectual aspects of labour'

(Leborgne and Lipietz, 1988, p.269). Multi-skilled, semi-autonomous work groups are developed, therefore enhancing worker involvement. Labour is organised by responsible autonomy, whereby workers are encouraged to adapt to situations by receiving higher status jobs with more authority and responsibility (Friedman, 1977). This model is therefore similar to Flexible Specialisation advocated by the Institutionalists. Leborgne and Lipietz argue that under this option, worker involvement is enhanced and that this involvement can take a number of forms. Firstly it may be individually negotiated (I in figure 2.1), i.e. by pay bonuses or career opportunities. Secondly it may be negotiated on a firm by firm basis between management and unions (F in figure 2.1), i.e. collective bargaining. A third type of involvement may take place at a sectoral level and a fourth at a societal level, whereby unions of workers negotiate on a regional or national basis (Leborgne and Lipietz, 1990; Lipietz, 1997).

Leborgne and Lipietz (1988, 1990) and Lipietz (1997) state that the impact on labour is further complicated by the wage contract, which can be either rigid or flexible. The rigid wage contract means that workers benefit from job security and stable wages (as in Fordism). Whereas the flexible wage contract leads to numerical flexibility, whereby workers experience fewer employment rights and may form part of a disposable labour force, being hired and fired at the will of the employer.

From this discussion Leborgne and Lipietz (1990) and Lipietz (1997) derive a list of possible replacements for the Fordist regime of accumulation. These can be seen in figure 2.1 and are described below. The first model involves a polarisation of skills via automation, plus rigidity in the wage contract. Workers are governed by direct control and this is a continuation of *Fordism*, which Leborgne and Lipietz argue was the main tendency in both Europe and the USA during the 1970s.

The second model involves a polarisation of skills via automation, plus a flexible wage contract. Companies utilise a numerically flexible workforce, expanding labour in times of high demand and laying off employees when demand falls. Again workers are governed by direct control. Leborgne and Lipietz refer to this scenario as *Neo-Taylorism* and view it as a further extension of Fordism and the Taylorist work ethic. They state that the adoption of this model would lead to an unsatisfactory social pattern, with a polarisation of skill and dualisation of both labour markets and society.

The third model concerns functional flexibility. It involves a move to more worker involvement, with workers enjoying the benefits of semi-autonomous group work, multi-skilling and job enrichment. Workers are governed by responsible autonomy and this involvement is negotiated at a societal level and exists alongside a rigid wage contract. Leborgne and Lipietz favour this model and argue that the closest example to it exists in Sweden. Indeed they name it *Kalmarism* in honour of the first car factory reorganised on the 'involvement' principle in Kalmar, Sweden in 1974.

The final scenario is based on intra firm level negotiated involvement and allows for the dualistic coexistence of both Kalmarism and Neo-Taylorism. Alongside the functional flexibility of increased worker involvement, multi-skilling, job enrichment and responsible autonomy based on a rigid wage contract, exists a situation whereby workers have little involvement and responsibility, being governed by the principles of direct control. These workers experience the drawbacks of numerical flexibility via the presence of a flexible wage contract. Leborgne and Lipietz argue that this model leads to the emergence of a dualistic labour market (i.e. according to gender) and state that a similar situation is occurring in Japan. Thus they refer to this model as *Toyotism*.

In his more recent work, Lipietz (1997) adds 'the rest of the world' to this model. Although this is a useful contribution to the debate, it need not concern us here, as we are solely interested in economic restructuring within the western world.

In addition, Lipietz (1997) argues that further changes have taken place since the publication of his influential work with Leborgne (1990) which have implications for this model of Post-Fordism. The crucial one being the fall of the Berlin Wall, which he argues led to an increase in flexible and skilled labour from Central and Eastern Europe. Lipietz suggests that the influx of flexible labour countered the advantages of negotiated involvement and particularly affected countries in the top right hand corner of the diagram (figure 2.1). Sweden, for example, has started to slide along the curve towards sectoral negotiation.

Both Leborgne and Lipietz therefore argue that a range of models could possibly replace Fordism. They state that at present no hegemonic model has developed and that in reality what has occurred in both Japan and Germany in the 1980s and 90s has been a mix of all these models. The fact that Leborgne and Lipietz (1988, 1990) and Lipietz (1997) look at the spatial aspects of economic restructuring is important in this context. They

Figure 2.1 Post-Fordism

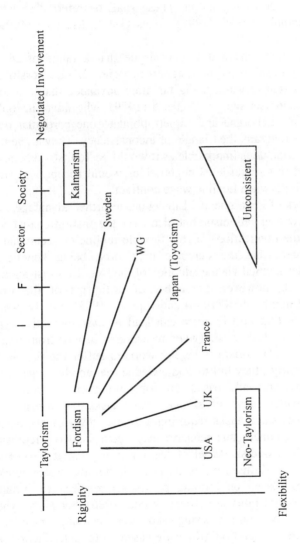

Source: Leborgne and Lipietz (1990)

acknowledge that the regime of accumulation occurs at different scales and times in different geographical areas, a factor which other Regulationist explanations of the restructuring process should take into account, as writers such as Peck and Tickell (1994), Tickell and Peck (1995) and Painter and Goodwin (1995) point out. Various authors have recently begun to look at the spatial implications of Post-Fordism but primarily in relation to the mode of regulation. These shall be referred to later and include, for example, Gough (1996), Jones (1997), Macloed (1999), and Macloed and Jones (1999).

Further, Leborgne and Lipietz argue that a range of additional scenarios in any position on the diagram in figure 2.1 are possible. This perspective is a step forward, being far more advanced than the work of previous Regulationists such as Aglietta (1979), who advocate only one possible outcome. Leborgne and Lipietz point to one particular point of exception on the diagram, the triangle of inconsistency. They argue that the scenario in this triangle is impossible as it would be 'foolish' to believe that unions involved in societal level negotiations would accept a situation of numerical flexibility via a flexible wage contract.

The work of Leborgne and Lipietz has a further advantage, not just over their fellow Regulationists, but also over the Institutionalist School. They examine the implications of the flexible regime of accumulation on labour and accept that the outcome may vary, being beneficial via Kalmarism or detrimental via the adoption of the Neo-Taylorist regime.

There are, however, a number of criticisms of the work of Leborgne and Lipietz (1988, 1990) and Lipietz (1997). Firstly, while the writers recognise that Post-Fordism can lead to two alternative types of labour organisation, Kalmarism (whereby workers benefit from functional flexibility) or Neo-Taylorism (whereby workers suffer the drawbacks of numerical flexibility), they fail to acknowledge that another type of labour organisation may prevail, based on job enlargement, with workers performing a wider range of similar status tasks but restricted from performing higher status tasks requiring a greater level of responsibility. As previously explained, this scenario may occur in two circumstances. Firstly, when the Swedish model of team working (what Leborgne and Lipietz refer to as Kalmarism) is introduced, but the wider workplace cultural changes (based on training provision) required to stimulate a dissolution of responsibility are absent (Wood, 1986). Secondly, when the Japanese variant of team working and accompanying manufacturing systems of JIT are in operation, which are based on the introduction of new technologies to enable operatives to perform a wider range of deskilled tasks, at a faster rate (Buchanan, 1994). Leborgne and Lipietz therefore need to incorporate this alternative form of work organisation (job enlargement) into their analysis, drawing upon the work of various authors such as Wood (1986, 1989), Buchanan (1994) and of other Regulationists such as Aglietta (1979).

A second criticism is that the possible replacements for Fordism provided by Leborgne and Lipietz (1988, 1990) and Lipietz (1997) (Neo-Taylorism, Kalmarism and Toyotism) are not explored in any substantial detail. The implications for labour relations are discussed but not in any great depth, whilst the production changes experienced under these models are virtually ignored.

Thirdly, and linked to the previous point, Leborgne and Lipietz present the various Fordist replacements in graphical form, but place countries on the diagram in a range of positions, without providing supporting empirical evidence that these models are emerging in reality. Sweden, for example, is placed close to the Kalmarism regime, yet there is little provision of evidence that it deserves to be so placed. The absence of concrete research and supporting empirical evidence is, in fact, true of Regulationist theory in general, as Gough (1996), Jones (1997), and MacLeod and Jones (1999) also point out.

Fourthly, Leborgne and Lipietz fail to explore regional disparities within nation states. For example, Lipietz (1997) places Italy on the diagram between Toyotism and Neo-Taylorism, yet there are wide regional disparities within the country. The regime of accumulation in the industrial districts of the Third Italy, for example, is completely different to that experienced in peripheral northern or southern regions. Gough (1996), Jones (1997) and MacLeod and Jones (1999) have also noted the failure of the Post-Fordist literature to explore regional uneven development.

The final, and in this context perhaps most important criticism, is that although Leborgne and Lipietz (1988, 1990) and Lipietz (1997) redress the Institutionalist problem of failing to examine, in detail, the implications of the search for flexibility on labour, they do not extend this to a detailed analysis of the possible implications for gender relations. There are many occasions where Leborgne and Lipietz mention gender, but they all too often fail to elaborate. Perhaps the best example of this is their statement (without any explanation or elaboration) that the dualistic coexistence of Kalmarism and Neo-Taylorism in the form of Toyotism may be determined by gender (Leborgne and Lipietz, 1990, p.13).

A Flexible Mode of Regulation Regulationist theory suggests that any new regime of accumulation is accompanied by a corresponding mode of regulation. However, as Tickell and Peck (1992, 1995) and Painter and Goodwin (1995) rightly point out, there has been substantially less research on this aspect of the theory. Nevertheless, it must be noted that this gap in the literature has started to be redressed in the 1990s by commentators such as Jessop (1993, 1994, 1995a, 1995b).

The majority of the research carried out in connection with the new mode of regulation concerns the changing role of the state. Most commentators examining this issue argue that the move to a Post-Fordist regime of accumulation has been accompanied by a decline in the Keynesian welfare state. This is explained by the fact that the small batch, semi-customised production of constantly changing products no longer requires the mass consumption which was made possible by this mode of regulation. Jessop (1993, 1994, 1995a, 1995b) argues that the Schumpeterian Workfare Postnational Regime (SWPR) has emerged as the new regulatory body of Post-Fordism. The SWPR has three distinctive features. The first feature centres on the 'hollowing out' of the national state; the second on a 'resurgence of local and regional governance' embracing various stakeholders; and the third a subordination of Keynesian social and regional redistributive policies in favour of supply side initiatives to promote international structural competitiveness.

Jessop (1994) suggests that there are three ideal-types of the SWPR: a) the Neoliberal SWPR which is based on a market guided transition, including deregulation, financial liberalisation, and privatisation; b) the Neocorporatist SWPR which is based on a negotiated approach; and c) the Neostatism SWPR which is a 'market conforming but state guided approach'.

Tickell and Peck (1992) and Moulaert and Swyngedouw (1989) similarly argue that the welfare state has disintegrated and suggest that this has resulted in a reduction of social security payments, i.e. the third feature of Jessop's SWPR. Bakshi *et al.* (1995) agree and suggest that there have been a number of broad changes in the British welfare state, each of which have implications for gender and race relations. The most important of these, in this context, are attempts to remove forms of regulation and state intervention, leading to increasing privatisation and commodification of welfare.

This latter point is also noted by Taylor-Gooby (1997) and, in relation to Lowland Scotland, by Jones (1997) and MacLeod and Jones (1999). Indeed, it is widely recognised that in Britain, since 1979, there has been a general trend towards deregulation. This is exemplified by Taylor-Gooby (1997) who argues that Britain has experienced privatisation, selectivity, an increase in the number of quangos, and weakened labour. As a consequence inequalities within the nation have widened. Indeed, McDowell, 1991 noted that 'incomes have become polarised, with the top one fifth of UK households experiencing a rise in the proportion of total disposable income between 1976 and 1986, while the bottom one fifth experienced a fall in the proportion of total disposable income during the same period'. Hoggett (1994) and Taylor-Gooby (1997) suggest that this has continued into the 1990s and that, due to state policy, class divisions have widened, contributing to rapid increases in inequality. Esping-Andersen (1994) supports this, pointing out that income inequalities have grown '....earnings in the lowest decile lost ground, relative to the median by 14 per cent in the UK' (p.14). Hence the gap between the 'haves' and 'have nots' in Britain has become wider than ever.

Moulaert and Swyngedouw's work (1989) can therefore be applied here. They argue that the regulation of the welfare state is being replaced by an entrepreneurial state for the well off and by a soup kitchen state for those caught in the doldrums of persistent unemployment. Tickell and Peck (1992) suggest that the result is the emergence of a more diversified, frequently changing demand, for semi-customised commodities from those on high incomes, while those on substantially lower incomes demand low cost, low quality commodities. This is perhaps one explanation of why mass production has continued to exist alongside this more flexible mode of production.

Bakshi *et al.* (1995) point out the welfare state itself led to gender inequalities in society, on the one hand treating women as a cheap source of labour, providing low paid, part-time work and on the other hand discriminating against women as users of the service. However, they recognise that its disintegration maybe even more damaging for women as long as they have the main responsibility for caring and domestic tasks. The removal or privatisation of welfare effectively means that the responsibility for provision of social services such as childcare, care for the elderly etc. are removed from the state and directed at the family and therefore ultimately at women. In the 1980s and early 1990s this was certainly the case, as McDowell (1991) pointed out. She suggested that the privatisation of welfare meant that some women were being forced out of paid employment and back into the home, while others faced the double burden of going out to work and taking on board the responsibility for the care of dependants.

However, the situation has changed recently in Britain. A combination of a new Labour Government elected in 1997 and a requirement to bring the country's social legislation in line with the rest of Europe has meant a greater emphasis on provision for workers who are also carers, this being exemplified by the government's promotion of policies such as the national carers' strategy, the national childcare strategy and 'family friendly' employment policies.

Despite the recognition of these changes in the mode of regulation, particularly in the welfare state, various commentators (Bakshi *et al.*, 1995; Gough, 1997; Painter and Goodwin, 1995; Peck and Tickell, 1994; Tickell and Peck, 1995) have argued that these changes are not sufficient to signify a new Post-Fordist mode of regulation but indicate that we are now experiencing a stage of transition in the mode of regulation and that a new one has not actually formed at present. Instead they suggest that the welfare state is in 'limbo' (Bakshi *et al.*, 1995, p.1552). Moreover, they argue that the nature of the mode of regulation varies geographically, which is a sensible suggestion given previous evidence that the regime of accumulation varies by locality (Leborgne and Lipietz, 1988, 1990) and Lipietz (1997). Peck and Tickell (1994) suggest that this uneven development indicates that the present situation is unstable.

Towards the latter part of the 1990s various commentators (Dunford and Perrons, 1994; Gough, 1996; Jones, 1997; MacLeod and Jones, 199; MacLeod, 1997, 1999; MacLeod and Goodwin, 1999) started to explore the mode of regulation and the role of space. In general, they argue that Jessop's analysis of the SWPR is useful but does not go far enough. Their main criticism is that it is abstract and not grounded in concrete research. However, although these authors criticise the theory of Regulation for its lack of analysis of spatial inequalities, they themselves do little to reverse this trend, simply arguing that more work needs to be conducted in this area and providing some limited evidence from Lowland Scotland (Jones and MacLeod, 1999).

As previously stated, even less research has been conducted on the wider social regulatory structures such as the church, the school, the family and the media. However, Harvey (1988) does attempt to redress this problem by examining the role that the media has played in the new mode of regulation. He argues that the media has reinforced the effect of a polarisation of incomes by generating a pattern of frequently changing fashion trends therefore encouraging individuals to constantly change consumption patterns. This work has not, however, been advanced or expanded upon since its publication over a decade ago.

One key criticism of Post-Fordist theory is that, not only does it needs to develop a more coherent theorisation of the mode of regulation but also, crucially, that the mode of regulation is separated from the regime of accumulation (Gough, 1996). In some respects this is correct but the complex nature of the subject area, by necessity, means that various researchers have been attempting to add elements to the debate, but understandably, no individual commentator has yet been able to provide a comprehensive account of the Post-Fordist regime of accumulation and mode of Regulation. Take this book, for example, it aims to 'genderise' the restructuring debate but cannot be expected, nor does it attempt to, provide an exhaustive account of all aspects of change accompanying the Post-Fordist era.

It can therefore be seen that Regulationist research concerning the new mode of regulation is limited and further more detailed research in this field must be conducted. The work of Bakshi *et al.* (1995), Gough (1996), Jessop (1993, 1994, 1995a, 1995b), Painter and Goodwin (1995), Peck and Tickell (1994), and Tickell and Peck (1995) requires further development and other avenues beyond the welfare state also need to be explored. One possible source of this research could be the work of the Institutionalists themselves who have carried out some research into the regulatory mechanisms of Flexible Specialisation and in particular the regulation of industrial districts, looking at regional level structures such as high trust environments and mechanisms balancing competition and cooperation. Although, as MacLeod and Jones (1999) point out, it is important to ensure that any changes in the regulation of localities are not 'institutionalised' but are explored within the context of the changing mode of regulation (p.579).

Conclusion: Towards a Model of Post-Fordism

The Institutionalist School and the theory of Regulation agree that Fordism is being replaced by a more flexible mode of production. However, there is a polarisation in their explanations for the rise and decline of Fordism and its replacement which is hardly surprising given that they each explore economic development and its restructuring from substantially different theoretical, ideological and political backgrounds.

The conflicts and contradictions between the two theories are perhaps at their greatest when examining the emergence of the Fordist replacement. The Institutionalists offer an indeterminacy view, arguing that a range of new technological paradigms are possible and that whichever emerges can be explained by a number of chance decisions taken at certain historical conjunctures. The Regulationists, on the other hand, have a more deterministic view of economic development, arguing that it is governed by the principles of the capitalist mode of production. Within the Regulationist School a diverse range of theories exist, with some observers such as Aglietta (1979) advocating that a regime of accumulation based on

Neo-Fordism is the only possible solution to the decline of Fordism, while others such as Leborgne and Lipietz (1988, 1990) and Lipietz (1997) provide a more convincing account, stating that the replacement regime of accumulation can take a variety of forms, which differ by locality.

For the Institutionalists the paradigm of Flexible Specialisation is centred around new technologies, which facilitate the flexible, small batch production of diverse, semi-customised commodities. Thus Flexible Specialisation advocates such as Piore and Sabel (1984) and Hirst and Zeitlin (1991) tend to focus attention upon production flexibility, failing to examine in any detail the implications on labour relations. The work carried out by Piore and Sabel (1984) and Sabel (1989) assumes in passing that Flexible Specialisation is necessarily beneficial to labour, allowing workers to experience the benefits of job enrichment and the wider advantages of functional flexibility. They fail to acknowledge that workers may also be adversely affected by the search for flexibility in the form of either job enlargement or numerical flexibility, suggesting that in these circumstances the restructuring can be more accurately classed as a modification of mass production rather than the emergence of Flexible Specialisation.

For the Regulationists, on the other hand, the reverse is true. Most Regulationist observers concentrate on the implications for labour relations, but fail to analyse changes in production organisation in any detail. Leborgne and Lipietz (1990) and Lipietz (1997) provide a good analysis of the implications of Post-Fordism for labour, revealing in diagrammatic form that workers may be affected in a variety of ways, benefiting from functional flexibility but also suffering from the disadvantages of numerical flexibility. However, like the Institutionalists, they too fail to acknowledge that the workforce may also experience another drawback - job enlargement, whereby workers are expected to perform a wider range of similar status tasks, hence enduring labour intensification.

The work of the Regulationists on the replacement of the Fordist regime of accumulation appears less advanced and developed than their previous research on the rise and decline of Fordism and more importantly, than the parallel work of the Institutionalists. Indeed, Piore and Sabel (1984) and Sabel (1989) suggest that Flexible Specialisation can take two principal forms, industrial districts and the reorganisation of multinational corporations, and provide a detailed analysis of these systems together with supporting empirical evidence. However, even the more advanced work of Regulationists such as Leborgne and Lipietz (1990) and Lipietz (1997) fails to provide a comprehensive account of the new regimes of accumulation. Although Leborgne and Lipietz offer a range of forms which Post-Fordism can take (Kalmarism, Neo-Taylorism and Toyotism), they fail to explore these in any detail. Moreover they locate a range of countries on various positions within their model but do not attempt to provide any supporting empirical evidence to justify these positions. They also place whole nations on the diagram without taking into account uneven development and regional inequalities.

Additionally, Leborgne and Lipietz largely ignore the corresponding modes of regulation, a factor which is surprising since the regulatory structures of accumulation are central to the theory of regulation. Some progress has been made in this direction (Bakshi *et al.*, 1995; Harvey, 1988; Jessop, 1993, 1994, 1995a, 1995b; Painter and Goodwin, 1995; Tickell and Peck, 1995) although with the exception of Harvey (1988) they concentrate solely on changes in the welfare state. This reveals that a great deal more empirical research on the emergence of Post-Fordism and on the corresponding modes of regulation is required by Regulationists in this context.

Neither the Institutionalists nor the Regulationists provides a comprehensive analysis of gender relations, indeed gender appears to be an issue largely missing from the restructuring debate. Consequently very few examples of working women are cited and little effort is made to utilise gender neutral language, with the worker constantly referred to as 'he'. Moreover when women are incorporated into the discussion they are often seen as marginal and as Jenson (1989b) points out, not like 'real' workers. The Institutionalists are perhaps the worst culprits here as they totally ignore the issue of gender. The Regulationists (Leborgne and Lipietz, 1988, 1990), on the other hand, do appear to recognise that women and men are often located in different positions in the labour market and therefore may be influenced by the development of Post-Fordism in different ways. They suggest that the extent to which the labour force experience the functional flexibility of Kalmarism or the numerical flexibility of Neo-Taylorism may be determined by gender. However all too often they 'skirt' around the issue of gender, failing to elaborate in any substantial detail. In one article the possible implications of Post-Fordism for gender relations is left until the final statement (Leborgne and Lipietz, 1988).

The absence of a discussion of gender relations in the Regulationist account of the restructuring process has also been recognised by Williams (1994) and Bakshi *et al.* (1995). The former suggests that Post-Fordist analysis does not account for social relations other than class, particularly in relation to the welfare state, but she does little to redress this. Whilst the latter, in contrast, make some attempts to reverse this trend with respect to the mode of regulation, exploring the gendered and racialised character of the welfare state and the way in which this is currently being redefined.

Thus it can be seen that neither the work of the Institutionalists on Flexible Specialisation, nor the work of the Regulationists on Neo or Post-Fordism, provides a comprehensive explanation of the restructuring process and the resulting replacement for Fordism. Indeed, both the Flexible Specialisation and the Post-Fordist theories have a number of strengths and weaknesses (illustrated in table 2.3). Whilst the analysis of the Institutionalist theory of Flexible Specialisation in this table is derived from a number of authors, it must be noted that the corresponding analysis of Post-Fordism is principally derived from the work of Leborgne and Lipietz (1988, 1990) and Lipietz (1997). This is primarily due to the fact that their work is the most advanced and well developed of the Regulationist School, in terms of the regime of accumulation.

Table 2.3 reveals that a more comprehensive and concise analysis of the restructuring process could be provided by a combination of various aspects of the two restructuring schools. This would be best achieved by taking the basic theory of the Regulationist School, developing their points of weakness, and adding insights from the Institutionalist supposition. Therefore in order to develop a more comprehensive model of Post-Fordism, the basic diagrammatic theory (figure 2.1) provided by Leborgne and Lipietz should be retained but modified. As the interaction between production and labour under the Fordist mode of production has been both well researched and empirically tested, Fordism can remain on the diagram in the original position, as can the triangle of inconsistency. However to the three forms of Post-Fordism originally advocated by Leborgne and Lipietz (Neo-Taylorism, Kalmarism, Toyotism) a fourth scenario needs to be added, based on job enlargement. Explanations for the existence of the three original forms of Post-Fordism are somewhat lacking and therefore substantially more research on these is required. Empirical evidence supporting the location of the various countries on the diagram is likewise absent and in order to adequately justify the position of the nations on the diagram this needs to be redressed. Moreover, there needs to be a recognition that regional disparities and inequalities exists within nations and that uneven development occurs. The empirical research of the Institutionalists could be utilised here, drawing upon the concept of industrial districts and the reorganisation of multinational corporations.

Table 2.3   The Strengths and Weaknesses of Flexible Specialisation and Post-Fordism

Flexible Specialisation	Post-Fordism*
Production Flexibility	
Production flexibility is analysed in detail looking at the small batch production of semi-customised commodities as a result of new technologies i.e. CNC, FMS, CAD, CAM.	Fail to analyse production flexibility in any detail.
Labour Flexibility	
Fail to provide an analysis of the effect of the search for production flexibility on labour relations. Assume that Flexible Specialisation is beneficial to labour via functional flexibility, failing to acknowledge that workers may be adversely affected by either numerical flexibility or job enlargement.	Provide a good analysis of the implications of production flexibility on labour relations, revealing that workers may be affected by flexible production in a variety of ways, principally by functional and numerical flexibility. However fail to explore an additional possibility in the form of job enlargement.
Regulation	
Despite the fact that regulation is not at the centre of the theory, research has been undertaken into the regional regulatory structures of industrial districts.	Claim that regulation is the backbone of the theory but only look at the regulatory mechanisms of the state, failing to examine wider regulatory institutions such as the media.
Empirical Evidence	
Provide empirical evidence to support the theory of Flexible Specialisation, i.e. evidence of industrial districts in Italy, the reorganisation of multinational corporations in Germany.	Fail to provide empirical evidence to support the theory of Post-Fordism, i.e. no evidence from the USA, UK, France, Japan, Germany or Sweden to support their location on the diagram with respect to the position of Neo-Taylorism, Toyotism, Kalmarism.
Gender	
Totally ignore gender relations.	Skirt around the issue of gender relations but often fail to elaborate in any detail.

*This is primarily drawn from the work of Leborgne and Lipietz (1988, 1990) and Lipietz (1997)

However the empirical evidence of these two models primarily concerns production flexibility and therefore more detailed research on the implications of this production flexibility for labour is required.

A further requirement of this proposal is an expansion of research into the regulation of these various forms of Post-Fordism. This could be derived from the work of the Institutionalists on the regional regulatory structures of industrial districts (although it is important to ensure that these are explored within the context of the changing mode of regulation) and also by an extension of the existing work on state regulatory mechanisms by Regulationists such as Bakshi *et al.* (1995), Jessop (1993, 1994, 1995 a, 1995b), Goodwin and Painter (1995), Tickell and Peck (1995).

This utilisation of the basic theory of Regulation, within which insights from the Institutionalist supposition can be added, is important as it enables an analysis of the implications of economic restructuring on gender relations. Regulationist theory examines historical concepts, viewing the restructuring process as an outcome of a number of social, political and economic struggles, thus recognising that all social relations are constructed. This is particularly significant here as gender relations are considered to be socially constructed, this being exemplified by one of the oldest themes of the women's movement, that 'women are made and not born' (Jenson, 1990a, 1990b).

However, within this Regulationist framework, further research concerning the implications of economic restructuring on gender relations is required. This is particularly important if a gender dimension is to be incorporated into the existing restructuring debate. Women and men are located in different positions in the labour market and consequently will not necessarily be affected by the move towards Post-Fordism and the accompanying search for both production and labour flexibility in the same way. Leborgne and Lipietz (1990) and Lipietz (1997) have already made some limited inroads in this direction with respect to the regime of accumulation, suggesting that the presence of either functional flexibility under Kalmarism or numerical flexibility under Neo-Taylorism may be determined by gender. However the implications for gender relations do not stop here. As has been previously pointed out, some authors (Wood, 1986) have explored the extent to which Post-Fordism stimulates the development of either job enrichment or job enlargement and the degree to which this is determined by gender. Some limited research has also recently been conducted into gender and the mode of regulation, particularly in relation the welfare state (Bakshi *et al.*, 1995).

However, neither of these issues is explored in any substantial detail and they are undoubtedly not the only implications of the move towards Post-Fordism for gender relations, indicating the need for more theoretical and empirical research in this whole area. This is addressed in the subsequent chapters of this book.

3 The Implications of Post-Fordism for Gender Relations at Work

Introduction

Regulationists and Institutionalists fail to systematically address changing gender relations as part of their account of flexibility. Mutari and Figart (1997) recognise this, arguing that 'most of the literature on flexibility is silent on the gendered impact and meaning of economic restructuring' (p.689). Although some progress has been made in this direction recently, much of the restructuring analysis remains 'gender blind'. Many commentators fail to use gender neutral language, with workers often referred to as 'he' and when women are cited, they are still portrayed as different, peripheral and not like 'real' workers.

This omission is unwise given that 'feminisation' of the labour force is occurring at an unrelenting pace. McDougall (1998) suggests that increased female participation has been one of the major changes in the structure of the labour force in recent years. The share of female employment in Britain rose from 41 to 46 per cent between 1981 and 1997, a trend which is predicted to continue (DfEE, 1998). It is therefore essential that more research concerning the implications of economic restructuring on gender relations is carried out, particularly as men and women are located in different positions in the labour market, work in different industries and often in separate locations within the same workplace (Jenson, 1989b). Moreover the workforce has become increasingly polarised in terms of gender, with many women concentrated in jobs which are classified as unskilled or semi-skilled. Consequently women workers have not necessarily been affected by Post-Fordism in the same way as their male counterparts.

Some attempts have been made recently to redress this gap in the literature. Bakshi *et al.* (1995) have begun to examine gender relations with

50

respect to the mode of regulation, exploring the transition of the welfare state. Christopherson (1989), Jenson (1989b), McDowell (1991), Walby (1989), and more recently, Halford *et al.* (1997), and Ledwith and Colgan (1996) have carried out research into economic restructuring and gender relations, however, their work is by no means extensive and tends to be limited to an analysis of the tertiary sector. Other authors such as, Banshop and Doorewaard (1998), Baugh and Craen (1997), and Kahn (1999) have conducted studies of the implications of team working for gender relations, but they too have examined the tertiary sector.

Some authors have attempted to examine the gender implications of restructuring in the manufacturing sector, for example, Pollert (1996) and Wallace (1999). However, in general there has been an omission of research in this context, and given that mainstream economic restructuring theories focus specifically upon manufacturing industries, the importance of this absence cannot be understated.

The aim of this chapter is to provide an analysis of economic restructuring, gender relations and manufacturing employment. Two main issues are examined, workforce flexibility and technological change. Feminist literature is drawn upon, particularly that concerned with labour markets and related issues such as the core/periphery model (Beechey, 1987; Hakim, 1990a; Walby, 1989), the social construction of skill (Phillips and Taylor, 1980; Jenson, 1989b) and the gendering of new technology (Cockburn, 1983, 1985; Lloyd, 1997; Wajcman, 1991; Webster, 1996). Examples are drawn from the implementation of one form of Post-Fordism: team working in the manufacturing sector, as this is the focus of the empirical investigation outlined in chapters five and six.

Workforce Flexibility

Post-Fordists (Leborgne and Lipietz, 1988, 1990) argue that there has recently been a search for greater production and labour flexibility, which has wide implications for workers in general and women workers in particular. Leborgne and Lipietz (1990) and Lipietz (1997) argue that labour flexibility can be achieved through: Neo-Taylorism; Kalmarism; and Toyotism. An analysis of these scenarios in the previous chapter revealed that labour flexibility takes two principal directions, via functional flexibility and via numerical flexibility. Functional flexibility is present under Kalmarism and involves reducing job demarcations between occupations and the development of polyvalent skills which can be adapted to match output. Numerical flexibility is prevalent under Neo-Taylorism and refers to changing the size of the workforce in response to changing demands for goods and services. This is often associated with the use of atypical or non-standard work, such as part-time, temporary, casual, self employed or fixed term contracts (Atkinson, 1984; Green, 1994; Wood, 1989; Meulders *et al.*, 1997). Leborgne and Lipietz additionally argue that as functionally flexible workers are not expected to bear the brunt of numerically flexible tasks, a mixture of the two may prevail in the form of Toyotism. As firms search for these different types of worker flexibility, the labour force becomes segmented. Leborgne and Lipietz (1990) indicate that this segmentation may be determined by gender, but fail to explore this issue further.

This form of dualism can be likened to Atkinson's now dated, but still relevant *Flexible Firm* (1984), whereby the labour market is divided into a core and periphery. The core is depicted by multi-skilling, polyvalency, highly skilled tasks, full-time work, job security, high pay, promotion prospects, reskilling and retraining, the availability of pension and insurance schemes. The periphery is characterised by semi and unskilled tasks, part-time work, temporary contracts, low job security, low pay, few employment rights, little chance of training and disposable labour. It is widely argued (Harvey, 1990; Jenson, 1989b; Walby, 1989, 1997; Wood, 1989) that functional flexibility characterises the core and numerical flexibility the periphery.

Christopherson (1989) confirms this, arguing that the search for labour flexibility has led to a need for a smaller but more skilled 'core' workforce and a less skilled and quite vaguely defined 'peripheral' workforce. This is evident in the Italian industrial districts, where a few core final firms are surrounded by a buffer of peripheral stage firms, which provide numerical flexibility, thereby protecting the core firms from economic fluctuations. In the Carpi textile industrial district for example, innovative final firms which trade directly with international markets and continually update, modify and redesign products have a multi-skilled workforce, who experience job enrichment, thus providing functional flexibility (Solinas, 1982). A large number of peripheral stage firms specialising in one operation, such as buttonholing, packing or ironing, provide these core firms with numerical flexibility. The workers perform low skilled, monotonous, repetitive work and are easily dispensed of when the core firms reduce or switch subcontractors (*ibid.*).

Brusco (1992b) refutes the existence of this core/periphery model suggesting that the relationship between final firms and subcontractors is reciprocal. This may be true in some respects as subcontractors and final firms often have a close working relationship, cooperating in order to produce the required commodity. Nevertheless, subcontracting firms are often utilised in a numerically flexible manner and can be classed as peripheral. The degree to which subcontracting firms are used in this way is determined, in part, by the number of final firm customers. The jobs of a subcontractor which is dependant upon one final firm are more precarious than those which 'spread their risk' working for a number of final firms.

Benetton has frequently been cited as a classic example of the core/periphery scenario (Belussi, 1992). An internal, skilled, core, labour force, who are predominantly white collar, male workers are responsible for the control and coordination of production and distribution operations, while female workers perform the peripheral, blue collar, repetitive and fragmented operations (*ibid.*). This has important implications for gender relations, supporting the claims of Leborgne and Lipietz (1990) that within the Post-Fordist model labour may be fragmented (in terms of functional and numerical flexibility) according to gender. Beechey (1987) and Walby (1989, 1997) confirm the occurrences of the Benetton model elsewhere.

This raises questions in relation to the implications of Post-Fordism on gender relations, suggesting that the search for labour flexibility may lead to the maintenance of existing gender segregation in the workplace, whereby women form the majority of the numerically flexible workforce (the periphery) whilst male employees enjoy the functional flexibility of the core. However, as indicated in the previous chapter, the debate is more complex than these authors suggest and cannot be discussed accurately in such a dualistic fashion.

Functional flexibility may be manifested in a number of different ways. It may prove beneficial to the labour force, enabling them to experience the advantages of job enrichment. However, if the ethos of functional flexibility is only partially adopted, workers may instead experience the drawbacks of job enlargement. This may occur when new work practices are implemented, either based on the Japanese model of team working or on a variant of the Swedish prototype without the accompanying cultural changes. This indicates that while some workers will enjoy job enrichment, benefiting from the functional flexibility involved in Post-Fordism, others will inevitably suffer, experiencing job enlargement.

It is therefore insufficient to discuss the extent to which men experience functional flexibility, whilst women experience numerical flexibility, as some authors have done. What is required is an examination of the degree to which Post-Fordism leads to various forms of flexibility; numerical flexibility or functional flexibility (either in the form of job enrichment or job enlargement). Moreover, the extent to which the prevalence of each is determined by gender requires careful consideration. In order to cast some light on these issues, the concepts of both numerical and functional flexibility require further exploration.

Numerical Flexibility

Numerical flexibility is often associated with atypical working practices, which can be defined as any form of employment that lies outside the traditional full-time employment model. It therefore includes shift work, weekend work, self employment, temporary work, homework and part-time work (OECD, 1994, Meulders *et al*, 1997). Atypical work has traditionally been precarious, being unprotected by legislation, enabling employers to achieve numerical flexibility, hiring and firing workers at their own discretion (Mazey, 1988).

Christopherson (1989), McDowell (1991), Meulders *et al.* (1997) and Walby (1989, 1997) focus upon the increase in numerically flexible work practices, concluding that part-time work, temporary contracts and homeworking have been expanding and are primarily undertaken by women with caring responsibilities. This has meant that many women have become part of the peripheral workforce.

Much of this research explores the issues surrounding Post-Fordism and gender relations from a theoretical perspective, providing statistical supporting evidence of the changing ratio of permanent, full-time jobs to more atypical employment practices. This evidence is drawn from nationwide surveys encompassing all industrial sectors, without the provision of detailed empirical evidence from a particular industrial sector. Moreover, where this type of empirical evidence is provided, the research is often limited to an analysis of the tertiary sector (for example Christopherson, 1989).

In order to examine this issue in more detail, three main issues are explored in this part of the chapter: the extent to which Post-Fordism has been accompanied by an expansion in numerically flexible work practices; the degree to which these jobs are performed by women; and the extent to which domestic and caring responsibilities influence this. The first two of these issues will now be explored together, followed by an examination of the third.

Post-Fordism, Numerical Flexibility and Gender: the Evidence During the twentieth century the balance steadily changed from traditional, permanent, full-time employment towards atypical employment practices, a trend which escalated after the 1970s (Hakim, 1990b). This trend was dominant throughout the European Union, but was particularly pronounced in Great Britain, where 38 per cent of all people in employment in 1993 were classified as belonging to the flexible workforce (Green, 1994). The number of workers employed on a full-time basis in the Britain fell from 85 per cent in 1971 (Office of Population, Census and Surveys, 1971) to just 65 per cent in 1993 (Office of Population, Census and Surveys, 1993). Simultaneously the number employed on a 'non-standard basis' increased. Thus in 1997, part-time workers in Britain accounted for 29 per cent of employees in employment, the comparable figure for self employed workers being 13 per cent. Moreover, both are estimated to grow even further, as a proportion of employees in employment, by 2007 (DfEE, 1998).

Most authors writing in this field recognise the growing importance of numerically flexible contracts. For example, a survey of firms by Cully *et al.* (1999) revealed that the use of numerical flexibility had increased in recent years. Dex (1999) likewise suggests that additional types of flexible employment, such as term-time only working, annual hours and zero hours contracts, are now becoming more evident.

One notable exception is Pollert (1988), who rejects the significance of the growth of numerical flexibility, arguing that it is nothing new and has always been present during the post war period. To this extent Pollert is correct, however she refuses to recognise that with the emergence of Post-Fordism from the 1970s onwards, the speed of this casualisation of the workforce has escalated. As Hakim (1990a) points out, these are not new forms of work, they are old, however the pace of change is new. Pollert's work is further impaired as she fails to acknowledge that the reasons behind the search for labour flexibility have changed in recent years with the demise of the dominance of Fordism. Since the 1970s the use of numerically flexible workers has been determined by different motives than those of the preceding two decades. This is reaffirmed by Beechey's study of Coventry's manufacturing industry, which concluded that during the 1950s and 60s part-time labour was utilised as a means of cutting costs, while in the 1970s part-timers were employed to maintain continuous production and to provide a flexible labour force (Beechey, 1987).

This growth of atypical work has implications for gender relations. Hakim (1990b) and Meulders *et al.* (1997) argue that throughout Europe non-standard work, particularly part-time jobs, are frequently held by female employees. The various types of atypical work practices (encompassing part-time work, temporary contracts and homeworkers) will now be analysed in order to examine the extent to which they constitute numerical flexibility and the degree to which they are occupied by women.

Part-time employment is usually defined as regular work, carried out during working hours which are distinctly shorter than normal (Robinson, 1988). Part-time work has been a key element in the move to atypical employment and has recently spread throughout the European Union (European Commission, 1992; Meulders *et al.*, 1997). However the dominance of part-time work varies enormously between different countries. It is almost non-existent in southern European countries like Italy, Greece, Portugal and Spain and is most pronounced in the Netherlands and the UK (Meulders *et al.*, 1997; OECD, 1998).

Part-time workers in Britain have traditionally been utilised in a numerically flexible manner, as Blanchflower and Corry (1989) confirm. However, recent legislation has meant that the ability of employers to use part-timers in this way has steadily been eroded. Until recently, British part-time workers have held precarious positions, enjoying fewer employment rights than their full-time counterparts (Hakim, 1990b; Social Europe, 1992). Traditionally employees must have worked at least sixteen hours a week with the same employer for two years to be eligible for employment rights, such as protection from unfair dismissal, paid maternity leave and redundancy pay. Additionally those who worked between eight and sixteen hours a week must have been with an employer for five years to qualify for security of employment (Walby, 1986).

Recent pressure from the European Union has, however, forced the British government to bring the UK in line with European equality directives and since February 1995 all distinctions in employment protection legislation based on the numbers of hours worked per week have been removed. Part-timers are now entitled to the same statuary rights as full-timers (Industrial Relations Service, 1995a, 1995b). The Employment Relations Act of 1999 has extended these regulations to provide part-timers with the right, from July 2000, not to be treated less favourably than comparable full-time workers in terms of pay, training, maternity and parental leave (DTI, 2000).

Compared to full-time workers, part-timers in Britain (until recently) have therefore enjoyed fewer employment rights, providing employers with a greater potential to utilise part-time workers in a numerically flexible manner. Consequently, it appears on the surface, that as part-time work has expanded in the last three decades both male and female workers have become numerically flexible and thus part of the peripheral labour market (Employment Gazette, 1993). A more in-depth analysis, however, suggests that women and men have not been influenced by this expansion of part-time work in the same way. Part-time work is traditionally occupied by female as opposed to male workers. Indeed the majority of the part-time work is available in the service sector, which employs a large proportion of women. In 1990, for example, there were nearly four times as many service sector employees working on a part-time basis in the UK than in the manufacturing sector (Anon, 1990; OECD, 1994), a statistic which retained validity during the latter part of the 1990s (DfEE, 1998).

The dominance of women in part-time employment is evident throughout Europe. In 1997 the proportion of women working part-time amounted to 32 per cent, the comparable figure for men being just six per cent (European Commission, 1998). This pattern is even more pronounced in the UK, with 45 per cent of women in paid employment in 1998 working on a part-time basis, compared to just nine per cent of the male workforce (Central Statistical Office, 1999).

Temporary working is slightly more complex. There are two main forms of temporary work: Temporary Work Agencies (TWA), where a worker is contracted out to a firm for a specified period of time; and fixed term contracts, where individuals are employed directly for a fixed period of time, i.e. with a specific termination date (OECD, 1994). Synonymous with part-time work, temporary employment has been growing recently. Although temporary jobs represent only a small proportion of total employment in the European Union (approximately 12 per cent in 1998), the proportion has steadily been increasing in virtually all member states (European Commission, 1998).

The UK has not been an exception to this trend, and in 1998 there were 1.7 million people in temporary jobs, representing 6.5 per cent of all those in employment. Over half of these were employed on fixed term contracts, 19 per cent in casual employment and 14 per cent worked for a Temporary Work Agency (Labour Force Survey, 1998).

Since 1991 both temporary and seasonal work has become particularly important in Southern Europe and has even spread to Italy which has traditionally had fewer temporary workers than the rest of Europe. For example, young Italian women have been hired for three months or less, once or twice in the same year in local government, education, the postal or telephone service, thereby allowing the public services to be flexible to changes in demand (Stratigaki and Vaiou, 1994).

Temporary work is capable of being numerically flexible. Temporary workers often have fewer employment rights and social protection, are subject to automatic dismissal procedures, have no entitlements to severance pay and therefore have little employment security (OECD, 1994).

The extent to which temporary work can be classified as numerically flexible varies between different countries and is primarily dependant upon the degree of government regulation. The greater the degree of government regulation, the less likely that temporary contracts will be used for numerically flexible purposes. Regulation for temporary workers has traditionally been minimal in the UK. Fixed term contracts can be renewed at will and Temporary Work Agencies are governed by minimal regulations. As a result temporary workers hold precarious jobs and can be dismissed easily by the employer (OECD, 1994).

However, legislation in this area is constantly being reviewed and indeed a new European Directive for fixed term workers has been formulated, the deadline for implementation being July 2001. This agreement will provide British workers on fixed term contracts with greater employment protection rights. It will forbid employers to treat fixed term workers in a less favourable manner than their permanent counterparts and will aim to prevent abuse of successive fixed term contracts (European Commission, 2000b). The position for temporary agency workers in Britain may also become more secure in the near future. The Employment Relations Act 1999 gave the government the power to review rights of workers who are not employees, including those working for temporary agencies. As a result, a consultation exercise is due to start towards the end of 2000.

There is some evidence to suggest that temporary workers are more likely to be female, with 13 per cent of women and 11 per cent of men in the European Union, in 1997, being employed on a temporary basis. Moreover, the percentage of women in temporary contracts was higher than for men in all member states (European Commission, 1998). Indeed, a survey of temporary workers in Great Britain found that just under 70 per cent were female (Tremlett and Collins, 1999).

Many temporary workers also work on a part-time basis, again this particularly affects women. In 1990 approximately 40 per cent of women on a fixed term contract in the European Union were also employed on a part-time basis, this compares to just 20 per cent for men (European Commission, 1992). Dex (1999) reveals a similar trend in the UK, with a higher proportion of women in temporary jobs, in 1996, working on a part-time as opposed to a full-time basis.

Homeworking is another important form of atypical work. In 1998 it was estimated that 6.9 million people in the European Union usually perform work at home, equivalent to 4.9 per cent of the population

(European Commission, 2000a). However, its precise incidence and range is difficult to asses (Rowbotham and Tate, 1998). This is partly because homeworkers are often not officially registered and partly due to difficulties with the definition of homeworkers.

Homeworkers are especially dominant in the Mediterranean countries. In Italy and Greece, for example, homeworking is a common phenomenon, being widespread across all industrial sectors in the former and predominant in the clothing industry in the latter (Stratigaki and Vaiou, 1994). The dominance of homeworkers in Italy is partly due to the Italian labour law which states that firms employing no more than ten employees and five apprentices are considered as artisanal and can avoid minimum employment rights, unfair dismissal laws etc. In order to keep below these levels and thus qualify, firms employ homeworkers (Solinas, 1982).

The UK also has its share of homeworkers, and although the precise number is difficult to gauge, there were an estimated 621,000 homeworkers in 1998, accounting for 2.4 per cent of all those in employment (Felstead and Jewson, 2000; Labour Force Survey, 1998).

The importance of homeworking has grown in recent years throughout Europe and Wajcman (1991) argues that the expansion of white collar homeworking since the 1970s has played a large role in this. The development of computer systems and telecommunications, in particular electronic mail, have made it feasible for large numbers of people to work from terminals at home.

Homeworking is a particularly important form of atypical work as it enhances numerical flexibility. Homeworkers often work on an informal basis, operate without an official contract, have few if any employment rights, such as social security benefits, sickness pay and have no security of employment. They can be dismissed without either motive or compensation, allowing firms to adapt quickly to changes in demand (Stratigaki and Vaiou, 1994; Rowbotham and Tate, 1998). In addition to these precarious employment practices, homeworkers are often paid on a piecework payment system and earn a lot less than comparable office or factory workers, earning in some instances just fifty pence an hour, as well as having to meet their own overheads/costs (Rigg and Miller, 1991; Wajcman, 1991; Phizacklea and Wolkowitz, 1995).

However, this insecurity of employment may change within the next few years. The European Union has recently recommended that all member states ratify the ILO Homework Convention of 1996 which provides a framework for protecting homeworkers, thereby helping to achieve a balance between flexibility of the labour market and security of employees (European Commission, 2000a).

It is widely claimed that the majority of homeworkers throughout Europe are women (Allen and Wolkowitz, 1987; European Commission, 2000a; Rigg and Miller, 1991; Rowbotham and Tate, 1998). Allen and Wolkowitz (1987) and Phizacklea and Wolkowitz (1995) reveal that the majority of homeworkers in Britain are women, with a high percentage being from ethnic minority groups. Belussi (1992) similarly points out that the majority of Italian homeworkers are women, aged seventeen to twenty-five.

It must however be recognised that some homeworkers are men, although they tend to work *from* home rather than *at* home. These men are often self employed professionals or managerial staff operating a small business from home, earning substantially higher wages than their female counterparts (Wajcman, 1991). The majority, but not all, of such professional homeworkers are male. In fact, in 1999, only 26 per cent of self employed people in employment the UK were women (Office for National Statistics, 2000).

Numerical Flexibility and Gender: the Explanations Women often perform a dual role in society in terms of work. They participate in paid employment in the formal labour market and in unpaid work (including domestic and caring activities) in the informal labour market. In order to accommodate these two roles, many women find it difficult to work on a full-time basis, working part-time, in temporary jobs, or at home.

Let's firstly examine women's role in domestic responsibilities. For many years, it has been widely recognised that society has been constructed in such a way that it is perceived the 'norm' for women to perform most domestic and household tasks (Bradley, 1999; Pollert, 1981; Westwood, 1984; Rigg and Miller, 1991; Showstack Sassoon, 1987). This is the case throughout Europe but has been most pronounced in southern European countries where traditional values concerning gender roles remain intact (Stratigaki and Vaiou, 1994). However, even in northern European countries where there has been some reversal of gender roles, domestic and household chores remain the prime responsibility of women. This makes it difficult for women to participate in the labour market on a full-time, permanent basis.

Pollert's (1981) research of women tobacco workers exemplifies this. The majority of the workers carried out most domestic duties, as well as taking the major responsibility for childcare, and thus viewed part-time work as a more viable option. Westwood's study (1984) reaffirmed this, with many of the women she talked to stating that they were too tired to sustain two full-time jobs - paid work and housework. As one woman explained 'we do two jobs, one here and one in the house. We'd earn a fortune if we ever got paid for both' (Westwood, 1984, p.164).

These research findings remain valid today, as Dex (1999) confirms. She suggests that, although the proportion of men performing domestic and household tasks has increased in Britain, it is still mainly women who are responsible for most of these duties. She points to a pilot study in 1995, for a national time use survey, which showed that mothers spent four times as long per day as fathers cooking and carrying out housework.

It is widely believed that men are guilty of having such stereotypical views, however, women themselves often reproduce these values. The women that Westwood (1984) spoke to felt that they were conducting 'proper' feminine work when they were doing housework and tended to bring their children up in the same gender stereotypical ways. Although this research was some sixteen years ago, and these gender stereotypical values are slowly being eroded, Bradley (1999), Dex (1999) and Williams (1997) reveal that these attitudes still exist amongst large sections of the population.

Alongside domestic tasks, it has also traditionally been perceived that women have the main responsibility for caring activities. Again some progress has been made in this direction and increasingly more men are participating in caring duties. However, the main burden for the care of children, the elderly, disabled and sick adults still rests with women (Daycare Trust, 1998, Williams, 1997). Indeed, Dex (1999) recently pointed out that mothers spend three times as long, per day, than fathers caring for children and adults. She explains that fathers still tend to fit family commitments around their working lives, whilst mothers usually fit labour market activities around their family responsibilities.

This division of caring labour, in terms of gender, restricts the terms and conditions on which women participate in paid employment and creates a number of conflicts over the balancing and use of time (Dell' Orto, 1993). Some women find it difficult to participate in paid employment at all and if they do manage to accommodate their caring responsibilities alongside paid employment they are more likely to be employed on a part-time or temporary basis.

The caring role of women involves two principal groups, the elderly and children although it also extends to include the mentally ill, those with learning difficulties, the long term chronically ill and the physically disabled (Crompton *et al.*, 2000; Drew, 1998; Graham, 1984; Finch, 1989).

As the population is rapidly ageing, care of the elderly is becoming an increasingly important issue (Dex, 1999; Phillips, 1998; Showstack Sassoon, 1987). In the UK, the number of people over the age of 65 has increased by one quarter between 1971 and 1991 and is estimated to rise even further during the next twenty years (Office for National Statistics, 1998). The number of very old i.e. those over 75 and those over 85 is expected to increase by 22 per cent and 25 per cent respectively between 2001 and 2021 (*ibid.*). Therefore people are living longer and are reaching an age where they need help and assistance in caring for themselves.

The 1995 General Household Survey revealed that, in Britain, one adult in eight were providing informal care and that one in six households contained a carer (Dex, 1999). Furthermore, the carers are most likely to be female, with women accounting for 60 per cent of all carers in 1995 (Office for National Statistics, 1998). This pattern is reflected in other countries such as Italy where care of the elderly is almost exclusively performed by families and the primary carer is almost always a woman, often a daughter or daughter-in-law (Dell' Orto, 1993).

There is often societal pressure on women to care for elderly relatives. It is deemed the 'right thing to do' if a woman, particularly a daughter, relinquishes her job to look after an elderly relative and the female carer receives public endorsement (Finch, 1989). Women are defined culturally as being more able to provide personal care for the elderly than men are. Indeed it is women, in general, who are expected to do the personal, intimate, dirty caring jobs.

In western society it is still the 'norm' for women to have the prime responsibility for the care of young dependants (Beechey, 1987; Dex, 1988, 1999; Walby, 1986; Williams, 1997). Both childbearing and rearing are perceived as exclusively female domains. Historically it was seen as damaging to the child if the mother was not there to look after it. This is exemplified by the work of John Bowlby, a social psychologist. In the 1950s he argued that the nature of the mother/child bond was central to the mental health of the future adult and his work was widely interpreted to mean that any separation of mother and child was damaging. This resulted in the production of a pamphlet in 1958 entitled 'can I leave my baby?'. The advice he gave suggested that apart from a brief shopping trip, the answer was no! (Riley, 1983, p.10). Over forty years later this issue is still one being debated in Britain. Indeed, a television documentary in 2000 focused on working mothers and the detrimental impact it has on their children (BBC, 2000).

This exemplifies the way in which gender roles are socially constructed in society and stereotypical views of both masculine and feminine roles are formed. Many women and men still tend to hold the view that childrearing is the main responsibility of the female and women often fail to question their role in the childrearing process, accepting it as an inevitable outcome.

Although it is now becoming more socially acceptable for men to participate in caring duties, it is still often difficult for both men and women to depart from these traditional gender roles. Men who wish to take the main responsibility for childrearing may be seen as strange and effeminate, while women who choose not to take the main responsibility for childrearing, can be viewed as masculine, uncaring and 'bad mothers'. This pressure to conform comes not only from society but from individuals themselves. Many women take the prime responsibility for childrearing as they are overcome by feelings of guilt.

One of the main arguments traditionally put forward in support of women being the prime carers is that their participation in paid employment is less significant than that of their male counterparts. Women are deemed as the natural carers and men as the natural breadwinners who have other, more important commitments in the formal labour market (Anon, 2000; Finch, 1989).

However in recent years there has been a growth in female participation rates in the labour force, with all European countries experiencing an increase in the number of women entering paid work since the 1970s. The only exception to this has been in the Scandinavian countries of Finland, Sweden and Denmark, where female labour force participation rates, although by far the highest in Europe, have fallen slightly in the 1990s (OECD, 1998; European Commission, 1998). As a consequence women are experiencing greater pressure, increasingly entering paid employment but remaining the prime carers. In attempts to perform these two conflicting roles, more women are searching for atypical employment, working less hours, often on a part-time basis or taking less permanent employment contracts.

Analysis of employment in the European Union reveals that mothers with a child are more likely to be in part-time employment than those without a child (Moss, 1990; European Commission, 1998). This is particularly pronounced in the UK where, in 1999, only 25 per cent of married or cohabiting women with no dependent children worked part-time, compared to 50 per cent of those with a youngest child aged between five and ten (Central Statistical Office, 2000). Moreover, due to their caring role, some women may be effectively housebound, unable to participate in paid employment away from their place of residence, hence resorting to homeworking.

The extent to and terms on which women are able to participate in paid employment, while performing both domestic and caring activities, is dependant upon the welfare provision available. The greater the provision of welfare services such as childcare, employment leave (maternity, parental and family), institutions for the elderly, home helps and so on, the higher the propensity of women to participate in full-time, paid employment. Welfare provision varies from country to country and hence so do the terms on which women participate in paid employment.

In some countries, such as Sweden, extensive welfare provision is available (Scheibl and Dex, 1998). Public facilities cater for a large percentage of pre-school children and Sweden has one of the highest percentage, in the western world, of children under six years old enrolled in public day and childcare institutions (Siim, 1991). Similarly Sweden has very generous paid leave provision for parents. As a result of these welfare policies there has been an increase in the number of women with children participating in the labour market, particularly on a full-time permanent basis and as previously stated Sweden now has one of the highest female participation rates in paid employment in Europe (OECD, 1998).

Welfare policy in Britain is substantially different. During the 1980s, and early 1990s, there was a reduction in welfare provision. For a number of years childcare provision in Britain was viewed as inadequate and amongst the worst in Europe (McDowell, 1991). However, in the last decade this has changed and there have been large increases in the numbers of young children placed in the care of day nurseries, childminders and out-of-school clubs (Scott, 1998; Yeandle, 1999a). The election of a Labour government in 1997 saw the introduction of policies aiming to provide better childcare. In 1998, the government launched The National Childcare Strategy with the aim of developing high quality, affordable childcare. It has also introduced a national minimum wage, which attempted to help support working parents, and has extended maternity leave, parental leave and time off for dependents. Furthermore, it has supported and encouraged the provision of 'family friendly employment policies' which are defined by Simkin and Hillage (1992) as 'a formal or informal set of terms and conditions which are designed to enable an employee to combine family responsibilities with employment'. Examples include flexible working arrangements, childcare, parental leave, and career breaks.

The expansion of childcare has meant that more women in Britain are participating in the labour force, and are returning to work after the birth of a child. However, the age of the youngest child is still important in determining women's participation in the labour market. In 1997, 57 per cent of mothers living as part of a couple with a child under the age of five were employed. This figure increased to 72 per cent for mothers with a youngest child aged five to nine, and 78 per cent with a youngest child aged over ten. However, a large proportion of these still work on a part-time basis, only 21 per cent of those with a youngest child under the age of five working full-time, compared to 41 per cent of those with a youngest child over the age of 16 (Dex, 1999).

Lewis (1992) explains the European variations of the participation of women in full-time permanent employment by the dominance of the male breadwinner model which advocates gender segregation of tasks i.e. that men are the breadwinners, whilst women are the carers and home-makers. Lewis argues that some countries such as Britain and Ireland have a strong male breadwinner model, France has a modified model, while the male breadwinner model in Sweden is weak. Wallace (1999) therefore suggests that Swedish women find it easier to participate in paid employment, particularly in full-time employment, than British women. However this has not eliminated all the problems for women in Sweden. Stereotypical gender attitudes towards caring and household tasks remain and therefore so does their role in unpaid employment (Forsberg, 1994; Lewis, 1992; Wallace, 1999).

It can be seen, therefore, that Post-Fordism has stimulated an expansion of numerically flexible work practices which, in turn, has had drawbacks for women employees in Britain who form part of the peripheral labour market. Furthermore, women will continue to occupy these jobs until stereotypical gender roles change and investment in welfare provision is improved further still.

Functional Flexibility

Institutionalists and Regulationists agree that functional flexibility is an outcome of the search for a flexible workforce. Piore and Sabel (1984) suggest that Italian industrial districts have led to functional flexibility, whilst Sabel (1989), Leborgne and Lipietz (1988, 1990), and Lipietz (1997) argue that the reorganisation of corporations on the basis of team working does the same. The key difference between the two theories is that the Institutionalists suggest that Flexible Specialisation necessarily leads to functional flexibility, whilst Regulationists argue that Post-Fordism may instead result in numerical flexibility.

Despite these fundamental differences, they both define functional flexibility in the same way, as beneficial to labour, leading to job enrichment. However, functional flexibility may instead lead to job enlargement, a factor which both schools of restructuring omit from their analysis. It has been suggested (Wood, 1986) that this may have implications for gender relations, with women's job's being enlarged whilst men's are enriched. However, as Wilson (1995) confirms, substantial research has yet to be undertaken in this area.

Post-Fordism: Job Enrichment or Job Enlargement Research in the early 1990s (Buchanan, 1994, Dawson and Webb, 1989, and Tomaney, 1990) indicated that Post-Fordism can lead to job enlargement as well as job enrichment, as the Regulationists argue. Dawson and Webb's (1989) study of the microelectronics industry revealed that the majority of assemblers, following the introduction of flexible production methods, worked on a range of products and carried out a variety of tasks but that the tasks were at a similar level.

The extent to which the workforce experience either job enrichment or job enlargement is determined by the way in which work is reorganised. This is evident when analysing the implementation of team working. The Japanese model emphasises technological innovation and therefore machines are introduced which shorten and simplify individual tasks, thus enabling operatives to perform a greater number of activities. Workers are expected to perform a wider range of similar activities, utilising several different machines as opposed to the one used on the production line. Management and supervisors retain control over the workforce, preventing them from performing higher order tasks requiring a greater degree of responsibility and judgement (Tomaney, 1990). The result is that the jobs of operatives are enlarged rather than enriched (Buchanan, 1994).

The Swedish model of team working should, in contrast, lead to job enrichment. In fact advocates of team working in the British clothing industry justify its implementation for precisely these reasons (NEDO, 1991b; Tyler, 1994). The emphasis is on operative as opposed to machine utilisation and therefore polyvalency is promoted, whereby workers carry out more tasks of a discretionary nature, such as decision making, problem solving and line balancing (Carrere and Little, 1989). Individual talents and knowledge are utilised and workers are appreciated as a valuable resource, enjoying greater autonomy. This can facilitate career progression, providing operatives with greater confidence and status, serving to encourage some to seek promotion to supervisory and management grades (Farrands and Totterdill, 1990).

However, the Swedish model will only have this enriching effect if management adopt a systematic approach to its implementation. There are a number of constraints which may prevent this 'ideal' model being developed and in these circumstances the workforce may instead experience job enlargement. These potential constraints encompass management style and training.

Management style can take two principal forms, responsible autonomy and direct control (Friedman, 1977). Under responsible autonomy managers give workers enhanced status, authority and responsibility in an attempt to gain worker loyalty. Direct control, on the other hand, is a strategy aimed at limiting the scope of labour power by the use of coercive threats, close supervision and by reducing individual responsibility.

If management are to adopt the full ethos of the Swedish prototype, the labour force must be controlled by responsible autonomy. It is only with this type of management that team members are able to work autonomously and reap the benefits of job enrichment (McLellan *et al.*, 1996). However, management may be wary of change and feel that by enhancing the powers of the labour force their own position will be undermined. They may attempt to implement team working while maintaining the traditional autocratic style of management necessary under line production, and retain direct control over their workforce (*ibid.*). In these situations companies merely pay 'lip service' to the Swedish notion of team working and team members are deprived of the enhanced responsibility, autonomy and control which is evident when the Swedish 'ideal' is adopted. Instead they experience job enlargement.

The second issue governing the extent to which team members experience job enrichment or job enlargement concerns training. Training of all members of staff is vital if it is to enrich the jobs of team members (Tyler, 1994). Operatives should receive continuous training and education in both technical and social skills. In the clothing industry, for example, team members should be trained to perform a wider range of machining tasks facilitating multi-skilling, while simultaneously acquiring the ability to perform more tasks of a discretionary nature (Carrere and Little, 1989). Moreover, it is essential that this training is provided by qualified and experienced personnel. This ensures that standardised techniques are adhered to and that the workforce experience an enrichment of their working lives (McLellan *et al.*, 1996).

Team working can, on the other hand, be introduced without comprehensive training. Management are often reluctant to invest into training workers who may subsequently leave the company. Indeed Weintraub (1987) argues that extensive training produces a number of increased risks and costs, and turnover often becomes a 'death knell' for the company. Reluctance to invest in training can result in two situations. Firstly, management may expect operatives to cross train each other. NEDO (1991b) in fact advocated that each team member should train their fellow colleagues in their main skill. Secondly, training may be provided but not to an adequate level. Management may refuse to train staff in wider social techniques, limiting education to pure technical skills. In both these situations team members are able to perform a wider range of operative tasks but their ability to perform tasks of a more discretionary nature is restricted. In these circumstances it is more likely that the workforce will experience job enlargement rather than job enrichment.

If team working is to enrich the jobs of operatives, training of both management and supervisors is also essential. Management require extensive training if they are to adapt to a new role which facilitates increased worker responsibility and autonomy. They must be trained to discard the day to day 'fire fighting' techniques utilised under line production, to trust the ability of their workforce, to become person managers and to be responsible for teaching individuals how to be involved and how to work as team members (Tyler, 1994). Supervisors likewise must be trained to become 'facilitators', 'coaches' or 'enablers' (Carrere and Little, 1989), instead of 'policing' operatives as in line production. They must learn how to devolve tasks to operatives for whom they were previously responsible (*ibid.*). However, if both management and supervisors fail to receive comprehensive training, they will be less likely to devolve powers and responsibilities to the workforce. As a result, team members will be expected to carry out more tasks of a similar nature leading to job enlargement but will not be given the opportunity to perform the more discretionary tasks involved in job enrichment.

The type of management style adopted and the quantity and quality of training provided therefore act as barriers preventing team members working within the Swedish prototype from experiencing job enrichment.

When analysing the impact of both the Swedish and Japanese systems of team working it is also important to examine the type of payment systems adopted, as this governs whether or not team members are financially awarded for obtaining more skills and influences the way in which both job enrichment and job enlargement affect the workforce. Team working is often accompanied by variations of flat rate or piecerate payment systems.

Flat rate infers that team members are paid a fixed amount each week, providing stable earnings and security of income. Piecerate means that operatives are paid 'by results', being financially rewarded for operating faster. Piecerate is often deployed under the traditional production line as it is believed to be the only method of staff motivation. The more able and quicker members of the workforce often benefit from piecework, earning relatively high wages (*ibid.*). However, piecework has its drawbacks: it fails to provide security of income, with operatives experiencing week to week fluctuations in take home pay, and it is unfair to those workers who are slower or are placed on slower operations.

Tyler (1994) suggests that ideally the introduction of team working should be accompanied by a flat rate payment system, however a variation of piecerate may often be retained. This, in many cases, involves the development of a group piecework payment system, whereby each team member is paid a common wage which is related to the overall group performance in terms of output. This has wider drawbacks for the workforce, with individual wages being dependent on the performance of team colleagues. Slower operatives may reduce the overall performance level of the team, leading to ill feeling, particularly amongst the fast performers, the so called 'high flyers'. Further peer pressure may also arise, with operatives who are genuinely ill being reluctant to take time off work and developing feelings of guilt for 'letting the side down' (McLellan *et al.*, 1996).

Job Enrichment, Job Enlargement and Gender: the Evidence There is some evidence to suggest that the way in which work is reorganised, and therefore the extent to which the workforce experience job enlargement or job enrichment, may be determined by gender. Dawson and Webb (1989), Elger (1991), Elsass and Graves (1997), and Wood (1986) suggest that women's jobs will be reorganised in such a way that they are enlarged, whilst the jobs of their male counterparts will be reorganised in a way which enriches. This again highlights the presence of the core/periphery model, whereby women are allocated peripheral activities.

Elger's (1991) study of electrical engineering sites concluded that while white male jobs were enriched following the introduction of flexible production methods, female jobs were enlarged. Similar evidence is provided by Dawson and Webb's (1989) study of the micro-electronics industry. They found that the introduction of Just In Time (JIT) and Total Quality Control (TQC) led to both up and deskilling. The upskilled work tasks were carried out by men, whilst the deskilled, routinised, computer controlled, tasks were allocated to women. Dawson and Webb state that:

> the reskilling of women assembly workers has largely been restricted to the adoption of Totally Quality Control (TQC) techniques to service on line quality control rather than the acquisition of technical knowledge to enable

the free movement of assembles across a wider range of tasks. Consequently, significant labour flexibility remains the preserve of the male dominated technician and graduate engineering workforce (Dawson and Webb, 1989, p.230).

Further evidence that work restructuring is not without gender bias is provided by Wood (1986) who examined the introduction of team working in the automobile industry and found that team working differentially affected men and women:

> for many of the male production workers, who were working individually, the scheme had basically facilitated regular small group (quality circle) meetings; whilst for the women who were working on short assembly lines at various points in the production process, it largely meant job rotation, that is increased mobility between very limited tasks, albeit on a basis worked out by the women themselves
> (Wood, 1986, p.426).

Similarly, Elsass and Graves (1997) suggest that women and 'people of colour' are likely to be marginalised under team working. They are often assigned low status jobs and seen as incapable of performing higher level tasks unlike their white male counterparts.

Job Enrichment, Job Enlargement and Gender: the Explanations Wood (1986) argues that team working has differential gender implications due to the distinct relationships that women and men have to technology. The issue of technology and gender is expanded upon later in this chapter, but is not sufficient alone to explain why women's jobs are more likely to be enlarged and men's to be enriched. Feminist theories concerning the social construction of skill are crucial here. The idea that skills are socially constructed is not new. Jenson has argued for many years that skilled work is defined by a variety of social mechanisms and that these skill differentiations are often identified in terms of gender. The jobs that men do are seen as skilled, whereas the jobs that women perform are often classed as unskilled, merely involving some sort of natural 'female talent' (Jenson, 1989b).

Pollert expands on this, arguing that qualities such as close concentration, accuracy and manual dexterity require skill and training, but are relegated to 'natural' and untrained 'aptitudes' when performed by women (Pollert, 1981, p.65). Gardiner (1997) suggests that this concept is still valid today. Skills that women possess are seen as natural feminine traits which are not acquired through a complex learning process and are therefore undervalued. Birmbaum summarises these points '...it is the sex of those who do the work, rather than its content which leads to its identification of skilled or unskilled work' (Truman and Keating, 1987, p.27).

This is exemplified by Truman and Keating, who point out that when machining in the clothing industry has been carried out by men it has been seen as skilled, but when performed by female workers it is classed as unskilled. These gender differentiations are justified by the separation of male and female workers, thus historically male machinists have been tailors manufacturing individual, high quality garments, whilst female machinists have manufactured standardised garments in large factories (Truman and Keating, 1987).

This concept of the social construction of skill can be explicitly linked to the debate concerning job enlargement and job enrichment and is evident when examining team working. Male employees are viewed as capable of working autonomously in small work groups carrying out polyvalent tasks and therefore tend to benefit from the search for flexibility via job enrichment. In contrast, female workers may be viewed as incapable of working more autonomously, suffering the drawbacks of job enlargement instead. This suggests that different forms of team working may be implemented in accordance with the sex of the employees. Hence, if the workforce is predominantly male, the Swedish prototype which enriches jobs may be introduced. However, if the workforce is predominantly female, either the Japanese or the variant of the Swedish model which stimulates job enlargement, may prevail. This process can be explained by two key factors, managers may be: a) unwilling to change their style of management when employing a female workforce; and b) unwilling to invest in staff training.

Firstly management style will be explored. Instead of changing their style of management to responsible autonomy when implementing team working, managers may retain direct control over their female workforce believing that they are not capable of handling a greater degree of responsibility, autonomy and control. Managers are often male and may feel that their masculine power is being threatened by empowering female employees, whom both they and the women themselves view as marginal and unskilled workers (Forsberg, 1994). In these circumstances women workers will be deprived of the benefits of job enrichment suffering instead the drawbacks of job enlargement.

Secondly the issue of training will be examined. Women are not only viewed as incapable of performing skilled work requiring any responsibility and discretion but are also often viewed as naturally 'unreliable', due to menstruation and pregnancy (Westwood, 1984). These stereotypical opinions of women and work have been eroded to some extent since this work was published, but still remain intact amongst large sections of the population.

The introduction of team working in companies with a predominantly female workforce means that management are less likely to invest in training and therefore job enlargement rather than enrichment may prevail. Management may refuse to adequately train female employees for two main reasons. Firstly, they may believe that it is not worth investing large amounts of resources into training a female labour force who may become pregnant and subsequently leave the company (Cockburn, 1983; Westwood, 1984), a view which is still often held today across British industries. As one male employer stated '...it costs £5000 for the boss to train a woman up and what if she then toddles off and has a baby?' (Cockburn, 1983, p.178). In these circumstances women workers will be expected to learn additional skills themselves or from a willing colleague. The second explanation can again be linked to the social construction of skill. As female workers are viewed as unskilled and peripheral in the workplace, managers may believe that although they are capable of acquiring more skills of a similar status they are unable to perform tasks of a more discretionary nature (Horrell *et al.*, 1990; Jenson, 1989b). In this case management may provide technical but not wider social training.

It is even less likely that managers of a female workforce will receive training themselves when team working is implemented. This is particularly true in Britain where management 'learn by doing' rather than by technical education and training. In fact the majority of British managers throughout the industrial sectors receive only minimal training, a fact which Nicholson and West (1988) point out and which retains validity in the 21st century. A large proportion of British managers possess no post-school qualifications at all and are very rarely provided with training, even when they change jobs. This has therefore created a culture in Britain whereby management resist training, believing that they 'know best' in terms of management technique.

The reluctance of managers to receive training may be especially severe if the workforce is female. Management often believe that they require less training to manage a female workforce, who are seen as less assertive, less confident, and less sure of their own abilities than men and therefore easier to control (Cockburn, 1985; Nicholson and West, 1988; Wajcman, 1991).

As a result of these conventional views of gender, skill and employment, work may be reorganised in a way which enlarges rather than enriches the jobs of female employees, which suggests that when team working is introduced with a female workforce, the prototypes which enlarge and therefore have a negative effect on the workers will be selected. This may be exacerbated by the payment system adopted. Some evidence indicates that women employees are viewed as marginal and peripheral workers and not really serious about paid work, carrying out certain activities just for 'a bit of pin money' (Forsberg, 1994; Wilson, 1995). Thus management may believe that the only way in which they can motivate their predominantly female workforce is by adopting a modification of piecework, via a group payment system. This will particularly affect the quicker team members, whose earnings may be reduced by the presence of slower operatives within the team. In order to counteract this, quicker machinists may find themselves working harder to raise the team's (and therefore their own) earning capacity.

These stereotypical views of women and work are perpetuated throughout society, in the mass media, in comics, magazines, on television, in advertisements, at school and at home, and are therefore difficult to break down. As a consequence women themselves may view 'women's work' as inferior, believing that they are not capable of performing the higher order tasks involved in job enrichment and that such tasks should be left to their male counterparts. This was noted some 20 years ago in Pollert's (1981) study of tobacco workers, where most of the female employees had a fixed idea of their future lives. They would get married, leave work and have children - after all work is really for men! Women's participation in the labour market and gender stereotypes have changed since this influential research was published, however as Elsass and Graves (1997) recently revealed, 'societal norms continue to create a hierarchy of roles that awards status and authority to white men' (p.947).

Trade unions have also played a large part in perpetuating these traditional views of gender and skill. They have conventionally placed 'skilled' labels on their male members in order to exclude women, keeping the labour supply low, wages high and therefore protecting the skill of the male craftsman (Coyle, 1982). Hartmann suggests that men have an interest in sustaining job segregation by sex, as it enforces lower wages for women and keeps them dependant upon and subordinate to men both at work and at home (Hartmann, 1976). Bradley (1999) reveals that trade unions are still male dominated in the late 1990s.

Furthermore even if women are viewed as being capable of performing the highly skilled work involved in job enrichment they are often constrained from doing so. Skilled, powerful jobs are often accompanied by overtime, evening and weekend work and as women tend to have the prime responsibility for household duties and caring activities, this serves to hold them back into unskilled, part-time work. Wilson (1999) suggests that women are seen as less committed to work due to their family responsibilities which restricts them from working long hours. Whilst Halford *et al.* (1997) conclude that children are seen as a drain on the commitment and loyalty of women to the workplace and some female workers chose opt out of motherhood for precisely these reasons.

Women are therefore in a catch twenty-two situation whereby stereotypical views pressurise them to take the main caring responsibilities, while (predominantly) male employers fail to provide adequate childcare facilities. Women are then told that they cannot have skilled jobs with responsibility because they will eventually leave to give birth to and rear children. The recent encouragement of 'family friendly employment' policies in Britain should help women to balance, more easily, work and family life but until societal stereotypes of gender and work change, these difficulties experienced by many women will remain.

It can therefore be seen that the way in which work is reorganised and the extent to which the workforce experience either job enlargement or job enrichment may be determined by gender. As men's jobs are enriched, women's will simply be enlarged. This process is evident when examining the implementation of team working. When the workforce is predominantly female the Japanese or the variant of the Swedish model which lead to job enlargement may be more likely to be implemented. This can be explained by the existence of stereotypical images of female employees as being unskilled, unreliable and unserious about paid work.

Technological Change

Fundamental innovations in micro-electronics have enabled the development of computer controlled technology which has resulted in Flexible Manufacturing Systems (FMS), such as Computer Numerical Control (CNC), Computer Aided Design (CAD) and Computer Aided Manufacturing (CAM), all of which facilitate the small batch, flexible production of high quality commodities so crucial to Post-Fordist production. A range of products can now be produced by a single machine with minimum cost and delay, simply by changing specification. This automated equipment enables the attainment of high levels of accuracy and therefore quality.

However, this technological innovation does not just concern the machinery and its implications for the production process but encompasses wider issues; how, by whom and for what means the machinery is utilised (Farrands and Talladay, 1994). Rapid technological development in recent years has fundamental implications for the labour process. The way it has been implemented has transformed the character of work, the control of the labour process and the structure of the workforce (Wajcman, 1991; Wood, 1989).

Institutionalists and Regulationists suggest that technological innovation is an essential component of the Fordist successor. However, to varying degrees, they both fail to examine its wider implications. The Institutionalists, in particular Piore and Sabel (1984), focus upon the production flexibility achieved as a result of technological advances. They do not, however, examine the implications on the labour force.

Regulationists such as Leborgne and Lipietz (1988, 1990) likewise recognise the importance of new technology in their model of Post-Fordism. They do begin to examine the way in which it is implemented and the implications on the labour force, suggesting that it can upskill some jobs and deskill others. Thus they state 'new technologies foster the separation between highly skilled intellectual designers and engineers, and poorly skilled operatives' (Leborgne and Lipietz, 1990, p.3). However, like their analysis of the workforce flexibility sought under Post-Fordism, Leborgne and Lipietz's examination of this technological revolution is problematic. They fail to examine the implications of technological change on the workforce in any substantial detail and omit a discussion of the specific implications for gender relations. In order to redress this, an in depth analysis of the implications of the technological change involved in Post-Fordism on the labour force in general and gender in particular is required.

Post-Fordism, Technological Change and Labour

Most research into technological innovation and labour has been conducted by labour process theorists, Braverman's publication of *Labour and Monopoly Capitalism* (1974) pioneering this debate. Braverman suggested that technological innovation is fundamental to capitalist society which, by its very nature, requires the continuous application of new technology in order to fragment and reduce the cost of labour. He therefore argued that new technology has a detrimental effect on the labour force, leading to a degradation of work, whereby the skill content is withdrawn from certain jobs. Moreover, he stated that there is a deliberate tendency for capital to utilise technology in this way as a furtherance of a general trend towards the deskilling of labour.

Braverman may be correct, in part, but his analysis is flawed to a certain degree as he fails to acknowledge that the technology introduced in order to deskill labour may simultaneously lead to the creation of jobs which involve a higher degree of skill. As Thompson (1983) pointed out, there is no technological inevitability about deskilling, new upskilled work can simultaneously be created.

It can therefore be inferred that the technological innovation characteristic of Post-Fordist production may have a dual effect on the workforce, deskilling some jobs and upskilling others, thus supporting Leborgne and Lipietz's initial claims. Very little research in this field exists, although a few studies were conducted in the clothing and textile industry towards the end of the 1980s (Cockburn, 1985; Truman and Keating, 1987; Wajcman, 1991) which confirm this process.

Cockburn's study (1985) of the introduction of FMS in the clothing and textile industry provides a good example of the way in which Post-Fordist technology can be utilised both to deskill and upskill. She studied the pattern room in traditional and Flexible Manufacturing Systems. In a traditional company, three prime activities are carried out in the pattern room: pattern making, pattern grading, and lay making, all of which were skilled activities. Cockburn found that in order to achieve greater flexibility and quality some companies had introduced CAD. As this was introduced, the skills involved were reduced but simultaneously highly skilled jobs were also created which involved the control and maintenance of the system, and resulted in the requirement of highly skilled computer analysts, programmers and engineers. Lloyd (1997) discovered an almost identical process when examining the impact of CAD on the skill levels of graders, markers and cutters, thus revealing that although Cockburn's work is dated, it remains valid today.

Truman and Keating (1987) came to similar conclusions when examining the introduction of micro-electronic sewing machines to achieve flexibility and small batch production. The machines are often pre-programmed to carry out and repeat specific operations, thus reducing the amount of skill and discretion needed by machinists. Gebbert (1992) also researched the introduction of these machines and concluded that the deskilling process had an additional drawback of labour intensification. One machinist was expected to feed two, three, or even more automated machine units, reducing the number of operatives required. At the same time as deskilling, Truman and Keating found that these electronic machines also led to the requirement of highly skilled computer programming operations which were not performed by the machinists but by other personnel, further withdrawing machinist control over the production process.

Wajcman (1991) found additional evidence of this dichotomy, with the introduction of numerical controlled machine tools. She discovered that when these machines were introduced in the clothing industry, the jobs of the machinists were deskilled, as they became mere 'button pushers'. But simultaneously new planning, control and computer programming jobs were created which were invariably performed by other employees in an office which was often located away from the shop floor.

This limited, and now dated, empirical research therefore provides further supporting evidence to the claims of Leborgne and Lipietz (1990) that the new technology involved in Post-Fordist production has a dual effect on the workforce, deskilling some jobs and upskilling others. However this research does not go far enough. It fails to recognise that the extent to and way in which technology is utilised, and therefore the way in which it affects the workforce, is dependant upon the way in which work is reorganised. This is exemplified by examining the way in which technology is utilised when different forms of team working are implemented.

Buchanan (1994) and Tomaney (1990) explain that the type of team working and the nature of its implementation has specific implications for the way in which the workforce is affected by technological change. An examination of the introduction of the Japanese style of team working reveals similar conclusions to those provided by Cockburn (1985), Truman and Keating (1987), and Wajcman (1991). Technological change is central to the Japanese philosophy of team working. Computer controlled technology is utilised in order to reduce the complexity and skill content of each task, enabling team members to use various workstations, performing a wider range of operations at a greater speed (job enlargement). As operative tasks become easier and team members are expected to be multi-skilled, they may be required to utilise several machines each, hence stimulating labour intensification. This is exemplified by the case of a garment company in the UK, where a typical team has twenty one workstations with seven operatives, thus each machinist operates three machines. Moreover, in some instances there can be as many as twenty four workstations to just five operatives (NEDO, 1991b).

The Japanese model of team working means that the majority of the power and control remains with management. As Sabel (1989) points out, increasing worker knowledge and autonomy is not a characteristic of the Japanese style of team working. It is therefore not surprising that the new, highly skilled, autonomous tasks created as a result of the introduction of the very technology which deskills operative tasks are not performed by the team members but by other personnel. This reveals that when team working is implemented, operatives suffer the drawbacks of deskilling and labour intensification, whilst others benefit, performing jobs with a high degree of skill content.

The Swedish model of team working, on the other hand, places importance on operative skills rather than technological change. Individuals are encouraged to become multi-skilled, performing a wider range of similar status tasks, but carrying out tasks of a more discretionary nature, hence increasing operative control and autonomy (Carrere and Little, 1989; Tyler, 1994). As a result, the division between production and control becomes less apparent. Functions such as planning and line balancing, which under traditional methods of production are the preserve of the 'technical elite', become the responsibility of the team members (Farrands and Totterdill, 1990; Totterdill, 1994). So even if some technological innovations are introduced which deskill operative tasks, it is likely that operatives will be trained to perform the newly created, highly skilled, autonomous, tasks such as computer programming and may consequently benefit overall from the technological change.

However if the Swedish model is introduced without either changes in management style or adequate training provision, it is unlikely that team members will be encouraged to perform tasks of a more discretionary nature and therefore they will not receive enhanced autonomy and control over their working lives. In this situation, team members (like those working on the Japanese model) will simply suffer the drawbacks of deskilling.

It can therefore be seen that the new technology involved in Post-Fordist production affects the labour force in a variety of ways, in some instances upskilling and in others deskilling. This process is not only determined by the type of machinery adopted but by the way in which technology is utilised, which is in turn determined by the nature and structure of work reorganisation.

Post-Fordism, Technology and Gender

For a number of years feminists (Cockburn, 1985; Jenson, 1989b; Wajcman, 1991; Webster, 1996) have argued that women are considered to have different aptitudes and attitudes to technology than their male counterparts. They suggest that the very definition of technology is gender biased. It is synonymous with 'masculine' images of industrial machinery, computers and cars but excludes 'feminine' technology concerned with cooking, childcare and so on. Wajcman (1991) argues that technology is identified with manliness and that this is not inherent in biological sex differences but is a result of the historical, social and cultural construction of gender. Women are seen as closer to nature, more emotional, less analytical and weaker than men are, and these associations play a powerful role in the ideological construction of women as inferior in terms of technological know how.

The crucial issue with regard to women's relationship to technology is how definitions of skill are established. Women's jobs are often said to be low paid because the work they do is unskilled, but the skill content of jobs is socially determined (Cockburn, 1985; Gardiner, 1997; Jenson, 1989b; Wajcman, 1991). A nursing job, for example, requires a high degree of training and ability as well as technical knowledge, however it is still not recognised as a technical job because it is deemed as 'women's work'.

Sewing machining is predominantly performed by women. This is perhaps one area where women are most at ease with machines and yet it remains seen as unskilled. It is viewed as a job that women have a natural aptitude for and consequently the technical skill required is devalued and underpaid. However, as Wajcman (1991) rightly points out, a sewing machinist can be a skilled job. To be a competent sewing machinist requires knowledge and experience of the machine.

Women's work has therefore been socially constructed as unskilled and as a consequence is undervalued. Definitions of skill are less related to technological competencies and associated more with ideological and social constructions. This process produces stereotypical images of women as technologically ignorant and incompetent and as a result they are viewed as incapable of invention. Until recently it was widely accepted that men are the main inventors. Moreover, when women have made discoveries their inventions have been accredited to men, particularly to their husbands (Wajcman, 1991). However women have invented or contributed to the invention of various things such as sewing machines, small electric motors and the Jacquard loom (*ibid.*). Furthermore, it is now recognised that women have played a major part in the development of computers and computer programming. Lloyd and Newell (1985) suggest that the first person recognised as a computer programmer was a woman.

Technology is therefore more than a set of artefacts, it also concerns knowledge and processes which are historically and socially constructed as masculine activities (Cockburn, 1987; Wajcman, 1991). As a consequence of these differential gender relations to technology, it has been argued (Cockburn, 1985; Jenson, 1989) that technology is gendered. Jenson explains these varying gender relations to technology by three principal factors: the design of machines; the assumptions made by managers; and the contribution made by women themselves to gender segregation in relation to technology.

Firstly, the design of machines can be looked at. Machines are constructed in a way that can easily be manipulated by men, this is primarily because the design itself incorporates assumptions about body size and strength. Cockburn (1983) utilises a study of the printing industry to illustrate this. She argues that the compositor's job is not just physically demanding by chance but that men have contributed to this outcome historically in two ways. Firstly, they have been influential in excluding women from the kinds of experience (including work) that develops physical strength and confidence. Secondly, they have been influential in designing labour processes. Men have used their 'political muscle' within trade unions to fight against excessively heavy tasks, but only when and to the degree which suits them. In certain instances men have found it advantageous to retain within their 'craft' particular tasks which are too heavy for the average woman.

The assumptions made by managers is another way in which technology is gendered. Milkman (1983) argued that within the electrical industry in the 1930s and 40s, managers determined whether a particular job was *feminine* or *masculine*. Women were employed to carry out the 'light' coil and armature winding, while their male counterparts performed 'heavy' winding. Moreover women worked on 'small' drill presses and men on 'large' ones.

Finally, women themselves make a substantial contribution to gender segregation in relation to technology. Stereotypical views that women are not able to deal with technology are reproduced in society through the education system, the family, and the media. As a consequence women themselves feel that they are not competent where technology is concerned. Indeed, women's own identity often contains a notion of *femininity*, which excludes the fact that technological skill or familiarity with the machine is feminine. Women are therefore less likely choose 'technical' occupations. This is exemplified Dennison and Coleman (2000), who reveal that only two per cent of young people entering skilled engineering occupations are female. Moreover, a recent governmental report reveals that women are underrepresented in Information and Computer Technology (ICT) occupations (Women's Unit, 2000).

Cockburn (1985) reports that women find themselves in a 'cleft stick' with regard to technological work, whereby if they are unfamiliar with technology they are viewed as 'real' women. Whilst if they become competent technologists they are seen as some kind of 'iron maiden', undesirable to men (Cockburn, 1985).

These gender inequalities towards technology start at a very young age. Children's toys vary depending on the sex of the child and the skills which children learn from these toys lay the foundations for mathematical, scientific and technological learning. Boys are encouraged to be assertive, to experiment with construction and therefore regard technical aspects of toys with confidence and familiarity. By contrast, girl's toys such as dolls are associated with caring and social interaction (Cockburn, 1983, 1985; Wajcman, 1991). Computers provide a good example of this process. As soon as they came onto the market they became gendered. Thus in the 1980s when they first became popular, a survey of British households owning microcomputers revealed that boys were thirteen times more likely than girls to be using them (Wajcman, 1991).

The education system further perpetuates these gender inequalities. Schools, the family and the mass media all transmit values and cultures which identify masculinity with machines and technological competence. At school the hidden curriculum ensures that teachers treat boys and girls differently according to their gender and as science has traditionally been taught by male teachers they provide gender role models which guarantee that fewer females participate in science based subjects (Wajcman, 1991). Gender is also important in the children's perceptions of themselves. Girls feel a need to behave in a certain way to be classed as feminine, and these feminine qualities are incompatible with the qualities supposed necessary for technological competence. This situation is exacerbated as pupils choose their GCSE options at the age of fourteen - at a time when they are most vulnerable and in attempts to prove their masculinity and femininity, choose gender appropriate subjects. Therefore boys are more likely than girls to study 'masculine' subjects such as physics, chemistry, computer studies, economics, and design and technology (Dennison and Coleman, 2000).

As a consequence of this gendering process of technology, women are seen as technologically incompetent and as incompatible with machinery. Technology is seen as an integral part of the male gender, on the other hand. As Cockburn argues, 'technology enters into our sexual identity: femininity is incompatible with technological competence, to feel technically competent is to feel manly' (Cockburn, 1985, p.12). This is particularly evident in the workplace. Thus some men are quoted by

Cockburn as saying, 'women are too temperamental to work with machinery'..... 'they [women] aren't happy with machinery like a man is' (Cockburn, 1983, p.177).

Wajcman (1991) argues that class is also an important issue here and that as women are not a homogenous group they do not have the same relationships to technology. There are obvious differences between the technical skills of women factory workers and of technically trained professional women. However Cockburn argues that despite these differences, both groups of women are found to be operating but very rarely controlling and manipulating machinery (Cockburn, 1985). Women therefore tend to be allocated the low status, low skilled controlled role of the operator, whilst their male counterparts control and reproduce the technology, occupying highly skilled jobs based on design, development, sales, installation and maintenance (Cockburn, 1987; Jenson, 1989b; Wajcman, 1991).

This is exemplified in Westwood's study of a hosiery company. The company made a sharp distinction between the jobs women and men could perform. The majority of the women workers were machinists whilst their sewing machines were serviced and repaired by mechanics, all of who were male (Westwood, 1984). Hence, the relationship to new technology, like the relationship to skill, is socially constructed. Men are not born 'handy' any more than women are born without the confidence to use a screwdriver (Jenson, 1989b).

This differential relationship of men and women to technology has led to some limited, and now quite dated, research into issues surrounding Post-Fordism, technology and gender relations (Chiesi, 1992; Cockburn, 1985; Crewe, 1990; Zeitlin, 1992). These authors appear to come to similar conclusions, suggesting that as the new technology involved in Post-Fordist production deskills some jobs and upskills others, the former will be allocated to women, whilst the latter will be performed by male employees. Zeitlin's (1992) study examines the introduction of CAD in pre-assembly stages of pattern development in clothing companies and concludes that it has led to a replacement of skilled men by women merely performing data entry tasks.

Further evidence is available if we return to Cockburn's (1985) study of the clothing and textile industry. As CAD was introduced into the pattern room, the pattern making, grading and laying jobs were deskilled. Subsequently, the number of women employed in these activities increased. Indeed, in the companies with traditional production methods, Cockburn found just three women employed in the pattern room, compared to eleven in the companies that had introduced CAD. As new technology was introduced into pattern room activities, the once skilled, male domain was replaced by a semi-skilled, female workforce. Moreover, the newly created, highly skilled jobs of computer analyst were allocated to men, with not one woman employed as a systems analyst in the companies with CAD technology (Cockburn, 1985).

Lloyd (1997) similarly looked at the impact of CAD on the skill levels of graders, markers and cutters in the clothing industry and, twelve years after Cockburn's study, discovered an identical trend. These jobs were deskilled following the introduction of CAD and were subsequently 'feminised'.

This is reaffirmed by Chiesi (1992) who found that the introduction of new technology in weaving and spinning occupations led to an abolition of some manual tasks, but also the creation of new tasks in the area of machine control. The manual tasks were previously performed by women, but the newly created job categories involving machine control were allocated to men. Moreover, in order to gain maximum benefit from the newly installed, expensive machinery three shifts (including a night shift) were set up. This had the direct effect of a substitution of men for women in the weaving department.

Crewe (1990) similarly found that the introduction of new technology in textiles and clothing firms in West Yorkshire reinforced and even intensified traditional divisions, as female jobs underwent a process of deskilling while male jobs were re-skilled. Many female workers who previously had skilled or semi-skilled status were reduced to machine-minders, whilst many men were upgraded from operators to skilled engineers or technicians.

This limited research concerning Post-Fordism, technology and gender is welcome but like the more general research concerning technology and labour, previously mentioned, it only partially examines the issues involved. Although the research considers the way in which Post-Fordist technology is gendered, it fails to acknowledge that the way in which it is utilised is also determined by the structure and nature of work reorganisation, which may itself be determined by gender. Again this can be exemplified by exploring the implementation of different forms of team working. Given the evidence that both technological change and the nature of work reorganisation may be determined by gender, two scenarios may emerge when team working is implemented with a female workforce.

Firstly, as female workers are often perceived as incapable of performing highly skilled work involving autonomy, discretion and control over technology there may be a tendency to install the Japanese rather than the Swedish model of team working. As this system is based upon the use of technologies which deskill, female team members may be encouraged to perform a wider range of simpler tasks, suffering the drawbacks of deskilling and labour intensification, becoming mere machine operators. The new, highly skilled, autonomous tasks created as a result of this technology may be allocated to male personnel, with female team members been viewed as incapable of performing these tasks. Therefore female operatives may experience deskilling and labour intensification, whilst other male employees benefit from this process, performing jobs with a high degree of skill content.

Secondly, the Swedish model of team working may be introduced but without the changes in management style and training necessary for the female workforce to experience a higher degree of autonomy and discretion. The Swedish model concentrates less on technological innovation and more on operative skills but in this situation if new technologies are introduced, female team members (like those working on the Japanese model) will be expected to perform a wider range of simpler tasks. The skill content of their existing tasks may therefore be reduced and they will not be allocated the discretion and autonomy necessary to benefit from the newly created, highly skilled activities such as computer programming. These tasks may be allocated to other male personnel who (unlike their female counterparts) are viewed as capable of controlling technology. Female team members may therefore experience deskilling and labour intensification, whilst other (possibly male) employees will be awarded the jobs involving a higher degree of autonomy and control over technology such as computer programming.

It can therefore be seen that the technological change involved in Post-Fordist production can have a dual effect on the labour force, deskilling some existing operative jobs whilst creating highly skilled job categories such as computer programmer or analyst. Moreover, the extent to which the workforce benefit from this upskilling or experience the drawbacks of deskilling and hence labour intensification is not only determined by the type of technology introduced but by the way in which it is utilised, which is in turn determined by the nature and structure of work reorganisation, together with the gender of the workforce. If the workforce is predominantly female, work will be reorganised and technology utilised in such a way that the jobs of existing female employees are deskilled whilst newly created highly skilled jobs are allocated to other male workers.

Conclusion

The Post-Fordist search for labour flexibility has profound implications for the labour force. It can have a dual effect, benefiting some workers whilst having detrimental implications for others. Some workers will enjoy the benefits of functional flexibility, job enrichment and the upskilling which is involved in the introduction of new technology. Others, in contrast, will experience the drawbacks of numerical flexibility, job enlargement and the deskilling and labour intensification which new technology likewise induces. Evidence suggests that the extent to which the workforce enjoy the benefits of the former or suffer the drawbacks of the latter is determined by the way in which work is reorganised and that this in turn may be determined by gender.

One way in which Post-Fordism has facilitated the search for greater labour flexibility has been through an expansion of numerically flexible working arrangements. This has resulted in an ever increasing proportion of the labour force working on a part-time basis, on temporary contracts or as homeworkers. Such contracts have traditionally been accompanied by fewer employment rights, resulting in many workers becoming part of the peripheral labour market. This has connotations for both male and female employees, but the latter are most profoundly affected. The majority of the numerically flexible workforce is female, with women constituting a high proportion of part-time employees, homeworkers, and those on temporary contracts.

Explanations for women occupying the majority of these numerically flexible jobs are related to their dual role in society, having the main responsibility for unpaid domestic and caring activities, whilst simultaneously performing paid work. This dual role often acts as a constraint to women wishing to enter the labour force on a full-time permanent basis. These constraints may be mediated by the provision of welfare services such as childcare facilities, home helps and so on. This has been the case in Scandinavian countries, particularly in Sweden where welfare provision and therefore women's participation in full-time permanent employment are high. However, welfare provision varies considerably from country to country and therefore so do the constraints to women working full-time. In some countries such as Britain, welfare provision has traditionally been low and therefore the constraints to women working full-time remain high. There is some evidence that this pattern has started to change recently with the current government's policies on family friendly employment and efforts towards expanding childcare provision. However, much progress is still required in this direction.

Another way in which Post-Fordism has facilitated the search for greater labour flexibility is via the expansion of functional flexibility. However, the term functional flexibility is more complex than authors concerned with the economic restructuring debate (Piore and Sabel, 1984; Sabel, 1989; Leborgne and Lipietz, 1988, 1990) would lead us to believe. These authors rightly point out that functional flexibility may manifest itself in the form of job enrichment but fail to recognise that it may also result in job enlargement.

The extent to which the search for functional flexibility results in either job enlargement or job enrichment is dependant upon the way in which work is reorganised. This is evident when examining the implementation of team working. If certain models of team working are implemented, particularly those based on the Swedish prototype, the workforce will experience the benefits of job enrichment. However, if the full ethos of this type of team working are not adopted or other variants of team working (such as the Japanese model) are installed, the workforce may instead experience the drawbacks of job enlargement and therefore labour intensification.

Within this chapter it has been suggested that the way in which work is reorganised and therefore the extent to which the workforce experience either job enlargement or job enrichment may be determined by gender. As male employees enjoy job enrichment and polyvalency, their female counterparts may be exposed to job enlargement and labour intensification. Again this process has been exemplified by an examination of the implementation of team working. It has been suggested that when the workforce is predominantly female, the Japanese or the variant of the Swedish model which lead to job enlargement rather than job enrichment may be more likely to be implemented. Feminist theory concerning the social construction of skill has been utilised to explain this form of gender segregation, with women being viewed as unskilled and therefore incapable of working autonomously and performing the higher order tasks involved in job enrichment.

Finally, it has been seen that the technological change involved in Post-Fordist production can also have a dual effect on the labour force, deskilling some jobs whilst upskilling others. However, the extent to which the workforce benefit from this upskilling or experience the drawbacks of deskilling and hence labour intensification is a complex issue. It is not only determined by the type of technology introduced, but by the way in which it is utilised, which is in turn determined by the nature and structure of work reorganisation, together with the gender of the workforce. If the workforce is predominantly female, work may be reorganised and technology utilised in such a way that the jobs of existing female employees are deskilled whilst the newly created, high skilled activities involving control and reproduction of technology are occupied by male employees. This differential effect of new technology in terms of gender can again be explained by the social construction of skill as well as by the fact that women are viewed as incapable of having any degree of technological 'know how' which is encompassed by the feminist theory that technology is gendered.

From the evidence provided in this chapter it can therefore be concluded that Post-Fordism has a dual effect on the labour force, benefiting some workers but proving detrimental to others. While it is acknowledged that all workers (both male and female) will inevitably experience the drawbacks of Post-Fordism, it appears that female workers may suffer the most, experiencing deskilling, job enlargement and labour intensification, while being forced into jobs which are numerically flexible and hence part of the peripheral labour market.

PART 2
EVIDENCE FROM THE
CLOTHING INDUSTRY

4 The Nottinghamshire Clothing Sector

Introduction

Up until this point we have been concerned with the theoretical implications of Post-Fordism for gender relations at work, which encompasses three main strands: numerical flexibility; functional flexibility; and technological change. In order to explore these issues in more detail, evidence from an empirical investigation which focuses upon the development of one form of Post-Fordism - team working, in the Nottinghamshire clothing industry - is drawn upon.

This chapter explores the nature and rationale for the empirical investigation, briefly outlining the research questions addressed, the characteristics of the Nottinghamshire clothing industry, and explanations for choosing it as the focus of the empirical inquiry. Details of the sample of companies utilised and the research methods deployed are also outlined.

Research Questions

The sector under investigation is a manufacturing industry which has a predominantly female workforce and consequently the questions addressed by the empirical inquiry vary slightly from the theoretical arguments raised in chapter three. These adaptations are explained below.

Numerical Flexibility

i) Leborgne and Lipietz (1988, 1990), and Lipietz (1997) suggest that Post-Fordism is accompanied by an expansion of numerical flexibility. The extent to which this is true in companies operating team working is examined by comparing its presence to that in companies operating the production line. In particular the way in which team working leads to a greater level of redundancies and part-time work is explored and the extent to which the latter can be classed as numerically flexible in the clothing industry is examined.

ii) The majority of numerically flexible jobs are performed by women, who experience the drawbacks of the peripheral labour market. Explanations for this are provided by Dex (1999), Pollert (1981), Rigg and Miller (1991), Westwood (1984) and Williams (1997) and are linked to women's role in domestic and caring tasks. In order to test the validity of this, the implications of numerical flexibility for female team members, particularly those with caring responsibilities, are examined.

iii) Feminist authors such as Finch (1989), Lewis (1992), McDowell (1991), Rubery et.al., (1998), Wallace (1999) and Yeandle (1999) argue that women's participation in numerically flexible jobs is determined by welfare provision. The lower the level of welfare provision, the greater the likelihood that women will be employed on flexible employment contracts. If team working is accompanied by an expansion of flexible working arrangements and childcare facilities, the constraints faced by working women will be mediated. The extent to which this process is occurring is therefore examined.

Functional Flexibility and Technological Change

i) Dawson and Webb (1989), Tomaney (1990) and Buchanan (1994) conclude that the Post-Fordist search for functional flexibility can be achieved by job enlargement as well as job enrichment. Other authors such as Cockburn (1985), Truman and Keating (1987), Wajcman (1991) and Webster (1996) suggest that the new technology utilised in the Post-Fordist economy can be used in a way which upskills some jobs and deskills others. In order to test these arguments it is necessary to see if team working enlarges or enriches jobs and uses technology in a way which upskills or deskills.

ii) Buchanan (1994) and Tomaney (1991) suggest that the way in which work is reorganised within Post-Fordism is one factor which determines if jobs are enlarged or enriched and if technology is used to upskill or deskill. In order to test these arguments it is necessary to examine the extent to which the model of team working determines this. Particular attention is paid to cultural change, in terms of management style and training.

iii) Various commentators suggest that gender also plays a role in this process. Dawson and Webb (1989), Elger (1991), Elsass and Graves (1997) and Wood (1986) argue that women's jobs tend to be enlarged, while men's jobs are enriched. Other authors such as Chiesi (1992), Cockburn (1985), Crewe (1990) and Zeitlin (1992) suggest that the way in which Post-Fordist technology is utilised is influenced by gender, resulting in the deskilling of women's jobs and the upskilling of men's jobs. These gender differential effects are related to the social construction of skill and the notion that technology is gendered (Cockburn, 1983, 1985; Jenson, 1989b; Truman and Keating, 1987; Wajcman, 1991).

Types of Post-Fordism which lead to job enlargement and utilise technology in a way which deskills may therefore be prevalent when the workforce is female and those which lead to job enrichment and utilise technology in a way which upskills may exist when the workforce is male. It is thus important to see if gender is one factor which influences the type of team working and the wider cultural changes which determine how the workforce is affected.

The Nottinghamshire Clothing Industry

Reasons for Selection

This sector and locality was selected for the focus for the empirical study for a number of reasons. Firstly, existing research on Post-Fordism and gender relations provides an overall analysis without exploring any particular industrial sector. Where evidence from a particular sector is available, it tends to be limited to an analysis of the tertiary sector (Christopherson, 1989; Banshop and Doorewaard, 1998; Baugh and Craen, 1997; Kahn, 1999; Ledwith and Colgan, 1996). Evidence from the manufacturing sector is limited (for example, Pollert, 1996; and Wallace, 1999). It was therefore felt important to reverse this trend, particularly as the mainstream economic restructuring theories (Regulationists and Institutionalists) have focused solely on manufacturing industries.

Secondly, the Nottinghamshire clothing industry was viewed as a good resource base - it has undergone considerable workplace restructuring and various public policy initiatives, based on the implementation of team working, have been developed.

Thirdly, the industry was chosen as it is an employer of a large number of women. Females account for 85 per cent of the employees in the sample of companies selected for this research.

There are, however, two main problems with this case study, which may not have been apparent had a different industrial base been chosen. The first difficulty concerns the extent to which the industry has ever been Fordist. Wilkinson (1993) argues that the clothing sector has not experienced Fordism to the extent that other industrial sectors have, and questions the extent to which the introduction of team working can be classed as Post-Fordist. In part, he is correct. Most industrial sectors during the post-war period have experienced Fordism, but by varying degrees, and if placed on a spectrum of intensity, the clothing industry would probably be placed towards the lower end. However, this does not necessarily infer that Fordism was never prevalent in the industry. It was but not to the same degree. Nor does it infer that the adoption of team working is not substantially different from its predecessor and cannot be classed as Post-Fordist. Nevertheless had the research been conducted in another industrial sector, better known for the presence of Fordism, the empirical investigation would have been open to less scrutiny.

The second difficulty is that the majority of employees within the industry are female, rendering a comparison of the implications of team working on male and female employees problematic.

Background and Characteristics

The clothing industry, along with the textiles sector, is a key employer in Nottinghamshire. At the time of the empirical investigation it employed approximately 24,000 people, although by 1997 this had fallen to 21,000 (Crewe, 1994; Haines and Oxborrow, 1997). The majority of these employees were female, constituting 62 per cent of the workforce in 1994 and a similar proportion three years later (Crewe, 1994; Haines and Oxborrow, 1997). Over half the workforce in 1994 were employed in large firms, however the majority of the companies were small, with over three quarters employing less than fifty people and only 6 per cent employing more than two hundred. This pattern remains the same at the end of the 20th Century. The clothing sector has traditionally been important in the region and still is, with garment producers out numbering textile manufacturers by a ratio of two to one (*ibid.*).

The Nottinghamshire clothing sector, like other industrial sectors throughout the western world has, during recent years, faced increasing competition from low cost countries in the far east, such as South Korea, Malaysia and Taiwan and more recently from former Eastern European countries. In order for it to survive, the industry has been forced to reorganise and restructure during the last two decades. This reorganisation has involved a pursuit of greater flexibility. There has been a change of emphasis away from the mass production of standardised, low cost, low quality garments, towards the adoption of smaller batch production of semi-customised, high quality garments with a degree of design content. Of particular importance to this pursuit of flexibility has been the realisation that quick response to fashion change is paramount and consequently the traditional two season fashion calendar has been replaced by four or five.

These trends are exemplified in the Nottinghamshire Textile and Clothing Sector state of the industry reports (Crewe, 1994; Haines and Oxborrow, 1997) which reveal that the average order sizes have been falling and that many companies are shortening lead times, highlighting the growing importance of quick response production. There has also been an increase in product diversity, signifying a move away from economies of scale towards economies of scope. The 1994 report revealed that one fifth of the firms had increased product diversity in recent years. However, although there were signs of some firms moving into higher value markets in 1994, this trend seems to have diminished recently, and in 1997 many firms still saw price as a critical competitive advantage (*ibid.*).

This restructuring has been aided by a series of public policy initiatives which, during the 1980s and 1990s, aimed to improve the competitiveness of the local industry. A key initiative has been the implementation of team working in traditional production line companies, the main instigator of this being the Nottinghamshire Work and Technology Programme.

The Sample of Companies

Two categories of firms were included in the sample, those operating the production line and those utilising team working. Where possible, companies which were simultaneously operating both the systems were included.

Companies were identified with the aid of the Nottinghamshire Textiles and Clothing Industry Capacity Register (Wigfield, 1994b). 25 companies agreed to participate in the study, 15 were operating the production line and ten utilising team working. Due to this small sample size it was necessary to visit companies outside the Nottinghamshire region and a further eight companies were identified by Nottinghamshire Work and Technology Programme employees. In total 76 per cent of the companies were located in Nottinghamshire. 12 per cent of the production line companies were located outside the region, compared to 37 per cent of those operating team working. The sample of companies were situated in a range of urban and rural localities.

Difficulties were encountered in gaining access to companies, mainly because the study involved in depth interviews with workers. As a result it was impossible to be selective in terms of employee size, products and location. Basically it was necessary to research those companies which were willing to allow access. In total 33 companies formed the sample, 17 of which utilise the production line as their principal method of production and 16 of which have some form of team work in operation.

The companies produce a range of products and have various workforce sizes. Nevertheless, it must be noted that companies with more than 50 employees dominate the interview sample (76 per cent), and none of the companies employ less than five workers. This tendency towards medium and large size manufacturers is particularly pronounced in team working companies, none of which employ fewer than 50 workers. This may indicate that the size of companies operating team working are, on average, larger than those utilising the production line, suggesting that the cost of implementing team working is beyond the reach of smaller enterprises. Moreover, smaller firms are inherently more flexible (particularly in terms of the workforce who tend to have a number of skills and can 'put their hand to almost anything') than larger ones and thus their need for the implementation of team working is less apparent.

Although the companies represent various geographical locations, product types and employment sizes, it must be noted that the sample is not large enough to attempt to identify or explain disparities which are determined by these criteria. However, the sample does represent a cross section of companies which are operating team working in the clothing industry, from which generalisations about the overall implications of team working for gender relations can be made. Indeed, all the companies which were known to be operating team working in Nottinghamshire have been included in the sample, together with an additional six companies from various other localities.

There are few differences in the methods of work organisation of the production line companies, but the way in which work is organised within the team working companies varies substantially. In order to illustrate this, the methods of work organisation utilised in both groups of companies are examined below.

Production Lines

The production line companies have a number of common characteristics, which are based on a rigid demarkation of operative functions. Operatives are generally seated at individual workstations which are located in long rows across the factory floor. Work is highly fragmented and operatives tend to remain on one operation, unless it is absolutely essential to move, i.e. due to absenteeism. As a result, they gain little knowledge about the broader process of garment construction and, particularly in larger companies, may never see the finished product that they are working on. Garments typically move in a unidirectional flow down the line, usually in bundles, and therefore work in progress is high.

Team Working

Existing literature indicates the presence of two principal models of team working, the Japanese and Swedish prototypes. However, the systems in operation in the sample of companies cannot easily be classified into these two categories. They all appear to utilise the former.

Sabel (1989) suggests that Japanese models utilise both the Kanban and Just in Time (JIT) philosophies (see chapter two for more details). However, the systems of team working in the sample of companies tend to emphasise one of these two philosophies, rather than both. Some companies operate the single garment system (often referred to as the Toyota Sewing System) and place more emphasis on the JIT philosophy, while other companies utilise the Kanban principle.

The Toyota Sewing System (TSS) originally developed in the Japanese car industry, and was pioneered in the mid-1980s as an application of Just In Time principles to garment assembly in the UK. Several multi-skilled operatives work at a series of workstations, often on a 'U' shaped module. Operatives work with single garments and work-flow progresses sequentially. They usually stand to sew, enabling quick movement between workstations, promoting flexibility and maximising communication (see figure 4.1).

In this system there are eight workstations and six operatives who are each responsible for between two and three workstations. Production is pulled back through the line, by the 'bump back' system. When the final operative (number eight), completes the garment, it is placed aside and the operative moves back down the line to operative number seven and takes control of the work, even if he/she is mid way through an operation. Operative number seven then becomes free and obtains work from operative six, operative six obtains work from number five and so on, until operative number one is free to commence another garment. To do this operative number one pulls more work on to the line, taking it from a stack of cut work (NEDO, 1991b; Tyler, 1994).

In contrast, the Kanban System is derived from the practice of using conveyance and production cards to direct work movements. A Kanban is the buffer of work between operations which is set at a

Figure 4.1 Typical Team Layout - Toyota Sewing System (TSS)

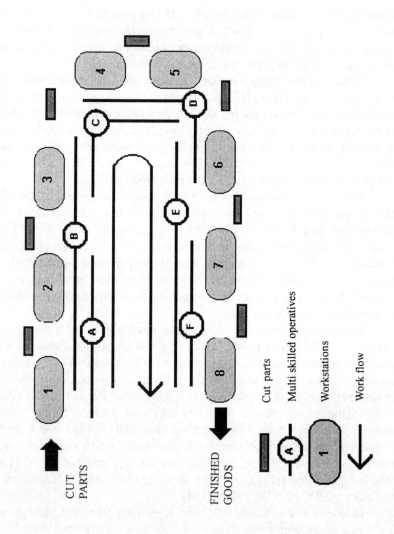

predetermined level and gives an operative authority to produce. Like the TSS, the Kanban system often takes the form of a 'U' shaped lay-out within which multi-skilled, self organised operatives work. Bundles of work are used rather than single garments and the maximum inventory in any buffer can be set at two, three, four or more bundles. When the Kanban is empty or only partly filled, the operator has the authority to fill it. When full, production on that operation must cease and the operative moves to another workstation where the Kanban is not full. The utilisation of bundles means that machining times at each workstation are longer than on the TSS and therefore operatives in general remain seated. At intervals operatives leave their seats and resume work at a different workstation (see figure 4.2).

In this system there are eight workstations and four operatives. Each operative is responsible for four workstations. Operatives move from workstations where the Kanban is full, to those where the Kanban is empty or only partially full.

Table 4.1 outlines the systems of team working in operation in the sample of companies. Ten operate a system based on the Kanban prototype. Six of these have all the characteristics of the Kanban model (Kanban control of work-flow, bundles of work and a seated workforce), with a further four having these characteristics but with some or all of the workforce standing to sew. Six companies operate the TSS model. Four of these have all the features of the TSS model (bump back control of work-flow, single garment and operatives standing to sew), whilst a further two operate the bump back system but utilise bundles of work rather than single garments. The size of the teams vary from three operatives to twelve (one company being the exception with more than twenty) and is determined to a certain extent by the model, with TSS companies tending to have slightly larger teams than their Kanban counterparts.

Research Methods

The research methods utilised are both qualitative and quantitative, and encompass: informal interviews with managers; focus groups with female machinists; and questionnaires for machinists participating in the focus groups. Pilot interviews were conducted in February 1994 in two production line and two team working companies. The final interviews were carried out between April and October 1994. For reasons of accuracy and reliability all interviews were recorded on audio tape and then fully transcribed.

Figure 4.2 Typical Team Layout - Kanban

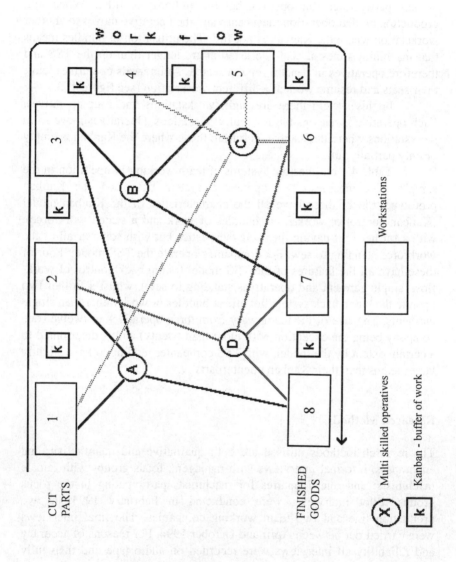

CUT
PARTS

FINISHED
GOODS

Workstations

(X) Multi skilled operatives

k Kanban - buffer of work

Table 4.1   **Characteristics of the Team Working Systems in the Sample of Companies**

Company	Kanban / Bump Back	Single Garment / Bundle	Stand / Sit	Number of operatives per team
1	Kanban	Bundle	Sit	5
2	Kanban	Bundle	Sit	5
3	Bump Back	Bundle	Stand	9-10
4	Kanban	Bundle	Sit	5-7
5	Bump Back	Single Garment	Stand	10-12
6	Kanban	Bundle	Sit	4-9
7	Bump Back	Single Garment	Stand	5-8
8	Bump Back	Single Garment	Stand	5-8
9	Bump Back	Bundle	Stand & Sit	5
10	Kanban	Bundle	Sit	4
11	Kanban	Bundle	Stand & Sit	5
12	Kanban	Bundle	Stand	5-6
13	Kanban	Bundle	Stand & Sit	3
14	Kanban	Bundle	Sit	20+
15	Kanban	Bundle	Stand	4
16	Bump Back	Single Garment	Stand	5-8

Operative Questionnaires

Ninety eight machinists completed questionnaires in 29 of the 33 companies. Fifty nine of them were working in 15 of the 17 production line companies and 39 were working in 14 of the 16 team working companies. Due to circumstances beyond the control of the author it was impossible to conduct questionnaires with all the machinists (126) who participated in focus groups.

All the respondents were female and represent a range of age groups, although there were very few elderly respondents within the 56-65 age group. There appears to be a clear distinction between the age of the operatives working on the production line and those working in teams, the latter tending, on average, to be younger. 80 per cent of the team members were below the age of 36, the comparable figure for respondents on the production line being just 39 per cent. This may be because older operatives are accustomed to the production line and its payment system and hence are more reluctant to change to team working. Moreover, the adoption of team working often involves operatives standing instead of sitting and this adjustment may prove more difficult for older operatives.

Most of the respondents (55 per cent) have worked in the industry between six to 20 years, with an additional 34 per cent working in the sector for more than 21 years, suggesting that once machinists enter the industry they very rarely leave. This can in part be explained by a lack of alternative employment opportunities and in part by the fact that many machinists have never experienced work elsewhere and are reluctant to undergo change.

A comparison of the length of time production line and team working operatives have worked in the industry reveals a contrast, with the latter working in the industry on average (measured by the mode) for just six to ten years, compared to 21 to 30 years for the former. This may be because operatives who are younger have less experience in the industry and of production line work and therefore are more amenable to working under new organisational methods such as team work.

Of the team working respondents, all but three (92 per cent) had worked on a production line previously. Nearly half those working in teams had done so for between one and two years and only three per cent had worked in teams for five years or more, thus reflecting the relatively recent emergence of team working in the Nottinghamshire clothing industry.

Focus Groups with Female Machinists

Thirty three focus groups were conducted with female machinists working on both the production line and in teams - that is one focus group per company. In total 126 machinists participated, 73 of these worked in the 17 production line companies and 53 in the 16 team working companies. The number of participants in each of the focus groups ranged from three to six.

Semi-structured Interviews with Managers

Managerial interviews were carried out in each of the 33 companies. The majority of the managers (61 per cent) were male and this pattern was true in both production line and team working companies, hence reflecting the dominance of men in managerial positions within the industry.

The interviews were designed to ascertain comparable details of both work organisation and gender relations in production line and team work companies. The interviews followed a set of semi-structured questions which were asked in roughly the same order. Certain issues were expanded on where necessary, sometimes instigated by the interviewer and sometimes by the interviewee. The structure of the interviews were similar for both groups of companies but obviously varied occasionally, particularly when discussing issues concerning work organisation. Managers were asked factual questions about the work organisation of the company and more subjective questions in order to ascertain their personal opinions, particularly with respect to gender relations.

Conclusion

The results of the empirical investigation are extensive and are detailed in the remainder of the book. Chapter five explores the debate concerning numerical flexibility, whilst chapter six examines functional flexibility, drawing upon issues concerning technological change where appropriate.

5 Team Working and Numerical Flexibility

Introduction

This chapter tests the theoretical arguments arising out of chapter three, in particular the expansion of numerical flexibility within the Post-Fordist economy. Evidence is provided from the empirical investigation of the introduction of one form of Post-Fordism - team working, in the Nottinghamshire clothing industry.

Post-Fordism can be accompanied by an expansion of numerically flexible working arrangements (i.e. part-time work, temporary work and homeworking). Much of the existing feminist theoretical debate surrounding the implications of Post-Fordism for gender relations at work focuses upon this issue (Christopherson, 1989; McDowell, 1991; Walby, 1989). These authors suggest that Post-Fordism leads to an increase in numerically flexible jobs, the majority of which are performed by women, who consequently experience the drawbacks of the peripheral labour market, being subject to 'hire and fire' work practices. They explain women's participation in these jobs by their role in domestic and caring tasks, and suggest that this situation is particularly evident in Britain due to the traditional lack of welfare provision, in particular childcare facilities.

The main criticism of this research is that the evidence is drawn from a general analysis of all industrial sectors and that case study evidence from particular industrial sectors is absent. Moreover, in the few cases where evidence from a particular sector is available (Christopherson, 1989), it tends to be limited to the tertiary sector.

This is a drawback in the existing feminist critique of Post-Fordism, particularly as manufacturing industries tend to have inherently different work practices than the tertiary sector. Indeed, numerical flexibility is far less prevalent in manufacturing than service sectors in Britain (Eurostat, 1990; OECD, 1994). Thus, the search for greater flexibility may be achieved by alternative methods in manufacturing industries, not necessarily through an expansion of numerical flexibility. The remainder of this chapter attempts to redress this imbalance, by providing empirical evidence from the implementation of team working in a traditional manufacturing industry, the clothing sector.

The chapter is divided into two main parts. The first explores the extent to which team working, as one form of Post-Fordism, encourages an expansion of numerical flexibility. The extent to which the presence of numerically flexible working practices is greater amongst employees working in teams than those working on the production line is explored. Particular attention is paid to the level of redundancies and part-time work, and the extent to which each can be classed as measures of numerical flexibility.

The second part examines the implications of these findings for females working in teams and specifically for those who also have caring responsibilities. The extent to which team working can mediate the constraints faced by these women is explored by analysing the degree to these companies are more likely to operate flexible working arrangements and provide childcare facilities than those operating a conventional production line.

This chapter relies upon qualitative evidence, which is drawn from both focus groups with machinists and informal interviews with management (see chapter four for an outline of the research methods), although quantitative data is utilised on occasions as supportive evidence.

The Presence of Numerical Flexibility

In order to examine the extent to which team working leads to a greater level of numerical flexibility, two criteria are examined: the level of redundancies in the industry and the amount of part-time work available.

Redundancies

The quantity and frequency of redundancies is one measure of the presence of numerical flexibility within the clothing industry. Widespread numerical flexibility means that employees have few employment rights and can be 'hired and fired' according to the level of demand, indicating a high level of redundancies.

In order to establish the prevalence of redundancies, managers were asked if they had made any workers redundant in the last few years. Redundancies within companies operating the traditional production line were extremely low. Just 13 per cent of these managers stated that they had made workers redundant recently. This is a remarkably modest level of redundancies for a period which had been marked by economic recession across most industrial sectors.

These managers explained the low number of redundancies by a high level of 'natural' labour turnover. Employees regularly leave for a variety of reasons, such as pregnancy, in search of higher pay or better working conditions. Indeed, managers argued that labour turnover is such a problem throughout the industry that labour recruitment has been the main problem, rather than unwanted redundancies. As one manager pointed out:

> We made some redundant probably three years ago.... I would say that the problem since then has been recruiting labour. At the moment it's a big problem trying to recruit labour.....it's the key workers on key operations who have given a number of years service and have been highly skilled, you tend to rely on those people and so when they go they take some replacing
> (Manager of production line company).

As the presence of numerical flexibility is believed to be higher in the Post-Fordist economy (Christopherson, 1989; McDowell, 1991; Walby, 1989), and given that team working can be classed as one form of Post-Fordism, one would expect redundancies to be higher in team working companies. There are two main reasons for this. Firstly, if team working leads to an expansion of numerically flexible employment contracts, employees will have few employment rights and as a result employers will have the power to 'hire and fire' the workforce according to the level of demand and therefore a high level of redundancies would be expected.

Secondly, it could be anticipated that in an attempt to increase the level of numerical flexibility, companies implementing team working will make permanent, full-time workers redundant with a view to re-employing them on a more flexible contract.

Initial observations provide supporting evidence to this effect, with 42 per cent of the team working managers stating that they had made workers redundant in the last few years. This pattern appeared to be the same in companies utilising both Kanban and TSS based systems of team work, revealing that managers of companies operating team working are three times more likely to make employees redundant than those in companies operating the conventional production line.

However, when the interviews are analysed in more detail, it becomes clear that the higher level of redundancies in team working companies does not necessarily indicate a higher degree of numerical flexibility, rather, it reflects the requirement for fewer indirect staff, such as examiners, when team working is initially installed. The team working companies which had made workers redundant in the last few years had done so as a direct result of the implementation of the new system of production. This was the case for both Kanban and TSS based systems of team work. A typical response from management was:

> When we changed over from line to Just In Time we tried to integrate [the examiners] and tried to train them up on machining. We offered it and if they didn't want it then they were obviously made redundant. But we did offer everyone a job. Just In Time didn't need examiners
> (Manager of team work company).

In the longer term redundancies in team working companies, like those in companies with the traditional production line, appeared extremely low, indicating that once the new system of manufacturing is implemented, managers are no more inclined to make workers redundant than those in companies operating the production line. This suggests, therefore, that team working does not stimulate a greater degree of numerical flexibility.

Explanations for the low level of redundancies in team working companies are similar to those previously stated for companies operating the production line, relating to the level of labour turnover. Advocates of team working (Farrands and Totterdill, 1990; Totterdill, 1995b; Tyler, 1994) suggest that one of the main benefits of its implementation can be a reduction in levels of labour turnover. They argue that team working can have numerous benefits such as multi-skilling, job enrichment, a fairer payment system and improved career prospects, thus facilitating labour retention. However, evidence from the discussions with managers of team working companies suggests that this has not been the situation, with only 31 per cent of the team working companies experiencing a fall in labour turnover. The remaining 69 per cent stated that labour turnover is still a problem despite the new system of production. Moreover two of these companies actually experienced increases in labour turnover following the implementation of team working.

There is also no evidence of team working companies making full-time, permanent, machinists redundant and re-employing them on more flexible, part-time or temporary contracts. None of the managers or machinists in the team working companies suggested that this process had occurred since the change in the production process. Indeed, many managers interviewed (80 per cent) indicated that if they required full-time machinists to work on a part-time basis they would simply instruct them to work less hours the following week, rather than re-employ them on a new contract. Indeed, formal contracts are rare in the clothing sector, which indicates that the workforce can be 'hired and fired' quite easily and therefore treated in a numerically flexible way. However, the high level of labour turnover means that this process is very rarely necessary.

Team working managers were also asked about future redundancies. Those in eight companies which had only partially implemented team working - thereby operating the new system of production alongside the traditional production line - agreed that machinists from the latter would be chosen for redundancy rather than those working in teams. This was frequently explained by the fact that team working would eventually be implemented throughout the company and therefore it made sense to make production line workers redundant rather than team workers. Team members had been trained to be multi-skilled and were seen as more valuable to the company than production line workers:

> I would take the redundancies off the lines if I was to make any, because they [team workers] are more skilled, we've invested time and money into them, they are more valuable as a workforce
> (Manager of team work company).

Some of these companies had implemented team working but had failed to invest in employee training, a practice which advocates of team working, such as Farrands and Totterdill (1990) and Tyler (1994) are highly critical of. Managers in these companies argued that although they had not invested time and resources into training their staff, the machinists had cross trained each other and were more skilled and therefore more valuable to the company than those remaining on the production line.

This evidence reveals that in the sample of companies, although team working initially stimulates a requirement for redundancies, a high degree of 'natural' labour turnover ensures that redundancies are not required in the longer term. Moreover, after the initial installation period, if redundancies are required in companies which have both systems of manufacturing in operation, they are more likely to come from the production line. The machinists working in teams in these companies are therefore able to enjoy the benefits of job security to a greater degree than their production line counterparts. Therefore, contrary to the arguments of various feminist commentators (Christopherson, 1989; McDowell, 1991; Walby, 1989), Post-Fordism, at least in the context of the introduction of team working in the clothing industry, appears not to produce a numerically flexible workforce which is treated as peripheral and can be 'hired and fired' at the discretion of the employer.

It must be noted, however, at this juncture that once individual companies implement team working throughout the factory, the benefits of job security presently experienced by team members in companies which are also operating the production line will be discounted. When redundancies are required in companies which are solely operating team working, it will no longer be those workers on the production line that are adversely affected, but those team members with the least number of skills. Therefore, in the absence of adequate training and with the subsequent requirement of 'self teaching', this will affect those workers who refuse to spend unpaid time cross training and learning new skills and techniques.

Part-Time Work

Part-time work is another indicator of numerical flexibility. As explained in chapter three, recent European legislation entitles part-time workers to the same statutory rights as full-timers, stifling the ability of employers to use part-time workers in a numerically flexible way. Nevertheless, at the time this empirical investigation was conducted, part-time workers could be used in order to achieve numerical flexibility. Prior to this legislation employees must have worked at least sixteen hours a week with the same employer for two years to be eligible for employment rights, such as protection from unfair dismissal, paid maternity leave and redundancy pay. Additionally those who worked between eight and sixteen hours a week must have been with an employer for five years to qualify for security of employment (Walby, 1986). Up until very recently part-time workers therefore enjoyed substantially fewer employment rights than their full-time counterparts and were subject to dismissal at the will of the employer.

According to feminist writers, Post-Fordism stimulates a greater amount of part-time work. As team working can be classed as one form of Post-Fordism, it could be inferred that its introduction in the clothing industry will lead to an expansion of the availability of part-time work.

Evidence from the interviews suggests that part-time work is relatively absent in the sample of clothing companies. This is highlighted by the focus groups, with just one fifth of the operatives (working on both the production line and team working) stating that they were employed on a part-time basis. All these part-time workers had family responsibilities, caring for children and/or elderly dependants, which acted as the main barrier to full-time working. This trend was the same for operatives working on the production line and in teams, highlighting the difficulties of the dual role faced by many working women:

> I started part-time because I'd got children, and they've grown up and now I'm older I don't want full-time. My mother has took the place of my children now, I'm running round after me mum
> (Production line operative).
> I work part-time because of the kids....I couldn't work these long hours and look after kiddies
> (Team member).

This supports the comments of feminist commentators such as Beechey (1987), Dex (1987, 1999), Rubery (1994) and Walby (1989, 1997) that part-time work is crucial to a large number of working mothers. However, despite its importance, part-time work is relatively scarce in the clothing sector, something which the above authors fail to comment upon. This absence is mainly because part-time working adversely affects the flow of the production process, causing problems for line balancing, creating bottlenecks when a part-time worker is absent and overall stifling the flow of production. Moreover, part-time work results in low levels of machine utilisation, with machines laying idle for long periods within the working day, as part-time operatives are absent from the factory.

The difficulties involved in employing part-time workers are evident amongst the production line companies, as the machinists point out:

> C: Part-time work is very difficult
> B: They don't like you working part-time
> D: I think it was possible at one time. But now they want full-timers, not part-timers
> C: [Because]... ..they want to get the production out
> (Focus group with production line operatives).

Managers of the production line companies likewise stressed the difficulties involved in employing machinists on a part-time basis and openly admitted to avoiding part-time work at all costs:

> Part-time workers affect the balance on the line, where normally if you had twenty girls all working full-time the work will flow, but because you have part-timers you end up having build ups at various stages
> (Manager of production line company).

Managers of three of the production line companies suggested that the difficulties experienced when employing part-time workers are so severe that they have a policy of recruiting machinists who are least likely to have childcare responsibilities and are therefore unlikely to require part-time work. These companies avoid employing machinists between the age of 20 and 45, instead preferring what they refer to as 'young girls', who have yet to have children and 'older ladies', whose children are now grown up. The age of the labour force is therefore one factor which affects the availability of part-time work amongst production line companies:

> We might show a preference for an older lady who has had a family as opposed to a younger person. I know it's a terrible thing to say but it's obviously something that you've got to take into account, not just for problems with part-time work but pregnancy as well
> (Manager of production line company).

Despite the problems involved in part-time work, almost half the production line managers (46 per cent) stated that they offer this type of employment to their workforce. These companies appear to be of a specific nature, in terms of company size and management attitudes/relations with machinists, both of which are interlinked. Managers of these companies had distinctly different attitudes to those in companies which refused to offer part-time work. Although most of them still viewed part-time work as problematic, they accepted that as the majority of the machinists are women who have the main responsibility for caring, part-time work is a harsh inevitability in the industry. They recognise that, due to the stereotypical feminine image of the machinist's job and the accompanying long hours and low pay, few men are willing to enter the trade. They therefore acknowledge that they have to make the most of their female labour and appear to view them as a valuable resource to the company, often stating that 'part-time labour is better than no labour':

> Our ladies have to work part-time because of their kiddies and ...... you have to accommodate that. Ladies need to work part-time, most of our workforce are ladies and so we have to provide part-time..... part-time labour is better than no labour after all...... they do a great job for us and so we have to treat them right
> (Manager of production line company).

There is no correlation between the sex of the managers and those expressing these opinions. Male managers are just as likely as female ones to recognise the value of part-time work to women employees. The size of the company, on the other hand, does play a role in this process. The majority of the managers who recognise the value of part-time work to their female workforce work in small companies, with fewer than fifty employees. This can, in part, be explained by the fact that managers of smaller companies often have closer working relationships with their staff, frequently working on the factory floor with the machinists in order to complete orders on time. As a result they have some affinity with the machinists and appear to value their work to a greater extent. An additional explanation is that small firms will go to great lengths to both recruit and retain labour, including the provision of part-time work. The loss of one member of staff has a much greater effect on production levels and the cost of recruitment a much greater effect on profit margins than in larger companies.

The evidence from the companies operating the conventional production line therefore suggests that female machinists working in the industry often require part-time work in order to combine paid work and caring responsibilities. However, due to the difficulties experienced in the production process, many managers are reluctant to encourage part-time work. The managers who do offer part-time working opportunities appear to be those in smaller firms, who value their female labour.

To date there has been little research conducted into the relationship between team working and part-time work in the manufacturing sector. However, it is agreed amongst both team working researchers and practitioners (McLellan, 1994; Hague, 1995; Totterdill, 1995a) that, as long as team members are multi-skilled, part-time work should be easier to accommodate in a team work environment. Team members will be able to cover for their part-time colleagues when they are absent, reducing the bottleneck problems experienced on the traditional production line.

When team working managers were asked about this, three quarters stated that they did not offer part-time working arrangements to machinists. This figure is much higher than the equivalent for managers of production line companies (54 per cent), suggesting that part-time working opportunities are lower, as opposed to higher, in team working companies. This is further reaffirmed by the focus groups with team members, just eight per cent of whom worked part-time, compared to 31 per cent of their production line counterparts. Similar evidence has also been discovered by Penn *et. al.* (1994) when analysing the availability of part-time work following the restructuring of the textiles industry in Rochdale.

In order to explain this relative absence of part-time work amongst team members, the age groups of the respondents have been analysed. As mentioned earlier, the age of the workforce may have an effect on the availability of part-time working opportunities. Women aged 20-45 are more likely to have children and therefore to want to work part-time. However, the lack of machinists working on a part-time basis in teams cannot be explained by this phenomenon. A greater proportion of the machinists working in teams (90 per cent) fall in the 20-45 age category, compared to those still working on the production line (63 per cent). This indicates that other factors are important in determining the relative absence of part-time work in team working companies.

Some team working researchers, such as Hague (1995), argue that these other factors can be attributed to falling rates of labour turnover following the introduction of team working. His view is that part-time work is easier to accommodate in a team work environment but as the problem of labour turnover lessens, machinists are in a weaker position to negotiate for part-time working arrangements. However, as stated previously, only one third of the companies operating team working reported that labour turnover had fallen since the introduction of team working and no correlation was found between the team working companies which refused to offer part-time working opportunities and those with lower levels of labour turnover.

The relative absence of part-time work in the team working companies appeared to be related to difficulties of incorporating part-time workers into a team work environment rather than low levels of labour turnover, suggesting that team working as a system of production, renders the availability of part-time work more, not less difficult. This is reaffirmed by evidence from the focus groups. When asked about the possibilities of working part-time, the machinists replied that it would be more difficult on team work than on the production line:

> B: I don't think the firm would allow it [part-time work] because they want all the teams to start and finish at the same time as regards full-time work
> C: It depends though if everybody's on the same hours, if they're all on different hours you're gonna be up and down aren't you, forget where you are and go and do one persons job and then they're gonna come in the morning and say 'oh I've got no work' you know. It'd be harder to fit in than on the line
> (Focus group with team members).

Half the team working managers had experimented with part-time workers and had attempted to incorporate a mixture of full and part-time team members. However, many of these (six out of eight) discovered that this created numerous problems, particularly relating to unfairness amongst team members. Full-time team members were expected to cover for absent part-time colleagues, having to work harder and undertake a wider range of tasks once the part-timer had completed their shorter working day. Moreover, team cohesion was stifled when part-timers were placed in teams with full-time workers and consequently they tended to feel excluded and not an equal part of the team:

> It [mixing full and part-time team members] just didn't work. Some girls were working a lot harder than others. Some were slogging all day, whilst others could take it easy and went home early. It just wasn't worth the hassle we got from the girls on full-time
> (Manager of team work company).

The six companies operating team work which had unsuccessfully experimented with a mixture of full and part-time team members consequently refused to allow machinists working in teams to be employed on a part-time basis.

Half the companies (eight out of 16) had only partially implemented team working, whilst continuing to operate on a production line basis. Two of the managers of these companies stated that they did allow operatives on the traditional production line to work part-time. These managers had chosen full-time workers to become team members, whilst retaining part-timers on the production line. This trend is exemplified by one of the operatives interviewed:

> If you are full-time you can't swap to part-time any more. I used to be a part-timer when I first came here and then when we went onto the teams they asked me to come in full-time and ever since I've been on full-time, I've stayed on it. There's no going back now, if you want to work part-time you've got to go back onto the line
> (Team member).

This suggests that when these companies implement team working throughout the whole factory, those currently working part-time may be asked to convert to full-time, indicating that in the long run there may be a fall in part-time working opportunities within the industry, as more companies take on board the principles of team working. Indeed, six of the eight managers of the companies which had installed 100 per cent team working refused to offer part-time working opportunities at all.

Only four of all the managers of team working companies (25 per cent) stated that part-time working opportunities were available to operatives working in teams. Two of these agreed with the assumptions of the team working commentators previously referred to (Hague, 1995; McLellan, 1994; Totterdill, 1995a), that the employment of machinists on a part-time basis appears less rather than more difficult than on the conventional production line. These two managers were both working in companies which had implemented a Kanban system of team working (companies two and four, table 4.1, chapter four). None of the managers of TSS based systems of team working stated that part-time working opportunities were easier to accommodate in a team work environment. This therefore suggests that the nature of the system of team working has an effect on the ability of companies to offer part-time work.

These two managers stated that, as a result of the implementation of a Kanban system of team working, part-time working opportunities are now available to their workforce. These companies are the two mentioned earlier, which have successfully incorporated part-time workers into teams with full-time team members:

> It must be easier to have them [part-timers] on team working than on line production, but it's still harder than having them all as full-time....it's much harder when you're trying to balance the line, if you've got part-timers because you've got truly a block in the line then when someone is off. If they are cross trained it is easier, it doesn't make any difference to the team, people just slot in there. It's easier to have part-time workers on teams....because at least someone can cover their job
> (Manager of Kanban team work company).

Contrary to the majority of the managers who were interviewed, these two managers have found it easier to accommodate part-time workers following the implementation of the Kanban system of team working. These companies do, however, have some common features which may explain why they have found it easier to offer part-time work, whilst others have found it more difficult. They have both provided comprehensive training for team members, encompassing both technical and social skills. The social aspect highlights the importance of working as a team. As a result, full-time team members are less resentful towards their part-time colleagues, who consequently feel an equal part of the team. Feelings of unfairness amongst full-timers are therefore dispelled. The technical training complements this, ensuring that team members are very highly skilled, hence enabling full-time team members to adequately cover for their part-time colleagues when they are absent. This therefore suggests that part-time work is only easier to accommodate in a team work environment if the workforce is trained to be multi-skilled, thus confirming what various team work commentators (Hague, 1995; McLellan, 1994; Totterdill, 1995a) have previously indicated.

The two remaining companies which offer part-time working opportunities have both experimented with a mixture of full and part-time teams. These companies both operate the TSS system of team working and although they provide technical training for their staff, they have failed to overcome the problems of accommodating part-time work.

It therefore appears that the availability of training and degree of multi-skilling are not the only factors determining the extent to which part-time work can be accommodated in a team work environment. The system of team working in operation also plays a major part in this process. Within the Kanban model, operatives leave their workstations when the Kanban is full and resume work at a different workstation with an empty or partially filled Kanban. Operative movements are therefore largely governed by the condition of the Kanban. However, operatives do have some discretion relating to the workstation they move to next. It may be that two workstations have empty Kanbans, in which case operatives then have the responsibility of deciding which one to fill. This system therefore requires a high degree of flexibility and consequently operatives need to be multi-skilled, which is facilitated by training, either on a formal or informal cross training basis. These multi-skilled operatives are then able to accommodate part-time workers, using their discretion to cover their workstations when they are absent.

The TSS style of team working is based on the bump back philosophy, whereby operatives have a pitch of three or four sequential workstations. When the final operative in the team completes a garment, he/she takes control of the work of the previous operative and so on until the first operative is free to commence another garment. Unlike the Kanban system of team work, the workstations which operatives can utilise are tightly prescribed, often by management or supervisors. As a consequence, operatives tend only to have the skills required to operate workstations within their designated pitch. Therefore even though machinists are trained and multi-skilled, they do not have the discretion to cover when their part-time colleagues are absent. The only way in which part-timers can be accommodated is if team members are trained to operate additional workstations which fall in the designated pitch of the part-timers. However, management are often reluctant to invest in any more training than is absolutely necessary (see chapter six for a detailed discussion of training):

> We've tried intermingling full and part-time workers on teams and it works
> if you've only got one [part-time worker] and you've got a very skilled
> team, where the girls can operate every workstation on the module, so that
> they can cover for that person....but of course however skilled they are, it's
> very rare that they can all perform all operations
> (Manager of TSS team work company).

Due to the difficulties of combining full and part-time team members, these two TSS companies have attempted to operate a limited number of part-time teams. The hours that these teams work tend to correspond with school opening times, from nine until three. One of these companies has also introduced a part-time team which they referred to as a 'mums' shift'. This team works from quarter past nine till quarter past three and does not work during the school holidays.

However, managers of these companies stated that the operation of part-time teams also caused considerable problems, that they are reluctant to operate them and that in their opinion part-time working in a team work environment has actually created more problems than it did on the production line:

> [Part-time work] has actually created more of a problem for us with team
> working because those teams are left idle whilst they've gone. We'd like to
> have all full-timers in here, we're not employing any more part-timers
> (Manager of team work company).

The main explanation for the difficulties experienced in operating part-time teams is that all workstations on a team are left idle for large proportions of the working day and as a result machine utilisation is low. This is less of a problem on the production line, where individual machines only are left idle. Low machine utilisation which is associated with part-time workers is particularly problematic with the TSS system of team work. As explained in chapter six, TSS requires heavy investment in new technology and therefore low levels of machine utilisation are undesirable.

Difficulties relating to low levels of machine utilisation could be eliminated by the operation of two shifts instead of one, with one team operating in the morning and another resuming duties in the afternoon. One of the TSS companies expressed a wish to implement such a form of shift work but faced obstacles - the shift pattern did not suit mothers who were required to accompany their children to and from school.

The managers of these two TSS based team working companies operating part-time teams stated that part-time work was more difficult to accommodate in a team work than a production line environment.

However, despite these difficulties encountered they continued to operate a small number of part-time teams. These companies did, however, have a specific feature in common. Like the managers of the production line companies, previously referred to, who offered part-time working opportunities despite the difficulties it caused, these managers too recognised the value of their predominantly female labour force and the importance of part-time working arrangements to them. In fact the managers of these companies appreciated the value of their labour force to such an extent that they offered part-time working arrangements despite the fact that they were operating 100 per cent team working. This suggests, therefore, that the extent to which managers allow team members to work part-time is also dependant upon individual manager attitudes towards women and work.

Having assessed the degree to which team working has facilitated the availability of part-time working arrangements in the clothing industry, it is also important to examine the extent to which part-time work within the sector can be used in a numerically flexible manner. Various feminist writers (Christopherson, 1989; McDowell, 1991; Walby, 1989) have argued that part-time work is used by 'Post-Fordist' companies as one way of achieving numerical flexibility. However, evidence from the companies indicates that part-time work within the clothing industry, in both production line and team working companies, cannot necessarily be classed as numerically flexible (and could not, even under the previous legislative framework), suggesting that these feminist theories cannot be directly transferred to the clothing sector.

Prior to the new legislation relating to part-time work and employment rights, these feminist authors argued that part-time work was numerically flexible on the basis that employees working less than 16 hours a week and with the same employer for less than five years were ineligible for employment rights such as protection from unfair dismissal, paid maternity leave and redundancy pay. However, all the part-time women who were interviewed stated that they worked more than 16 hours a week, working approximately six hours a day, therefore working only slightly fewer hours than their full-time counterparts. Part-time working hours tend to be from eight or nine o'clock in the morning till three o'clock or three thirty in the afternoon. These hours correspond with school opening hours and enable working mothers to take their children to and from school. This therefore reveals that the part-time workers who were interviewed were eligible, even under the previous legislation, for employment rights and could not be classed as numerically flexible.

It could be argued that part-time workers can be used in order to achieve numerical flexibility in another way, irrespective of the number of hours worked. The hours of individual part-time workers could be altered on a weekly basis in order to effectively meet demand. However, there was no evidence of this practice in any of the companies.

It can therefore be seen from the evidence provided in this section that, although team working can be classed as one form of Post-Fordism, the extent to which it stimulates more part-time work in the clothing sector is limited. The majority of companies which have implemented team working have found that it is more difficult to offer part-time working opportunities than on the production line. Furthermore, the extent to which team working companies offer part-time work is governed by the system in operation, together with a number of complex interrelated issues relating to managerial cultures and attitudes.

These conclusions, together with the evidence that part-time work within the clothing industry could not necessarily be classed as numerically flexible (even before the legislative changes) and the fact that team working does not stimulate a greater level of redundancies (in the long term), therefore cast doubt upon the transferability of the theories of various feminist writers, particularly those relating to the expansion of numerical flexibility in the Post-Fordist economy, to the clothing sector.

Implications for Gender Relations

This section explores the way in which the withdrawal of part-time work in team working companies affects the predominantly female workforce. Feminist literature explores the implications of part-time work for women, examining both its potential values and drawbacks (Beechey and Perkins, 1987; Dex, 1987, 1999; Robinson, 1988; Rubery et al., 1994; Walby, 1997). This literature suggests that although women often require part-time work due to caring responsibilities, particularly in Britain where childcare facilities have traditionally been minimal, part-time workers are exploited. They have lower pay, less chances of both training and promotion, and until recently fewer employment rights. It is therefore argued that, as the majority of part-timers are female, the provision of part-time work in Britain has facilitated gender segregation in the labour market.

From this it could be inferred that women who are forced to work full-time rather than part-time, following the introduction of team working, will benefit from higher pay, job security, more training and improved chances of promotion. However, once again these feminist concepts cannot be directly transferred to the clothing industry. It has already been pointed out that part-time work in the sector is not numerically flexible and that part-time workers have traditionally had the same employment rights as full-timers. Moreover, there was no evidence from the interviews with either management or machinists that part-time workers receive lower wages than their full-time counterparts.

Nevertheless, employers may still view part-timers as marginal workers who are the first to be chosen for redundancy and the last to receive training or promotion. There were hints of this from the interviews with managers, who agreed that part-time workers could be the first to be made redundant. Furthermore, the amount of training and promotion opportunities available in the industry is limited, not only amongst part-time workers but amongst full-timers too, as chapter six reveals.

The feminist writers mentioned above rightly point out that part-time work can lead to greater gender segregation in the labour market, but the extent to which this is accurate in the clothing industry is debatable and is, in any case, beyond the scope of this book. Machinists who worked part-time on the production line and are expected to work full-time in teams, may therefore gain very little and, indeed, none of those interviewed agreed that there were benefits. On the contrary, they experience immense difficulties.

Chapter three discussed the way in which the role of caring has been constructed in our society as a feminine activity (Beechey, 1987; Dex, 1999; Pollert, 1981; Walby, 1986; Westwood, 1984; Williams, 1997). Women face pressure to conform to this stereotypical gender role. Thus, as long as the task of caring remains the responsibility of the female, and until childcare provision in Britain adequately meets demand, women who previously worked part-time on the production line but are now forced to work full-time in teams, are being made to work much harder. Effectively, they have two full-time jobs: one at home, and one at work.

This process is reaffirmed by the interviews with machinists working both on the production line and in teams. The majority of whom took it for granted that they should have the main responsibility for childcare, and although they made it clear that working full-time and rearing children was not an easy process, very few of them actually advocated a need for more male involvement:

> D: I would say it's almost impossible working full-time
> A: It's impossible because of school holidays
> D: Unless you've got a partner who's at home or somebody who lives virtually next door who can have them

(Focus group with production line workers).

The women expressed concern about the lack of part-time work within the industry, frequently arguing that working mothers face enormous problems which could quite easily be solved if management were prepared to grant them permission to work part-time:

> B: I think they ought to start doing part-time
> A: I couldn't work full-time and go home and look after a family
> C: .....they don't do any part-time work here and I think they should. Because there's a lot of women left to have babies and they're really good machinists and because they can't come back part-time they're loosing good machinists [who have had] years and years of experience and they just can't come back because it's too much and they go somewhere else to look for another job
> (Focus group with team members).

This requirement for part-time working arrangements within the industry was widely recognised by the machinists. In some cases women had left the company in order to give birth to their child and on return had been refused part-time work on the grounds that it caused the company 'too many problems'. Some explained that in these circumstances they had been more or less forced to leave the company and search for alternative employment opportunities. However, in the words of one female machinist 'it's the same everywhere, they just don't want part-timers'.

As a result some women stated that they had no alternative but to work from home. Their partner's wage was often not enough to support the family and they expressed feelings of uselessness being a 'housewife'. These women said that they had worked at home for a period of time, until their children were of school attending age. Homeworking is not, however, the ideal solution and creates specific problems of its own:

> The youngest must have been six before I went back to work because I did it at home but that becomes a bit of a bind at times working at home because you don't sit yourself down, somebody comes in and say's 'are you going out?' and off you go and then you'll not get it done.... so you need to be very strict with yourself. I mean when you've got little children, you know you're able to earn some money so it's better than not having anything at all, but you have to do it either when they've gone to school or when you've got little ones around you when they've gone to bed, for two or three hours, so you're working odd hours with that and you have to push yourself more than you do here
> (Production line operative).

Other machinists had faced similar difficulties and with no alternative means of earning an income made a conscious decision to work full-time and cope as best they could with the problems it created. These machinists utilised close female friends and/or relatives as childminders in order to overcome the difficulties of full-time work. This therefore provides supporting evidence to the theoretical explanations of authors such as Dex (1999), Finch (1989), Twigg and Atkin (1994), and Williams (1997) that care is frequently provided on an informal basis by close female relatives who, due to gender stereotypical roles present in society, feel obliged to provide the necessary care:

> I managed by taking them to grandma's.....my mother-in-law had them in the school holidays.
> (Production line operative).
> My mum looks after her while I come to work. I take her early in the morning and pick her up about fourish after work. My mum takes her to school and then picks her up and it works really well
> (Team member).

These solutions were not, however, the answer to all the machinists' problems. Some women found the task of combining full-time work and childcare too big a burden, particularly those without any relatives at a close proximity. These women stated that they were forced to leave paid work altogether for long periods of time, at least until their children reached school attending age:

> Well mine [children] are grown up. I didn't work till they were, I didn't do a job until my youngest was nine. I didn't have nobody to look after them
> (Production line operative).
> I didn't go to work when they were younger I stayed at home....I left work and looked after them till they all left school. What else could I do. I didn't have anybody to help me out
> (Team member).

These sentiments were mirrored by machinists presently without children, who stated that they could see themselves ending up in a similar situation in a few years time:

> I would have to pack work in because I've got no parents and neither has me husband so there would be no messing about really, it would be a case of I'd have to stop
> (Team member).

However, some machinists argued that these stereotypical gender roles were changing and that in the future child rearing may become both a masculine and feminine activity. When asked if they thought that men were now taking more responsibility over childcare duties and if this would make it easier for women to work full-time in the future, the women appeared divided and at times the discussion got fairly heated. Some stated that working women would always have considerable problems and that men were not contributing to the child rearing process more than they had previously. Others were more optimistic arguing that gender relations had changed substantially during the last few decades. These women, nevertheless, expressed a desire to see further changes and remained adamant that working women with children continue to be restricted in terms of career progression. The following extract from a focus group reveals the extent to which the women had mixed opinions:

> C: I think a woman tends to fit her life into a family, round her husband and her children
> B: ....it's more difficult for a woman, and even though it's supposed to have changed, women's lib and all of this I think it will be the same for ever and a day
> A: Because men always expect you to wait on them, it don't matter if you're full-time or not
> C: Well its like if you've got children, who's expected to stop at home? It's the woman it's not the man
> D: That's it, you work here all day and then you go home and you've got tea to prepare and you've got pots and....
> A: Sit down about nine o'clock
> D: Mind you things are changing though now aren't they, or have changed. I mean my lads have grown up and their wives work, their family life's different to mine, because their wife's career is just as important, both of them. So it don't just revolve around what husband's doing, it's what wife is doing as well. Whereas it didn't with me.........but there's women in here that's capable of doing a lot more, capable of doing office jobs and career jobs, to go a lot further than what they are, but they're fitting it in with their children aren't they and their families and everybody around
> (Focus group with production line operatives).

It is therefore clear from the evidence provided here that gender relations are socially constructed in our society in such a way that women have the main responsibility for the care of dependants, in particular children. Thus in the absence of part-time work in the clothing sector, particularly in team working companies, female employees face the difficulties of two full-time roles, one as a mother and one as a worker.

Nevertheless, the reduction of part-time work in most team working companies does not necessarily have to have a detrimental effect on women. As long as existing stereotypical gender relations remain, women will continue to find it difficult to work the full-time hours required by many team working companies. But the introduction of team working could be accompanied by other strategies aimed at relieving the difficulties faced by women working full-time. Two such strategies are the provision of flexible working arrangements and childcare facilities, policies being promoted by the Labour government taking office in 1997. If these are introduced alongside team working, women in companies whose managers refuse to offer part-time work may benefit from its implementation.

Firstly, to look at flexible working arrangements. The interviews with managers of production line companies reveals that flexible working arrangements in the clothing industry are extremely limited. None of the production line companies offered flexi-time or encourage job-share, which are the most basic of the strategies available. Allowing the workforce to start or finish slightly earlier or later each day is as flexible as it gets:

> We don't have job share, we normally say to part-timers 'you must work thirty hours within our opening times'. The full-timers can either start at seven thirty or eight o'clock and finish at four thirty or five o'clock and that's it, it's not real flexi-time as such
> (Manager of production line company).

As flexibility is one of the principal characteristics of team working, one would expect the companies operating this system of production to offer a greater degree of flexible working arrangements than those still utilising the production line. However, the pattern was similar for both groups of companies. None of the team work companies offered either flexi-time or job-share. A manager of one team working company did suggest that a policy of flexi-time was in operation. But in a pattern similar to that seen in the companies still utilising the production line, this policy merely allowed each team to start or finish work slightly earlier or later each day. Thus the implementation of team working does not appear to alter the situation:

> I mean that's [flexi-time] one thing team working can't facilitate, I say to them 'look you've got thirty nine hours there ladies, the doors are open from then to then, as long as we've got the work, let's go'
> (Manager of team work company).

This lack of flexibility within the industry is further highlighted by an examination of holiday entitlements. Almost all the sample of companies (both production line and team working) had extremely inflexible holiday arrangements, closing for just two weeks in July or August, therefore ensuring that the workforce all take their holidays simultaneously.

Managers in a few companies appeared slightly more flexible than others and allowed their employees a couple of floating days. Discussions with machinists in these companies reveal that flexible holiday arrangements enable working mothers to attend school events such as sports day or Christmas plays and to remain at home when their children are ill. However, these machinists still believed the policy to be insufficient and the benefits are limited.

The task of quantifying the precise number of companies offering floating days has proved difficult. Even though they were pressed for answers, managers appeared quite vague when asked for further details about holiday arrangements. There do not appear to be any differences between companies utilising the production line and team working in this respect, nor between companies operating different models of team working. From the evidence available, it is difficult to asses if the companies which do offer a limited number of floating days have any other characteristics in common (such as the sex of the manager, the size of the company etc.). In any case, as this policy has only limited benefits to the workforce, such an analysis would not prove very useful. This situation may improve to a certain extent in the near future. All employees are now legally entitled to a reasonable amount of unpaid time off work to deal with emergency care, for example when a dependent falls ill.

In common with other manufacturing sectors in Britain, flexible working arrangements are therefore seen to be absent in the clothing industry. This situation may begin to change with the Blair Labour government promoting policies designed to encourage family friendly employment strategies (see chapter three for a more detailed account). Until such changes take place the predominantly female workforce will continue to be adversely affected. Women, particularly those working full-time, would benefit from flexible working arrangements. Flexi-time would enable them to escort their children to and from school, and accompany them on visits to the doctor or dentist.

This unwillingness to offer flexible working arrangements can partly be explained by the fact that the managers of both production line and team working companies fail to recognise the problems caused by the lack of flexibility. Both male and female managers, and even those who had earlier stressed the value of part-time work to their female workforce, failed to recognise the importance of flexible working arrangements. The latter appeared to believe that the availability of part-time work was a sufficient measure to enable women with childcare responsibilities to continue working in paid employment. They seemed unable to understand that some women with childcare responsibilities may wish to work full-time and that one way of facilitating this is via the availability of flexible working arrangements.

From this evidence it is clear that flexible working arrangements are relatively absent within the clothing industry and that the introduction of team working does not encourage or enhance their provision. This lack of flexibility is unacceptable within an industry which has such a large proportion of female workers, particularly to those with caring responsibilities. Furthermore, it may cause particular difficulties to women working in teams, who are less likely to be in a position to work part-time.

Having discussed the availability of flexible working arrangements, the provision of childcare facilities will now be explored. None of the 33 companies operating either the production line or team working provided any kind of childcare or crèche facilities for their workforce. This lack of provision was acknowledged by both managers and machinists alike, but was an issue of most concern to the latter, prompting passionate, heated discussions.

Although the machinists working on both systems of production appeared resigned to this situation, many were aggrieved by the absence of alternative facilities outside the workplace, in either a public or private sphere. When asked about the adequacy of childcare facilities in this country, the machinists unanimously stated that childcare facilities were inadequate, in terms of quality, quantity and price. A typical response is outlined below:

> C: No, there aren't any
> All: No.
> D: Definitely not.....there isn't any
> C: Well if there is they're expensive aren't they?
> D: ......you'll be paying out as much are you're earning and that's stupid
> B: There used to be nursery schools
> C: Well I mean your nursery schools don't take em till after three so you've got at least three years haven't you
> E: Unless your families are gonna have them.......I waited till they went to school and then I got a part-time job
> (Focus group with production line operatives).

This reaffirms the arguments put forward in chapter three that childcare in Britain is grossly inadequate and until recently has been amongst the worst in Europe. This situation is currently in the process of change, in light of the Blair Labour government's encouragement of good quality affordable childcare, through the National Childcare Strategy. A number of studies of this policy are being undertaken, for example Crompton *et al.* (2000), however, it is too early, as yet, to assess its full impact.

As the clothing industry is a notoriously low paid sector, the quantity of childcare places available was not the only concern of the machinists. The cost of the facilities understandably also provoked much anxiety, with the majority of the women (working in both production line and team work companies) stating that this factor provided the biggest single barrier to crèche usage. Many agreed that, financially, it would not be worth their while to utilise a childminder and that if they were not able to draw upon an informal network of friends or relatives to take care of their children, they would inevitably be forced to cease paid employment, at least until their children reached school attending age:

> B: I don't think it would pay anybody in this trade to come back to work and pay a childminder. Well it wouldn't be worth their time, their effort and they just wouldn't gain anything at the end of the day
> A: They just wouldn't gain anything because you see a childminder now, if you have one full-time for a week it's about £80, but then they'd perhaps only come out with £20 at the end of the week so it just wouldn't be worth it
> (Focus group with production line operatives).

These sentiments were mirrored by machinists working in teams:

> C: I haven't got no children, but I think it's disgusting what they charge
> A: Say you take home a hundred and twenty pounds a week, you've got to pay forty, fifty pounds out straight away for childminders, so it really works out that you're better claiming social then you are working
> (Focus group with team members).

The enormous expense of childcare facilities was likewise recognised as a problem by management, particularly by female managers who, despite their higher income than the average machinist, faced similar problems. When asked if childcare facilities in Britain were adequate, one female manager replied:

> No I think it's very difficult, I think it's the cost more than anything for most women, certainly in this trade which is renowned for quite low pay. Usually people with children in our trade generally find that it's family and friends.....the childminder is expensive, it's more than me mortgage. And I know that a lot of girls here couldn't afford to pay the amount I have to pay in childminding fees but you know obviously I do earn a lot more than most of the girls here, but it's still a lot for me really
> (Female manager of production line company).

The high cost of childcare facilities was a reoccurring theme throughout the focus groups and machinists working on both the production line and in teams argued that managers could alleviate this problem by providing on site crèche facilities. Some women stated that the provision of on site crèche facilities was of such importance that they would even be prepared to pay for the privilege, whilst others more sensibly suggested that the company contribute towards the costs. Women in one company, who were no longer allowed to work part-time following the introduction of team working, felt so strongly about childcare provision that they had made numerous suggestions to management:

> At the last meeting somebody said about so much towards childminding fees and they said they would look into it, but it's been asked before......I don't know why they can't pay for a crèche for the amount of people that have got children and then pay so much.....you know because if someone's paying forty pounds a week and if you charge them twenty quid, they're saving twenty straight away
> (Team member)

All the female managers who were interviewed recognised the importance of childcare facilities to their predominantly female workforce. These managers suggested that childcare facilities were particularly important to mothers working full-time. Many of the male managers, on the other hand, failed to recognise the importance of childcare facilities. This even extended to the male managers, referred to earlier, who recognised the value of their female employees and therefore offered part-time work. These managers appeared to believe that the availability of part-time work is a sufficient policy for working mothers and, consequently, women with children who work on a full-time basis are not catered for.

Despite the fact that the majority of the machinists, as well as some of the managers, identified a lack of adequate childcare provision outside the company sphere and recognised the importance of workplace childcare provision, the managers who were interviewed all remained adamant that such facilities would not be provided in the foreseeable future. This pattern was similar in all the companies, in those operating both production line and team working, as well as those with male and female managers. In fact, pressure from the workforce to provide such facilities appeared to have no impact whatsoever, with a large number of company managers stating they had been approached by machinists about the possibility of providing childcare but that it was not a feasible option. The most frequently cited explanation as to why was the financial cost involved:

> They've looked at the cost aspect of it but at that specific time it didn't work out cost effective enough but it depends what sort of level of machinists they're looking to bring back, I mean if and how much we're going to charge. If it's going to be free you could possibly look at getting ten or twelve excellent machinists back on which would obviously mean not having to recruit raw trainees
> (Manager of team work company).

The high monetary cost of providing childcare facilities was often attributed to the existence of extensive legislation, with management arguing that the official requirements of a workplace crèche are so considerable that the whole process is unaffordable. In particular, management cited the nurse to child ratio, health and safety regulations and insurance requirements as the principal constraints:

> We don't have crèche facilities, legislation has now made that totally unrealistic financially for a factory of this size. Health and safety, you're only allowed one for every six kids, you need one trained nurse, I mean it just becomes a nightmare
> (Manager of production line company).

Childcare facilities in Britain generally, and in the clothing industry in particular (at least at the time of the study), were therefore inadequate for the needs of machinists. As team working expands throughout the clothing industry and the availability of part-time work diminishes, women will be increasingly forced to work full-time. In the absence of adequate childcare facilities and flexible working arrangements, this will inevitably result in an expansion of the reliance of women upon the caring capacity of the family, particularly female relatives. However, not all women within the industry will be able to make use of such informal caring relationships, particularly those who have moved away from their place of upbringing and their close relatives. This suggests that only those women who have relatives living close by and who have retained their roots will be able to remain in paid employment:

> It was a problem for me, my mum and dad lived away at the time so I couldn't leave them with anybody so I just had to leave work till they were old enough
> (Team member).

Conclusion

This chapter has explored the hypothesis advocated by various feminist authors that Post-Fordism leads to an expansion of numerical flexibility which is damaging for female labour. By an examination of the introduction of one form of Post-Fordism - team working, in the clothing industry - it is clear that although this may be true in the tertiary sector, it does not necessarily hold up in a manufacturing context.

The presence of numerical flexibility is low overall in the clothing industry. This is highlighted by a low level of redundancies, a lack of part-time employment opportunities and the fact that part-time work within the clothing sector has not traditionally been utilised in a numerically flexible manner. Furthermore, this chapter has shown that the implementation of team working does not reverse this situation, suggesting that Post-Fordism is not necessarily accompanied by an expansion of a numerically flexible workforce.

The failure of team working to stimulate a greater degree of numerical flexibility is evident when exploring the level of redundancies. If the workforce is treated in a numerically flexible way and are 'hired and fired' according to demand, a high level of redundancies would be expected. Although the installation of team working initially stimulates a requirement for redundancies, a high degree of 'natural' labour turnover ensures that redundancies are not required, in the longer term. Furthermore, after the initial installation period, in companies operating team working alongside the traditional production line, machinists working on the latter system are more likely to be made redundant. This indicates that in companies operating both systems of production, if anything, those working in teams will be less rather than more subject to numerically flexible work practices.

The inability of team working to stimulate numerical flexibility is also evident when examining part-time work. The majority of team working companies have found that it renders part-time working more rather then less difficult than on the production line. Moreover, it has been discovered that the level of part-time work in the clothing industry is not, in any case, a good indicator of the level of numerical flexibility, with part-time employees working only a few hours less than their full-time counterparts and therefore enjoying similar employment rights.

Some team working companies do offer part-time work and it has been shown that this is dependant upon the system of team working in operation, together with a number of complex interrelated cultural issues. The two companies which have found it easier to employ part-time machinists since the implementation of team working have been those which have adopted the Kanban system and which have provided comprehensive training for their workforce.

The other team work companies have found it more difficult to offer part-time work than on the production line and therefore only a limited number of them allow machinists to work on a part-time basis. These companies provide part-time work despite the difficulties involved, primarily because they have managers who recognise the importance of female labour and their requirement for part-time working opportunities. However, for most team working managers, the problems of incorporating part-time work outweigh any concerns they have about the needs of female employees. Some companies which have only partially implemented team working do offer part-time working opportunities to operatives still working on the production line. Nevertheless, many of the managers of these companies have made it clear that when they adopt team working throughout the factory, part-time working will no longer be available.

The reduction in the availability of part-time work in the majority of team working companies obviously has connotations for gender relations. It means that team members are more likely to work full-time, creating difficulties for many women employees, particularly to working mothers who have the main responsibility for childcare. This is exacerbated by the fact that managers of team working companies refuse to encourage either flexible working arrangements or childcare facilities, both of which would help mediate the adverse implications of the reduction in part-time work. Despite the fact that most machinists would like flexible working arrangements and childcare provision and that some managers also recognise the importance of the latter, both policies were absent in the companies visited. This may begin to change in light of the Blair Labour government's encouragement of family friendly employment policies, but it is presently too early to provide conclusive evidence with respect to this.

In conclusion, the evidence discussed in this chapter suggests that the hypothesis that Post-Fordism leads to an expansion of numerical flexibility, which is consequently damaging to female labour, can be refuted, at least in the context of the implementation of team working in the clothing industry. In some instances team workers are less likely to be made redundant which may benefit female labour and, in the majority of companies, they are less likely to be in a position to work part-time (which, in any case, cannot be classed as numerical flexibility). Moreover the relative absence of part-time work may prove damaging, particularly to working mothers with childcare responsibilities.

6 Team Working, Functional Flexibility and Technological Change

Introduction

This chapter tests the theoretical arguments outlined in chapter three relating to functional flexibility and technological change within the Post-Fordist economy. Evidence is provided from the empirical investigation of the introduction of team working in the Nottinghamshire clothing industry.

Chapter three explored feminist theories of Post-Fordism and gender relations at work and revealed that, alongside numerical flexibility, the simultaneous development of functional flexibility and the significance of technological change are important issues.

Functional flexibility is a complex phenomenon. Buchanan (1994), Dawson and Webb (1989), and Tomaney (1990) suggest it has a dual effect on the workforce, stimulating job enrichment and job enlargement. Furthermore, the Post-Fordist, flexible technologies can have the same effect. Cockburn (1985), Lloyd (1997), Truman and Keating (1987) and Wajcman (1991) suggest that these technologies can be used to deskill and upskill.

It was indicated in chapter three that the extent to which the search for functional flexibility results in either job enlargement or job enrichment, and the way in which technology is utilised, are dependant upon the way in which work is reorganised. Buchanan (1994) and Tomaney (1991) suggest that the Swedish model of team working will lead to job enrichment, with an emphasis placed on operative skills as opposed to technological innovation. They suggest that even if new technology is introduced with this model, it will be utilised in a way which upskills. However, if the full ethos of the Swedish prototype are absent or other variants of team working (such as the Japanese ideal type) are installed, the workforce may instead experience job enlargement and new technology will be used in a way which deskills.

Dawson and Webb (1989), Elgar (1991), Elsass and Graves (1997), and Wood (1986) suggest that the way in which work is reorganised, and therefore the extent to which the workforce experience job enlargement or job enrichment and either upskilling or deskilling as a result of technological change, may be determined by gender. Male jobs will be enriched whilst female jobs are enlarged, leading to labour intensification. Some feminist writers (Cockburn, 1985; Gardiner, 1997; Jenson, 1989b; Truman and Keating, 1987) explain this by the social construction of skill. Women are viewed as unskilled and incapable of working autonomously and performing the higher order tasks involved in job enrichment. Other commentators point out that the jobs which are upskilled as a result of technological change are assigned to men and those which are deskilled allocated to women (Chiesi, 1992; Cockburn, 1985; Crewe, 1990 and Zeitlin, 1992). Cockburn (1985), Jenson (1989b), Lloyd (1997), and Wajcman (1991) explain that this is related to the 'gendering' and social construction of technology. This process was exemplified in chapter three by an examination of the implementation of team working. It was suggested that the likelihood of the implementation of the models of team working which lead to job enlargement and deskilling, rather than enrichment and upskilling, may be higher when the workforce is female.

Existing research in this area is relatively absent and this chapter aims to redress the gap in the literature. This is achieved by testing the hypothesis that 'models of team working which lead to job enlargement and which utilise new technology in a way which deskills are more likely to be implemented than those which lead to job enrichment and which utilise technology in a way which upskills when the workforce is predominantly female'.

As explained in chapter four, the models of team working implemented in the sample of companies cannot easily be classified into either the Japanese or Swedish ideal types but are instead categorised into those utilising the Kanban or Toyota Sewing System (TSS) Japanese philosophies. This chapter will therefore explore the extent to which these two systems of team working determine whether the jobs of the workforce is enlarged or enriched and deskilled or upskilled as a result of technological change.

The chapter is divided into three sections. The first explores a number of criteria, thereby enabling a comparison of the quantity and status of tasks undertaken by production line workers and team members. The link between the skill content of tasks and technological change is also explored and the way in which different systems of team working play a part in this process is examined.

The second section looks at the implications of this process for team members. A number of criteria are explored in order to assess the extent to which the quantity and status of tasks undertaken by machinists affects the quality of their working life.

The third section explores the validity of the job enlargement versus job enrichment dichotomy. This incorporates a discussion about the relevance of the deskilling versus upskilling dichotomy which is said to result from technological change. It also examines in further detail the nature of and explanations for the models of team working implemented, and investigates the role that gender plays in this process.

The chapter utilises both qualitative and quantitative evidence, drawing upon the operative questionnaire results, the focus groups with machinists and the interviews with managers (see chapter four for a more detailed analysis of these research methods).

The Quantity and Status of Tasks

Advocates of team working (NEDO, 1991b; Farrands and Totterdill, 1990; Totterdill, 1994; Tyler, 1994) justify its implementation in the clothing industry on the basis that it enhances the quality of working life. Team working can promote the development of a multi-skilled workforce, which possesses a range of transferable skills that extend beyond those performed on the production line to encompass tasks of a more discretionary nature. However, they argue that these benefits will only be experienced if cultural change simultaneously takes place, with management style being based on responsible autonomy rather then direct control, and a comprehensive training programme initiated.

These commentators fail to outline the resulting implications if team working is implemented without the required cultural change. McLellan *et. al.* (1996) have begun to redress this, arguing that the result will be job enlargement rather than job enrichment, as Buchanan (1994) and Tomaney (1990) suggest.

Multi-skilling

The term multi-skilling can be interpreted in a variety of ways. Academically it is used to refer to the process whereby workers enjoy an expansion of technical and social skills, experiencing polyvalency.

Technical skills mean that team members perform a wider range of similar status tasks, operating a variety of machines and performing different sewing operations. Social skills mean that machinists participate in higher order tasks such as problem solving and decision making. Amongst managers and operatives within the clothing industry, however, the term multi-skilling is used to mean the ability to perform a wider range of similar status technical skills. As the empirical research for this book relies on interviews with both employers and employees within the clothing industry, the latter definition of multi-skilling is utilised here.

The questionnaire results suggest that the majority of all machinists view themselves as being multi-skilled. Nevertheless, there are minor disparities between the two groups of machinists, with slightly more team members (87 per cent) identifying themselves as being multi-skilled, in comparison to production line workers (62 per cent). Team members were also slightly less inclined to agree that they only had 'one good skill' (three per cent), in comparison to 19 per cent of production line workers.

On the production line there is a correlation between the size of the company and the degree to which machinists believe they are multi-skilled. All the production line machinists working in companies with less than fifty employees agreed that they are multi-skilled. As the size of the company increases, the likelihood of machinists agreeing with this diminishes. This can be explained by the fact that small production line firms are inherently more flexible; they have a limited number of machinists who have to learn a wider range of skills than those in larger companies. The extent to which this is true in team working companies is difficult to detect as variations in company sizes are less pronounced (see chapter four).

The number of skills possessed by team members is also greater than that of production line workers. The average number of skills enjoyed by the former being four, double that of the latter. Once again there is a correlation between the size of the production line companies and the skill levels of the machinists. The smaller the company, the greater the number of skills possessed by machinists. Again, this can be explained by the 'flexible' nature of small firms.

The quantity of skills is not, alone, an adequate indicator of the existence of multi-skilling. Machinists may possess numerous skills but unless these are regularly utilised, they cannot be classed as polyvalent. The number of skills performed by machinists each day is therefore a better indicator. The focus groups confirm that team members are more likely to be multi-skilled than their production line counterparts. Although the majority of the latter stated that they were multi-skilled, all except four said that they remain on one sewing operation each day. This even extended to those machinists, previously mentioned, who work in small production line firms and have a wider range of sewing skills. Although these machinists do possess a number of skills, they very rarely change operations each day, unless an operative is off ill.

The four production line machinists who said that they change sewing operations each day all work in the same company, producing wedding dresses. Due to a combination of both the small size of the firm and the wider variety of sewing operations involved in the 'one off' dresses, they change operations more frequently than production line machinists in other companies.

For team members, on the other hand, the regular performance of a range of tasks is the rule rather than the exception, with 83 per cent stating that they change operations each day:

> A: We do about three jobs every day
> C: ....You don't stop on one job all day.....before you might have been on one job for a couple of months and then moved. But you do learn more jobs on JIT
> E: In an hour there are certain jobs you'd be moving every five minutes, every ten minutes
> (Focus group with team members).

The difference in the replies of production line and team working respondents reveals the subjective nature of the concept of multi-skilling. The majority of all machinists believe they are multi-skilled, yet production line workers generally perform one main task each day, whilst team members regularly change operations.

The frequency which team members change operations each day varies between companies, as does the skill content of each operation and the ability of machinists to decide when and where to move. Each of these are dependant upon the nature of the system of team working implemented, as well as the degree of cultural change.

In six companies machinists move workstations frequently each day, changing operations every few minutes. These were all working in companies which had implemented the TSS model, which is based on the bump back philosophy, whereby workers have a pitch of three or four sequential workstations. Consequently, operative movements between workstations are frequent and regular.

In order to facilitate this, the TSS managers said that they had invested in technical training and new technology. Technical training is explored later in this chapter and so a detailed discussion shall not detain us here. It is sufficient to point out that technical training enables machinists to operate a wider range of sewing machinery. Investment in new technology based on programmable sewing machinery, which reduces the skill content of individual tasks, was initiated in all six TSS companies. This shortens the sewing time involved in each operation and enables operatives to perform a greater number of tasks:

> The machines were slowed down and therefore the operators could handle the work more efficiently, and so acquire a skill quicker.....a lot of them have been deskilled, in the past on a conventional way if it had been a big job where you had to make your collar, turn it out, top stitch your collar, then attach it, attach the first side, close it again and close the second side. Now we have a separate machine which would make the collar, then we'd have a second machine to turn it through, then top stitch the collar, then a third machine would attach the first side and then the fourth machine would close the second side, so it has actually been deskilled
> (Manager of TSS team work company).

However, this technological change does not only deskill, it upskills as well. The sewing machines are often programmable and require additional higher level skills involving computer programming and the alteration of pre-set programmes. But machinists do not seem to participate in these accompanying upskilled tasks, which are instead carried out by other predominantly male personnel, usually mechanics. The machinists stated that computerised sewing machines had enabled them to perform some limited programming tasks but these simply involved the 'pressing of a few buttons':

> B: You don't actually do that programming they'll set it up and then you'll perhaps alter the simple things
> A: ....you change the stitches and things
> B: The mechanics do the complicated things and we do the easy ones, like measurement or drop
> C: You have two programmes or three programmes and you just hit a button to change each programme as you go along
> (Focus group with TSS team members).

Thus the computerised programmable sewing machines which are introduced in TSS team working companies are utilised in a way which deskills the jobs of the machinists, whilst upskilling the jobs of the mechanics. This may be because machinists are provided with technical training to operate a range of sewing machinery but not in programming activities. One reason for this is related to the way in which technology is gendered, an issue which is explored in more detail later.

This deskilling is exacerbated by the fact that managers retain overall authority and therefore machinists have little autonomy over their actions. All TSS team members stated that they are able to utilise all the workstations in their designated pitch but that their pitches are not self-determined, and are instead prescribed by their managers or supervisors.

A different picture emerged in the ten other team working companies, all of which operated a variant of the Kanban model. Team members move less frequently (between one and four times a day). They change workstations only when the Kanban is full, in contrast to the TSS model, where operation changes are required each time a garment is completed. As the frequency of machinist movements are lower, investment in new technology is not required and therefore deskilling does not prevail to the same extent:

> We have got computerised machines, but we'd got them before we went onto team working.....I don't think it [team working] really changes it
> (Manager of Kanban team work company).

These managers suggested that, if anything, the introduction of team working had reduced the requirement for technological change, rather than increased it. They advocated an expansion of employee skills and stated that they had introduced new technology which deskills sewing operations only if absolutely necessary:

> We haven't introduced much new technology, although we have introduced some.....we've tended to go for operator skills rather than high-tech machinery
> (Manager of Kanban team work company).

Although these Kanban companies focus less on the introduction of new technology which deskills individual tasks than companies operating the TSS model, when new programmable sewing machines have been introduced once again the computer programming tasks which have a higher degree of skill content tend to be performed by the predominantly male mechanics. This can again be linked to the absence of technical training focusing upon programming activities at an operative level and the way in which technology is gendered.

Nevertheless, unlike TSS team members, most Kanban team workers appeared to gain a greater degree of responsibility and discretion than they had on the production line. In all except one Kanban company

(company 14, table 4.1, chapter four) the style of governance had changed, with managers devolving some of their duties to team members. However, this was limited and merely meant that in accordance with the condition of the Kanban, machinists were allowed to decide when and to which workstations to move to. Thus, if two workstations had empty Kanbans, machinists had the responsibility of deciding which one to fill. This can be contrasted with the experience of TSS team members, whose movements are constrained within their individual pitch, which is in turn determined by management.

The experiences of Kanban team members are not, however, homogenous and two different scenarios emerged. Machinists in the majority (seven out of ten) of these companies had not received any technical training to enable them to operate a range of workstations. Managers did not prioritise training to the extent that TSS mangers did; frequent and regular operative movements are far less crucial to the Kanban philosophy. Nevertheless, operative movement between workstations is still required and both the machinists and managers recognised the importance of multi-skilling to the Kanban team work philosophy:

> A: Team working is all about being multi-skilled
> C: You've got be multi-skilled to earn your money, you can't get your bonus if you can't do a few jobs
> (Focus group with Kanban team members).

The majority of the companies operating team work (both TSS and Kanban systems) have introduced a system of payment which is related to performance, whereby the team receive a bonus for reaching certain levels of production (payment systems are explained in more detail later). In order to operate at the optimum speed and therefore reach the production targets set, machinists are required to perform different operations within the team. However, unlike the TSS team members, machinists in the majority of the Kanban companies are not formally trained for the required multi-skilling. As a result machinists in all except one (again company 14, table 4.1, chapter four) of these seven companies explained that they had been forced to cross train, teaching their fellow team members their 'best' skill. This is invariably conducted during lunch breaks and is unpaid.

The level of multi-skilling amongst machinists working in the majority of the Kanban based companies is therefore limited and dependant upon the willingness and ability of team members to cross train each other. As a result many of these machinists indicated that they move workstations only when absolutely necessary, preferring to remain on the workstation that they are most familiar with and that they can operate the quickest.

This situation can be contrasted to that in the minority (three) of companies which have implemented the Kanban model of team working. Managers of these companies have provided technical training for team members enabling them to operate a variety of workstations and as a result cross training is not required. Machinists working in these companies have been able to utilise the limited amount of authority devolved from management to decide when and to which workstations to move to. So as well as performing a wider range of similar status tasks they have also experienced an increase in delegated responsibility, at least in some respects.

It can therefore be seen that team working does encourage a degree of multi-skilling, with machinists performing a larger quantity of sewing operations than on the production line. However, the way in which this affects the workforce is determined by the nature of the model of team working and the accompanying cultural change.

General Levels of Responsibility

The general level of responsibility experienced by machinists is an indicator of the status of tasks they perform. A high level of machinist responsibility suggests that they have some discretion and autonomy and are able to perform higher order tasks.

The majority of team working managers and machinists agreed that team members had more responsibility than on the production line, 81 per cent of former and 60 per cent of the latter arriving at this conclusion. This slight discrepancy in the views of these two groups of personnel is because on occasions managers stated that they had assigned more responsibility to machinists, when in reality they had not. Two main reasons have been identified for this: in some situations managers were intent on portraying their company and hence team work as beneficial to the workforce, whether or not it was; and in other cases managers and machinists had different ideas of the definition of responsibility. What managers believed to be a devolution of responsibility, machinists classed as the mere ability to think and in their words 'use our brains'. Although many machinists viewed this ability to 'think' as beneficial, they quite rightly did not classify it as a greater degree of responsibility.

All the machinists who agreed that they had more responsibility than previously were working in the Kanban companies. The machinists working in TSS based teams, on the other hand, unanimously agreed that they had no more responsibility than before. This suggests that the Kanban model is more likely to stimulate a greater degree of responsibility than the TSS model. However, the nature of this additional responsibility requires exploration.

Self Organisation within the Team

Self organisation within the team suggests a greater degree of machinist responsibility and autonomy and has implications for the status of tasks performed. All the team members who stated that they had experienced a greater degree of responsibility than previously attributed this to the requirement for self organisation within teams. As members of a team, they have the prime responsibility for its operation and performance. Each team is expected to manage itself, with minimal intervention at a supervisory level and as a consequence team members are often required to make decisions which would have been the responsibility of the supervisor under the production line. These decision making responsibilities encompass team discipline and performance levels.

The requirement to make these decisions is in itself an indicator of enhanced machinist responsibility. However, this responsibility is reinforced further still as the level and quality of each team member's performance is dependant upon that of their peers, thus ensuring that each team member is responsible not only for their own actions but for those of their colleagues. This aspect of team working was viewed by the Kanban team members as the main factor contributing to their higher levels of individual responsibility:

> D: You've got more responsibility when you're working as a team than when you're working on your own because you're not just looking after yourself
> B: With there being four of you it's not just yourself you're working for, it's everybody
> (Focus group with Kanban team members).

The experiences of the TSS team members were different. All suggested that self organisation within teams was not a feature of this model of team working. Managers and supervisors retain overall control and therefore supervisors have the main responsibility for the organisation of the team rather than team members.

So while Kanban teams are expected to manage themselves, with minimal intervention, TSS teams rely on both supervisory and managerial direction. As a consequence TSS team members are very rarely expected to make the decisions that their Kanban counterparts are; team discipline and performance levels are controlled by supervisors who regularly and frequently 'patrol' the teams that they are responsible for:

> We don't get any more responsibility, they interfere. It's not so much management, but it's supervisors. They tell you what to do....they're up and down, up and down all time, watching
> (TSS team member).

This contrast between Kanban and TSS team members is reinforced by the nature of team meetings. In order to facilitate collective team decisions, thereby ensuring optimum team performance, both TSS and Kanban team members stated that they have been instructed to conduct team meetings, either amongst themselves or if the issue cannot be resolved, jointly with managers or supervisors. This can be contrasted with production line machinists who unanimously stated that team meetings were unheard of, highlighting a degree of additional responsibility delegated to machinists working in teams.

However, the levels of responsibility involved in team meetings varies between the companies and the model of team working determines this. TSS team meetings are held on a regular basis, ranging from once a day in some companies to once a month in others. They are invariably instigated and directed by the supervisor responsible for the team and are often referred to as team briefings, which is perhaps a more accurate title. All the TSS team members stated that they regularly attend team briefings/meetings and that their supervisor also attends, without exception. The purpose of these team briefings is diverse; they are used to keep supervisors and managers informed of the progress of the team, to identify and solve any problems relating to either the production process or associated with team cohesion, to discuss performance levels, production targets, style changes and so on.

The TSS managers agreed that team briefings are often instigated at a supervisory level but were additionally keen to point out that machinists are also able to call team meetings with managers and/or supervisors if required. The machinists disagreed, stating that although this was theoretically true, the reality was quite different. None of the TSS team members had ever attended a team meeting that was not instigated by either a supervisor or manager. This again confirms the limited amount of responsibility devolved to TSS team members.

In contrast, Kanban team meetings are informal and ad hoc. Kanban team members are responsible for the organisation of the team and one way in which they facilitate this is via team meetings. Machinists meet on the basis of need and the responsibility of deciding when and where to meet and what issues to discuss lies with them. The nature of the meetings varies according to the issues to be discussed. If a problem arises which is particularly severe, the entire team stop work to meet. If the problem is minor, only the machinists concerned discuss the issue. This again indicates that Kanban team members have a greater degree of responsibility for team organisation than their TSS counterparts.

However, this increased responsibility is more limited than it at first seems. Although most Kanban team members are responsible for calling team meetings, like their TSS counterparts, they are unable to initiate team meetings with either supervisors or managers. Theoretically they can initiate such meetings, but they stated that they were frequently discouraged from doing so. This is exemplified by the fact that Kanban team members are invariably paid for time spent in meetings called by management, but when they request such a meeting, they are not paid for lost production time:

> If you ask for a meeting you don't get paid for it, but if they ask you, then you get paid for it
> (Kanban team member).

Furthermore, Kanban team members agreed that when they arrange meetings, management are often reluctant to attend and when they do show up, they very rarely act on any of their comments or anxieties:

> B: You can ask to see him [manager] and he will see you
> A: ....don't mean he'll take any notice
> D: [Then we] think that was a waste of time
> (Focus group with Kanban team members).

It can therefore be seen that the extent to which team working leads to a greater degree of machinist responsibility, with respect to self organisation within the team, varies between companies and is determined by the type of team working introduced.

Solving Production Problems and Line Balancing

The frequency of stoppages in most production line companies is high due to bottlenecks, and supervisors usually bear the burden of these difficulties.

Farrands and Totterdill (1990), NEDO (1991b), and Tyler (1994) argue that team working can lead to a transfer of responsibility for solving production problems and line balancing from supervisors to operatives. They argue that this not only benefits the workforce, enabling them to enjoy the benefits of enhanced responsibility, but is advantageous for the company, leading to a reduction in stoppages; supervisors on the production line are a lot slower to intervene than team members are.

Farrands and Totterdill (1990) stress that the responsibility for line balancing and other production problems will be transferred to operatives only if company culture simultaneously changes. This requires a management style based on responsible autonomy rather than direct control and the introduction of a comprehensive programme of training. Managers and supervisors need to be trained to accept this devolution of responsibility and to facilitate machinist action when required. Meanwhile machinists need training to participate in these activities.

When asked about this issue in the questionnaire, there were slight disparities between the replies of the production line machinists and the replies of team members. The latter were slightly more likely to participate in problem solving activities (30 per cent), than the former (22 per cent). Moreover, 39 per cent of production line workers said that they do not solve production problems, compared to just 16 per cent of team members.

Evidence from the focus groups reveals a similar pattern, with more of the team members than the production line workers agreeing that they solve production problems. When asked about the nature of the problem solving activities that they are engaged in, both production line workers and teams members mentioned line balancing activities.

It therefore appears that only a minority of the machinists participate in problem solving activities, all of which involve line balancing tasks. Moreover, team members have only a slightly higher propensity to participate in these activities than their production line counterparts. However, it must be noted that the nature of the production line companies and the system of team working also play a part in this process.

The production line machinists who participate in problem solving and line balancing activities work in small companies, employing up to 25 workers, and these actions are often unauthorised. Indeed, managers are usually unaware of any action that machinists have taken:

> A: When we see work building up, or if there's a problem, if the fabric's not been cut right, you stop blockages on the line if you can, then you can get the work out quicker

C: No one tells you, you just pick it up as you go along. You soon learn to spot problems instead of getting the supervisor, that takes time
A: He [the manager] hasn't got a clue what's going on
(Focus group with production line operatives).

Similar evidence was discovered by Farrands and Totterdill (1990). It may appear strange that machinists are willing to take such action when they are not instructed to do so, but production line workers are generally paid on a piecework basis and therefore as wages are linked to productivity, it is in their (financial) interest to avoid potential situations, such a bottlenecks, which may affect the level of productivity.

This then raises an additional question: why is it that machinists employed in small firms carry out these unauthorised activities and those in larger companies, who are also paid on a piecework basis do not? There are two main explanations for this. Firstly, as Farrands and Totterdill (1990) point out, machinists in smaller firms generally have a higher skill base than those in larger companies and therefore tend to have a greater awareness about the process of garment construction, which enables them to recognise problems before they arise. Secondly, supervision tends to be less formal in smaller companies. Many of the small firms have one supervisor who is primarily engaged in machining activities, but intervenes if required to oversee any difficulties. Supervision is informal and ad hoc, therefore, machinists are often able to take unauthorised action, rectifying line balancing problems before they ever require supervisory attention.

Machinists in larger production line companies, on the other hand, are more likely to have one skill and therefore possess little knowledge about the broader process of garment construction. Moreover, supervision tends to be more structured and formal. A combination of these two factors means that any difficulties that arise tend to remain undetected by the operatives and are instead discovered by the supervisor.

Team members who participate in problem solving and line balancing activities also work in companies of a specific nature. Similar to those machinists who experience a greater degree of responsibility for self organisation in the team, these machinists all work in the Kanban companies. They agree that team working has enabled them to perform problem solving tasks and that, prior to its implementation, these activities were the sole responsibility of the supervisor:

A: You feel more aware of what the problems are
B: Before you used to be more like a zombie than an actual person

C: You have more responsibility now for problems....we never did that on line work
(Focus group with Kanban team members).

It is hardly surprising that these machinists have started to participate in problem solving activities only after the introduction of team working. They all work in quite large companies, with 50 or more workers, where problem solving activities are traditionally performed by supervisors.

Following the implementation of the Kanban model, managers in these companies had recognised the need for a devolution of responsibility. Moreover, two thirds of the team members who agreed that they now had responsibility for these issues worked in just two companies (companies two and four, table 4.1, chapter four). As explained in chapter five, these are the only two companies which operate the Kanban model of team working and provide technical and social (including problem solving) training for their machinists, as well as providing training at a supervisory level.

The technical training enables machinists to perform a wider range of machining tasks. They gain broader knowledge about the garment construction process and are able to recognise production problems as they arise. The social training informs them how to identify and intervene in the production process to prevent bottlenecks. Meanwhile, the supervisory training means that supervisors are encouraged to work with and facilitate the teams, instead of policing and directing machinist action, as they had done on the production line. This ensures that supervisors both accept and assist the transfer of responsibility for problem solving tasks to operatives.

It can be seen therefore that there is one vital difference between the production line workers and the Kanban team members who participate in problem solving activities. The actions of the former are unauthorised by managers and supervisors, while the latter are sanctioned. Farrands and Totterdill (1990) and NEDO (1991b) have also discovered that following the implementation of team working, problem solving activities become authorised. They argue that the very fact that these activities are authorised indicates that machinists experience a greater degree of responsibility than on the production line. However, the validity of this argument is questionable: both groups of machinists perform the same problem solving and line balancing activities and therefore it is difficult to measure the extent to which those working in teams have a greater degree of responsibility for these tasks.

For the majority of the team members (approximately 70 per cent), the situation is different. They do not participate in line balancing or problem solving activities. These machinists were working in two types of team working companies. Over half were working in Kanban companies, which had neglected to provide a comprehensive programme of training at either an operative or supervisory level. The absence of operative training meant that machinists were unable to participate in problem solving activities, while the absence of supervisory training meant that supervisors retained their 'production line' method of surveillance, instructing team members about the best course of action to take, intervening when production problems arose, and making decisions with respect to line balancing issues. Two of these machinists working in just one company had received technical training and gained broader knowledge about the garment construction process, which enabled them to recognise production problems. Nevertheless, a lack of social training meant that they were reluctant to intervene in the production process and an absence of supervisory training meant that supervisors were reluctant to devolve responsibility for these tasks.

The remaining team members who stated that they did not participate in problem solving or line balancing activities were all employed in the six TSS companies. Within this model, managers and supervisors tend to retain overall authority and control. So despite the fact that all these companies had provided supervisory training, technical training at an operative level, and five of the six companies had also provided social training for team members, the responsibility for solving production problems, including line balancing, remained at a supervisory level. As a result of their technical training, machinists have greater knowledge about the process of garment construction and are able to recognise problems as they arise. However, once they have identified a problem, rather than take action themselves, they are instructed to inform a supervisor.

It can be seen therefore that the responsibility for problem solving and line balancing often lies at a supervisory level. Team members have only a slightly higher propensity to perform these tasks than their production line counterparts, and this is primarily evident in Kanban companies which provide comprehensive training. Moreover, the extent to which this differs from small production line companies is questionable.

Responsibility for Quality

It is suggested (for example Tyler, 1994) that one of the principal benefits of team working to the manufacturer is an improvement in the quality of production. This is facilitated as team members become more responsible for the quality of the final product and therefore indicates a widening of machinist responsibilities.

However, the questionnaire results reveal little difference in the replies of the two groups of machinists, with the majority of production line workers and team members agreeing that they regularly check the quality of their work (over 80 per cent) and that the achievement of a high level of quality is an important requirement (over 60 per cent).

Nevertheless, the evidence from the focus groups with team members suggests that the importance of quality increases following the implementation of team working. All the team members, working in both Kanban and TSS based teams, agreed that although quality was important when they worked on the production line, it is even more important in a team working environment. This can be explained by two main factors. Firstly, the standard and quality of work of each team member is dependant upon that of the others. Each machinist has a responsibility to ensure that the level of quality is acceptable to enable their fellow team members to adequately perform the next stage of the production process. On the production line, however, machinists are both unaware and unaffected by the performance of the next person in the production process and therefore, if they can get away with it, are more inclined to produce work of a lower standard. Secondly, if the quality of work is below standard in a team work environment the team responsible can easily be identified and the garment returned to the team as a whole for correction. On the production line, where numerous machinists perform identical operations, it is far more difficult to trace the individual culprit and therefore machinists are more likely to submit work below the required standard:

> B: When I was on production line..... you can earn money and you just pile it out, leave it for the next person, it could be totally all wrong. Whereas now you've got to make sure your job's right, when you've finished to pass for the next person
> A: So you're not getting it back or holding that girl up
> (Focus group with team members).

Although team members stressed the importance of quality within the focus groups, they also indicated that speed is still important. As we will see later, the payment system often changes with the implementation of team working but remains performance related; a group payment system with a bonus replaces the individual piecerate. However, team members stated that they are no longer able to prioritise speed over quality. Sub-standard or faulty garments are returned to the team for repair, reducing the output of the team and affecting their ability to reach the production targets required to achieve the bonus. This can be contrasted with the situation in the production line companies, where some machinists are able to prioritise speed over quality in the knowledge that faulty garments are very rarely returned to the individual responsible.

Although the team members unanimously agreed that quality is more important in a team working environment, they questioned the degree to which this is an indication of a greater degree of responsibility. They have always been responsible for quality, the difference being that on the production line they could choose to avoid the responsibility but when working in teams they cannot:

> It's no different than on line.....you got away with it before, if something wasn't quite right you put it in and didn't worry, now it comes back to you (Team member)

Team members undoubtedly place greater importance on quality than their production line counterparts and this is obviously beneficial to the company, but the extent to which machinists benefit from this process is questionable. By placing a greater emphasis on quality, team members do not feel that they enjoy a greater level of responsibility. Moreover, as speed remains important due to the nature of the payment system, team members experience the additional burden of balancing the speed of production with the quality of the final commodity.

Setting Production Targets

Machinist participation in setting production targets suggests a degree of worker responsibility and autonomy. When asked about this in the questionnaire, production line machinists were slightly more inclined to agree that production targets are set by management (59 per cent compared to 41 per cent for team members) and slightly less inclined to agree that they themselves participate in setting production targets (26 per cent compared to 30 per cent for team members). Thus, overall the majority of all respondents believe that they have little responsibility for the setting of production targets and that these activities are primarily performed by management.

Evidence for this lack of machinist participation in the setting of production targets is even stronger when analysing the focus group data. Both production line workers and team members unanimously agreed that responsibility for this activity remains solely in the hands of management. They all agreed that production targets are formulated without their consultation and when on occasions they had attempted to contribute to this decision making process, their suggestions were completely ignored.

Furthermore, the introduction of team working does not appear to reverse this trend, as the following focus group shows:

> B: We don't have no say over production targets, none over style changes, no. That's up to planning
> C: You've no say, you do the work and that's it
> B: Just like on the line, it's not changed, you had none then and none now (Focus group with team members).

A detailed analysis of the focus groups with team members reveals that the situation is identical for those working in both Kanban and TSS teams. The inability of team workers to participate in this activity is perhaps most clearly exemplified by the situation in three companies, all of which operate the TSS model. These three companies have a system of flashing lights and electronic music to enable the identification of teams requiring assistance. This is complemented by a board, located adjacent each team module, displaying production targets. Each team's progress towards their production targets is displayed electronically on this board. The target the team needs to meet to achieve its bonus is shown, as is the number of actual garments made, enabling each team member to see at a glance if they are ahead of, on, or behind target. This system is clearly designed to inform machinists of the production targets set rather than involve them in the decision making process. Some managers of other team working companies (both TSS and Kanban) also expressed a desire to introduce such a system in the near future.

Style Change

Machinist participation in style change decisions is another indicator of worker responsibility. The managerial interviews reveal that the personnel responsible for making such decisions varies substantially between production line and team working companies. Production line managers unanimously stated that machinists had little input into the decision making process during style changes, with senior personnel (managers or supervisors) being responsible for both initiating style changes and deciding the most effective method of constructing a new style. In some cases the new style specification is set out in writing for machinists to follow and in other cases, often in larger companies, supervisors demonstrate the most effective method.

In contrast, all except one team work manager (company 14, table 4.1, chapter four) stated that machinists now have a certain degree of responsibility for making such decisions, which they did not have previously. Machinists are now expected to make decisions on a range of issues relating to the new style: deciding the number of team members required; which team members should operate certain workstations; and the most effective method of constructing the new style.

However, all except two of these team working managers had kept some control over this process, and decisions during style changes were made by the machinists in coordination with the supervisor:

> The managers at the moment balance the line for how they see it going through the line best. The manager then issues that out to the supervisor who looks at it, gets the machines that she needs, implements them into the correct order for it to flow through and then each girl is then shown her own job and then the work just flows off so...once we've actually written down what we want. What we think is the best way, we tell them and then they come back and tell us, "oh no we don't do that, we'd rather do it this way". We'll say "OK have a go, send it through that batch but if there's any problems come back to us"
> (Manager of team work company).

The only two team working managers who agreed that machinists had been assigned complete responsibility for style changes worked in companies two and four, which were mentioned previously. These are the only two companies which operate the Kanban model and provide technical and social training for machinists, as well as training at a supervisory level. As a result, supervisors are willing to devolve responsibility for these tasks to operatives, whilst the operatives are able to deal with the extra responsibility. The following discussion has been extracted from an interview one of these managers and implies a large increase in the teams' responsibilities:

> Before the supervisors would be actively involved, they'd plan it, they'd work out how many people we need..... whereas now it's just, here's the short, here's the machines, that's what the garment should look like, there's your work, bye, bye, effectively and they seem to prefer it that way. We used to have a lot of supervisors now we don't really have any, they just get on with it
> (Manager of Kanban team work company).

When the machinists were asked about their role in the decision making process during style changes, the replies appeared quite different from those of management. Although all (except one) of the team working managers had stated that machinists were now able to exercise more discretion during style changes than they had previously, only 11 of the 53 machinists who participated in the focus groups agreed. These 11 all worked in the two Kanban companies, two and four. So, despite their manager's claims that they had been assigned complete responsibility over style changes, these machinists disagreed, stating that the added responsibility was limited. They suggested that management were only really paying 'lip service' to the idea of worker empowerment and although they were consulted, all too often their decisions were ignored and only very rarely taken on board. A typical statement from these machinists was:

> C: They decide who does what when we have a change of style and you get on with it
> D: But management do listen a bit. We have some say when new styles come in because we can decide which girls go on which jobs and things like that
> A: Yeh, but they don't always listen
> C: Not as much as I'd like. I think we should have more say
> (Focus group with Kanban team members).

The remainder of the team members (79 per cent), on the other hand, stated that they had no more responsibility over these issues than when working on the production line. These machinists worked in two different types of companies. One group worked in TSS teams and though they had received both social and technical training enabling them (in theory) to participate in the decision making process during style changes, the system of team working ensured that these activities remained at a supervisory level. The second group of machinists worked in Kanban teams and had been informed that they would participate in the decision making process during style changes. However, unlike those working in companies two and four, neither machinists nor supervisors received any training. As a result machinists did not have the skills to perform the tasks and supervisors were reluctant to devolve responsibility for the tasks to them.

It can be seen therefore that only team members in companies operating the Kanban model, alongside a comprehensive training programme, believe they have more discretion with respect to style changes, and even then they claim the responsibility is more limited than their managers suggest.

Relations with Managers and Supervisors

Machinist relations with managers and supervisors is the final indicator to be examined in this section: the more equal the relationship, the greater the degree of machinist responsibility and empowerment. Many of the questionnaire respondents believe that they have a good relationship with their supervisors, agreeing that supervisors 'respect them' (46 per cent for production line workers and 57 per cent for team members) and 'let them get on with their jobs' (68 per cent for production line workers and 77 per cent for team members), with only a minority believing that supervisors 'think they know best' (17 per cent for production line workers and 28 per cent for team members) and 'interfere in their work' (less than ten per cent for both groups of workers). This pattern appears to be the same for all machinists, suggesting that the introduction of team working has little (if any) effect on machinist/supervisor relations. Evidence from the focus groups supports this, with the majority of both production line and team working machinists (62 per cent and 64 per cent respectively) agreeing that supervisors interfere only when necessary.

It was evident and worth noting that, when asked about issues of power and control, the machinists attitudes changed slightly. Nearly all production line workers (88 per cent) suggested that the relationship is an unequal one; supervisors are very much in control. In the words of one production line machinist 'they let you know who the boss is'.

Most team members (77 per cent) agreed. Their actions were controlled by the supervisor when they worked on the production line and team working made no difference. The remaining 23 per cent (12 machinists) said that the supervisors' role had changed following the introduction of team working. Supervisors were less likely to act as 'policers' and more likely to act as 'enablers' or 'facilitators'. All but one of these machinists worked in the two companies, two and four, which operate the Kanban model and have provided both social and technical training for team members, as well as training at a supervisory level.

Unlike the TSS model, the Kanban system enables a transfer of responsibility to team members, which is realised only when supervisors are trained to facilitate additional machinist responsibility and when machinists are trained to deal with this. The extent to which the machinist/supervisor relationship has changed in these two companies is exemplified in the following focus group:

> D: You decide between you what you do, she's [supervisor] just there to help
> B: Before you worked on the line and you shared a supervisor
> D: She'd normally tell you, do it like this, or you do it this way, now you decide between yourselves which way you do it and you tell her. We do have a bit more say
> (Focus group with Kanban team members).

The questionnaire results reveal that the majority of both production line and team working machinists believe management to be 'approachable', but only 39 per cent of both groups agree that 'management take notice of them'. This indicates that although machinists believe they can approach management, only a minority of them feel that their comments are taken seriously. Moreover, the implementation of team working does not appear to alter the situation.

Evidence from the focus groups further highlights the unequal relationship between managers and machinists. The production line and team working machinists all reflected on their inability to influence managerial decisions and the latter unanimously agreed that the introduction of team working had failed to alter this situation. This was the case even in the two companies, two and four. Although the role of the supervisors has clearly changed in these two companies, the managers remained the same. They were clearly in control:

> A: We have more say when it comes to supervisors, the difference between us is not as big. But managers, they're the same as ever
> B: Supervisors - they do listen now and take notice, but the manager, he say's oh just get on with it, that's what you're paid for, we've given you more powers, you're empowered now, you have more responsibility, don't try and take advantage, I'm still the boss you know
> (Focus group with Kanban team members).

Such managerial attitudes are not surprising. The culture of British managers has traditionally been based around direct control, with the workforce being dictated to and possessing little discretion and autonomy. This has been particularly evident in the clothing industry, where Taylorist principles of work organisation have dominated. Farrands and Totterdill (1990) and Tyler (1994) quite rightly argue that training can help managers adapt to a new style of governance involving a devolution of power, although, none of the sample of companies examined here have introduced such a programme of training.

It is therefore clear that power and authority lie at a supervisory and managerial level in both production line and team working companies. Devolution of responsibility is evident only in companies which have introduced a Kanban system, together with comprehensive operative and supervisory training but even then, the devolution of responsibility is limited:

> It's not power. You can think for yourself at last.....You've not got supervisors thinking for you. You're using your own brains at last. The power stops with management. I mean the production manager just said to the team this morning, "you'll have to do all those again, you're not getting any more till you've done them again". The team said, "we won't earn anything, we said we'll put it right in out own time". The factory manager said, "well it's too late, you'll have to do them now". So much for empowerment
> (Kanban team member).

The evidence provided up until this point reveals that the way in which the quantity and status of tasks performed by machinists changes following the introduction of team working is a complicated issue which is determined by the type and nature of the system of team working implemented (as Buchanan, 1994 and Tomaney, 1990 point out), together with the degree of accompanying cultural change.

Implications for the Workforce

In order to assess the extent to which the working experiences of machinists have changed following the implementation of team working, this section explores a number of criteria which encompass the following: interest and enjoyment; hard work and peer pressure; promotion opportunities and career progression.

Interest and Enjoyment

Most questionnaire respondents, working in both production line and team working companies (56 and 59 per cent respectively), view work as interesting. However, production line workers are twice as likely to believe that work is boring. This is further reaffirmed by the evidence of the focus groups, which suggest that machinists working on the production line are more inclined to believe that work is boring than their team working counterparts.

The main explanation for this is that production line machinists are more likely to perform one task each day, whereas team members perform a wider range of tasks, thus enjoying more variety at work:

> You're just a robot. It's continual same thing, over and over again.....it's boring. I wouldn't be bored if I was doing garments from start to finish. When you're doing forty-five dozen a day, just putting sleeves in, it does get boring
> (Production line operative).

There are, however, difficulties in comparing the replies of the two groups of machinists. The extent to which machinists feel work is interesting is subjective and depends on their work experience. Those working on the production line have never experienced team working, whilst those working in teams have experienced both systems of production and so their comments are based on different experiences.

In order to overcome these problems of comparison, team members were asked if team working is more or less interesting than the production line, and all but four (working in company 14, table 4.1, chapter four) agreed that work was now more interesting. There are two main explanations for this. The first and unanimously agreed explanation amongst both TSS and Kanban team members relates to the point just mentioned, i.e. that team working requires a range of sewing operations each working day and therefore entails more variety at work. The second explanation was provided only by Kanban team members and relates to levels of responsibility. All Kanban team members (except the four previously mentioned) agreed that alongside the performance of a greater variety of machining tasks, responsibility for the organisation of the team, in terms of its discipline and performance, means that work is more interesting than previously. The 11 machinists who work in the two Kanban based companies, two and four, additionally pointed to their participation in the decision making process during style changes, line balancing and problem solving activities as a further explanation.

The variety at work involved in team working has wider implications for the workforce. As they perform a range of sewing tasks, and in the case of the Kanban team members have a greater degree of responsibility, machinists not only find work more interesting but also more enjoyable. The overwhelming majority of team members (92 per cent) agreed that they enjoy variety at work. The remaining eight per cent all work in the company previously mentioned (company 14, table 4.1, chapter four).

Some benefits are therefore derived from the performance of numerous machining tasks, with work becoming more interesting and enjoyable following the implementation of team working. Indeed, the majority of team members (79 per cent) believe that being multi-skilled is beneficial to them. As a direct result of this greater degree of interest, four fifths agreed that, in general, they enjoy team working.

Hard Work and Peer Pressure

The degree to which machinists work hard is difficult to quantify, but this was a reoccurring theme raised by both production line workers and team members. However, there are disparities between the two systems of production, with team working intensifying work. This is confirmed by the questionnaire, with 72 per cent of team members agreeing that they work harder in a team than on the production line.

Evidence from the focus groups supports this, with all (except the four machinists working in company 14) stating that the work required in teams is harder than on the production line. Explanations for this are twofold. Firstly, team members perform a wider range of sewing operations, thereby experiencing labour intensification. Although the number, frequency of movements, and skill content of individual operations vary between TSS and Kanban companies, this pattern appears to be the same for both systems.

The TSS model involves the introduction of new technology which deskills. Although this means that each sewing operation involves a lower degree of skill content than previously, TSS team members find it harder work as they have to frequently move between numerous operations:

> C: JIT means that you have to work harder now, you have to do more jobs
> A: It's a lot harder now.....a lot more jobs to do, a lot more work, it's go, go, go all the time, all day long, they don't half push us
> (Focus group with TSS team members).

Kanban team members also change operations and find this harder work, but in a different way to their TSS counterparts. They are not under as much pressure to move regularly and frequently between workstations. However, they are required to move and the relative absence of new technology which deskills individual operations means that the skill content of the tasks required at each workstation remains unchanged:

B: Team work is harder
A: It is hard work, you've got to learn a lot of jobs instead of just one or maybe two
B: We have to work a lot harder than on line.....moving between jobs
(Focus group with Kanban team members).

The second explanation for team working requiring harder work was only expressed by Kanban team members and relates to levels of discretion and responsibility. As previously outlined, these machinists experience a greater degree of responsibility, particularly for the organisation of the team and as the following machinist points out, this responsibility exacerbates the amount of work required in comparison to the production line:

We have to work a lot harder now than on the line. Changing jobs, doing new operations, organising the team. It's harder work now, a lot harder (Kanban team member).

The eleven machinists working in the two Kanban companies, two and four, which have developed operative and supervisory training, have additional duties. They are not only required to work harder, performing a range of sewing operations and being responsible for the organisation of the team, but they have the added workload of participating in problem solving and line balancing activities, as well as making decisions during style changes.

It was explained in chapter three that payment systems play an important role in this debate. If machinists receive higher wages for performing more tasks of either a similar or higher status, then although they are having to work harder, at least they are being rewarded financially for doing so. However, the questionnaire reveals that team members are not rewarded for their harder work. Although 28 per cent agreed that they were better paid in a team, the majority (72 per cent) were either receiving the same or lower wages than when working on the production line.

This is reaffirmed by the focus groups. A minority of team members received higher wages than previously, whilst over three quarters were no better off financially than they were on the production line. Thus a substantial proportion work harder, performing a wider range of tasks but are not financially rewarded for doing so, hence experiencing labour intensification.

The degree to which machinists are adversely affected by this varies according to the company within which they work and the nature of the model of team working. TSS team members perform a wider range of similar status tasks, without financial remuneration:

A: When they changed it to pressing on the end of the line as well we said, "well we'll be getting a pay rise on top of what we normally earn because we're going to be able to press as well as machine" the same with the pressers, but we didn't. So we do more work for the same pay
B: We've got to press, do our own job and other jobs and no more dosh
(Focus group with TSS team members).

Kanban team members suffer even more. They not only perform a wider range of similar status tasks, but also carry out higher status tasks, all for similar levels of pay:

B: I think we should get paid more
C: On conventional you did one or two jobs and that was it, now here you've got to learn about eight and you've got more responsibility than on the line and I get paid less, a lot less
(Focus group with Kanban team members).

The type of payment system is also important, determining the degree to which machinists believe they have to work harder in teams. Traditionally, piecework has been the dominant payment system in the apparel industry, whereby workers are paid by results. This type of payment stresses the importance of speed rather than quality and is widely recognised as not being compatible with team working. Therefore as team working is introduced, it is often argued (Farrands and Totterdill, 1990; NEDO, 1991a, 1991b; Tyler, 1994) that it should be accompanied by a flat wage. This relieves machinists of the intensity of work associated with piecework and allows them to prioritise quality over speed.

The interviews with both management and machinists reveal that team working has often been accompanied by a change in the payment system. Individual piecework was the dominant payment system in all except one of the production line companies, but not in the majority of the team working companies. However, the payment systems in the latter remain performance related, most of which are based on a flat wage, with a group bonus for attaining certain levels of performance.

The team working managers were all reluctant to adopt a payment system without some element of performance related pay. Managers are wary of change. They believe that the only way that the workforce can be motivated is by linking wages to performance and so although they are prepared to adopt a flat wage when implementing team working, they incorporate a bonus system to ensure that the workforce have an incentive to work hard, thereby maintaining a high level of productive efficiency.

Just over half the team working managers agreed that performance related pay was particularly important with a female workforce, therefore providing similar evidence to that outlined in chapter three. This view was held by both male and female managers, as well as managers of TSS and Kanban companies. These managers believe that women and men attend work for different reasons, the latter in order to 'earn a living', and the former for a variety of other reasons. They believe that women are less motivated than their male counterparts and require an additional incentive in terms of performance related pay to encourage a high level of production:

> Men are the breadwinners, women don't work for the money....you always need to motivate your workforce, be it your males or your females. Your ladies need that extra incentive to get their heads down and go, go, go all day. It's important to have a bonus to keep them going....I think with your males you might get away with a flat wage, they're already motivated (Manager of team work company).

The retention of performance related pay under team working exacerbates the extent to which machinists experience labour intensification. As they are expected to perform a wider range of tasks than previously, their speed on each additional operation inevitably falls, at least in the initial stages. This is particularly true in Kanban teams, where machinists are expected to move less frequently than their TSS counterparts. Less frequent movement means they are less familiar with, and therefore slower on, other operations. Machinists are therefore in danger of earning less as the team struggle to reach their production targets and obtain a bonus. In order to reverse this downward effect on wages, machinists often work harder to increase their speed on second and third operations in an attempt to obtain their bonus and avoid a loss of earnings during operation changes.

This situation can be avoided if production targets are lowered or if machinists are compensated financially in the initial stages of performing an additional operation until they build their speed up again. However, neither of these policies were found to be in operation in any of the companies and as a result team members found themselves working harder to increase their speed and protect their earnings:

> C: We're always doing different jobs now, so our money's dropping all time
> D: We feel we'd be better off on a set wage

B: None of this bonus. We just can't earn it. They just expect you to go on a new job and earn your money and it's not like that. If somebody's off and I go in for Jackie and she can be off on holiday for a fortnight. Well within that fortnight I will get up to earning me money on that job again. Now it might be another year before Jackie's off and then they'll expect me to go back onto that job and still earn that money
(Focus group with Kanban team members).

As the payment systems in most team working companies are based on a group incentive scheme, further added pressure and anxiety amongst the workforce is generated. Each team member is paid a common wage which is related to the overall group output. Individual wages are therefore dependant on the performance of other team members, causing pressure to attain a certain level of output in order to achieve the bonus, not only for themselves but for their colleagues too. As explained in chapter three, this causes particular problems when operatives are absent from work or when certain operatives are slower than others. This may reduce the overall team performance level, sometimes causing them to forfeit the bonus, without which many machinists argued they are unable to earn a 'decent' wage. This is particularly evident if the bonus is paid for the achievement of daily rather than weekly targets, with one absentee on one day reducing the possibility of attaining the weekly bonus:

A: You can't always earn your bonus
C: The bonus is paid at the end of the week
A: It's not that bad, but if you lose it one day and you can't make it up, you lose the lot. So if you get a 75 per cent on a Monday and somebody's off for the rest of the week and the other three girls are trying to make it up for that Monday while she's off, you lose that Monday's
(Focus group with team members).

As a direct result of this payment system machinists feel pressurised to reach production targets for fear of letting their colleagues down. This is reaffirmed in questionnaire, with team members slightly more likely to feel pressurised by production targets and feel a need to strive to reach these targets than their production line counterparts (84 and 65 per cent respectively).

Peer pressure causes problems when machinists are ill They feel guilty for 'letting the side down' and are reluctant to take time off work. This can be avoided by the alteration of production targets to reflect the level of absenteeism. However, such allowances were very rarely made in any of the companies. Thus, almost all the team members (92 per cent) were reluctant to have any time off work:

> A: There's been odd days where if I'd have been on conventional line I might have thought "oh sod it", I can't be bothered
> D: It's not just working for yourself, you've got three other people to take into consideration. It makes you feel real bad, guilty, so whereas before you might stay at home, now you come in
> (Focus group with team members).

69 per cent of the team members stated that they feel guilty when off sick, compared to just half the production line workers. Moreover, three quarters of the latter said that it does not matter if an operative is off sick compared to 51 per cent of the former.

It can be seen therefore that the presence of group incentive payment schemes in a team work environment often leads to excessive peer pressure. This can incite ill feeling within the team, with machinists feeling resentment towards those who are absent, or who are slower than themselves. This ill feeling was particularly present amongst the fast performers, the so called 'high flyers', who in attempts to obtain the team bonus have to work harder to make up for the lower production of their team colleagues:

> D: You've got certain people on the line who don't want to work, but want the money at the end of the day and expect people who do work quick to cover the work for them. We're having a problem at the moment, we're about eighty odd garments down, which are behind one girl only and she should be capable of doing it. So we can't reach the bonus, so our wages have just dropped about fifty quid
> A: The management, don't do owt. They time them to see if they are up to standard on what they're supposed to be doing and they're fast when they're timed, so they are up to standard but when they go, they slow back down again. So the management can't do anything about it, so really it's left to us to sort it out
> C: If somebody doesn't work as hard you get less pay, and it's not always your own fault. Whereas if you're on your own it's up to you what you do
> (Focus group with team members).

Although fast performers are particularly adversely affected, there are some beneficiaries of the system. As stated previously, a minority (less than one third) of the team members receive higher wages than previously. These, in general, tend to be the slowest machinists, earning relatively low wages on the production line but receiving higher wages in teams, with quicker team colleagues increasing average productivity.

Promotion Opportunities and Career Progression

Farrands and Totterdill (1990) argue that team working encourages career progression. Team members should be able to perform a wider range of similar and higher status tasks, enjoying more responsibility and autonomy, thus providing them with greater confidence to seek promotion opportunities. Management confidence in the workforce will grow, ensuring that they are more willing to facilitate promotion than previously. Totterdill (1996) argues that for these reasons managers are encouraged to recruit from the factory floor for managerial positions rather newly qualified graduates. However, he suggests that this can only occur if there is a complementary programme of vocational education and training.

The evidence from the questionnaire appears to support this view, with team members more inclined than their production line counterparts to believe that there will be promotion opportunities at the company (31 per cent and 16 per cent respectively) and less inclined to believe that they would have to leave the company to obtain promotion (20 per cent and 52 per cent respectively).

This disparity may, however, be linked to the size of the companies rather than the system of production. Team working companies are, in general, larger and, as the managers unanimously agreed, larger firms tend to have more promotion opportunities than smaller ones. This is exemplified by a small production line manager:

> We have two levels, there are a number of people on the bottom and we have one person, the supervisor, who's paid more money, who they go to if they've got problems. But the only way you would get promoted from the bottom upwards is if she left. That's purely because we're a small company (Manager of production line company).

This is further confirmed by the fact that all the production line and team working machinists who agreed that promotion opportunities might arise worked in larger companies, employing over fifty workers.

When analysing both the questionnaire results and the focus group material in detail, the impact of team working, in terms of promotion opportunities, appears limited. Very few of the machinists working on both the production line (12 per cent) and in teams (16 per cent) stated that they wanted promotion. The majority of both groups of machinists stated that promotion does not interest them, most of whom appeared to doubt their own ability to handle the work involved. Thus, when team members were asked if they have any career aspirations, the following was a typical reply:

> B: I wouldn't like to be a supervisor, not here anyway. I couldn't tell me friends what to do
> C: I couldn't tell anyone what to do, I'd end up with 'em all running wild
> D: It's not easy all that responsibility, you've got to be a certain type
> (Focus group with team members).

Explanations for these feelings of inability can be linked to the social construction of skill and existing gender divisions within society, which ensure that women are viewed, by both themselves and others, as peripheral workers who are not serious about their careers. This issue is addressed later in this chapter and is widely documented elsewhere (Pollert, 1981; Westwood, 1984; Tomlinson, 1996) and therefore a detailed discussion need not detain us here.

The managers perpetuated these views, agreeing that many machinists would be reluctant to accept promotion and that, in any case, it is very rarely available:

> The only channel we've got is to be supervisor.....and then garment technologist, they might get into production managers job..... so there is a channel really for the exceptional ones, but it is a slow process
> (Manager of team work company).

This was a typical response of most managers working in both team working and production line companies, revealing that promotion opportunities are limited in the industry and that team working fails to reverse this trend. Indeed, the majority of team working managers stated that its introduction had not improved the promotion chances of machinists:

> There's very little promotion possibilities, they can go to be a training officer or some form of supervisory role, so there's very little opportunities for anybody, line or teams. It doesn't make any difference. It's about the same as it was before. Team working's not really had an effect on promotion
> (Manager of team work company).

As Totterdill (1996) points out, this may be reversed by the provision of a complementary programme of vocational education and training alongside the introduction of team working. Machinists will, as a result, have adequate skills for managerial positions and the confidence to seek promotion regardless of existing stereotypical perceptions of gender and work. Thus, when the limited number of managerial positions do become available, they may be filled by machinists from the factory floor rather than external graduate candidates. However, there was no evidence, in any of the companies, of the presence such education and training to facilitate career progression. Moreover, it could be argued that such provision would increase the chances of promotion for machinists irrespective of the system of production.

It can therefore be concluded from this section that machinists working in Kanban and TSS teams experience both benefits and drawbacks. They tend to find work more interesting and enjoyable than the production line, performing a wider variety of tasks. Nevertheless, these benefits must be weighed against the drawbacks of having to work harder without either greater financial remuneration or improved chances of promotion.

The Validity of the Job Enlargement Versus Job Enrichment and Upskilling Versus Deskilling Dichotomies: Explanations

This section explores the validity of the job enlargement versus job enrichment, and deskilling versus upskilling dichotomies. The nature of, and explanations for, the models of team working implemented, and the role that gender plays in this process are then examined, facilitating an explanation for the way in which team working affects the female workforce.

Buchanan (1994) and Tomaney (1991) indicate that the Swedish prototype of team working leads to job enrichment. New technology is rarely used and when it is, it is utilised in a way which upskills. But if the full ethos of the Swedish model are absent or other variants of team working (based on the Japanese prototype) are installed, the workforce may instead experience job enlargement and technology will be utilised in a way which deskills. The evidence provided in this chapter, however, reveals that the situation is more complex and offers two criticisms of these authors.

The first concerns the way in which the team working firms are divided into two distinct groups: those operating the 'Swedish' model and those operating either the 'Japanese' model or a variant of the 'Swedish' prototype.

All 16 team working companies surveyed utilise either the TSS or Kanban principles which originate in Japan. On the basis of the theoretical assumptions this would seem to indicate the prevalence of job enlargement and deskilling, rather than job enrichment and upskilling. However, the companies can be classified into three broad groups, each of which has different implications for the workforce.

At one end of the spectrum, 37 per cent have implemented a TSS model. Team members move frequently between prescribed workstations, performing a larger quantity of sewing operations than on the production line. Technological change which reduces the skill content of each sewing operation is a central component. On the basis of existing definitions this indicates the existence of job enlargement and deskilling.

50 per cent of the companies can be located at a central point on the spectrum, operating a Kanban model but without the provision of a comprehensive training programme. Machinists perform a wider range of similar status sewing tasks, however unlike the TSS model, technological change which deskills is not a feature of this system. Team members additionally perform higher status tasks requiring a greater degree of responsibility (primarily concerning the organisation of the team). On the basis of existing definitions, this indicates the existence of job enlargement and a degree of job enrichment.

Two companies (13 per cent) have implemented a Kanban model alongside a comprehensive training programme, and can be located at the other end of the spectrum. Machinists perform a wider range of similar status sewing tasks, but additionally experience a greater devolution of responsibility, being responsible for the organisation of the team, as well as line balancing issues, solving production problems and making decisions during style changes. However, even in these companies, the devolution of responsibility is limited. On the basis of existing definitions, these workers experience both job enlargement and a greater (although limited) degree of job enrichment.

It is therefore clear that the debate should not be dichotomised in terms of job enlargement and deskilling versus job enrichment and upskilling, nor in terms of Swedish versus Japanese prototypes. Models of team working which utilise Japanese manufacturing principles are not homogenous systems which have a single effect on the workforce, enlarging their jobs and utilising technology in a way which deskills. Although this appears to be true of the TSS model, the Kanban system can also enrich jobs, the degree to which this occurs being determined by the nature and extent of the training provided. Moreover, technological change which deskills is not a feature of this system.

The second criticism of these two dichotomies concerns definitions and their implied implications. It is suggested by Buchanan (1994) and Tomaney (1990) that job enlargement and deskilling is a detrimental process, forcing the workforce to experience labour intensification. Job enrichment and upskilling, on the other hand, are viewed as beneficial.

These arguments are too simplistic. Consideration also needs to be given to the wider implications for the labour force. Machinists working in all three models of team working viewed work as more interesting and enjoyable, irrespective of the extent to which their jobs were either 'enlarged' or 'enriched', 'deskilled' or 'upskilled'. Thus, although Kanban team members enjoyed the additional variety and responsibility involved in organising the team and (in the case of those working in companies which have adopted a comprehensive training programme) making decisions about style changes, problem solving and line balancing, TSS team members who carried out a wider range of lower skilled sewing operations also enjoyed greater variety of work, finding it more interesting and enjoyable.

Furthermore, machinists working in all three models of team working experienced a degree of labour intensification, often being forced to work harder for similar financial remuneration. Team members who experienced the greatest degree of job enrichment and upskilling rather than enlargement and deskilling suffered the most in this respect, being expected to perform a greater variety of similar and higher status tasks for the same pay. The prevalence of labour intensification without financial remuneration is exacerbated as team members are not rewarded by any other means for their harder work, being no more likely to gain promotion than their production line counterparts.

The evidence therefore questions the validity of the job enlargement versus job enrichment, and deskilling versus upskilling dichotomies. While the greater degree of operative autonomy involved in job enrichment and upskilling should be welcomed, the possibility of drawbacks, particularly in terms of the absence of financial remuneration, should also be taken into account. Likewise although discussions of the implications of job enlargement and deskilling should not omit the drawbacks of the resulting labour intensification, neither should they ignore the advantages involved in the performance of a greater variety of tasks.

We have seen that the way in which the workforce is affected by team working is determined by the model implemented, together with the degree of accompanying cultural changes, particularly alterations to management style and training provision. The system of team working has implications for the way in which management style and training provision change, though other factors are also involved. The remainder of this chapter explores these factors in order to assess in more detail the way in which team working affects the working lives of employees in the clothing industry.

Management Style

The system of team working determines the way in and the extent to which management style changes. Within TSS companies, the style of governance remains based on direct control, but the Kanban model is more conducive to a change towards responsible autonomy. However, responsible autonomy has only been partially adopted in the Kanban companies surveyed, and is more evident in those providing supervisory and operative training (both technical and social). Although, even in these companies it is restricted: the responsibility and discretion devolved to team members is limited to certain tasks and managers retain overall control, only paying 'lip service' to worker empowerment. This can be partially explained by the absence of managerial training but other factors may also be involved, concerned with gender relations.

The hesitation of management to devolve responsibility is understandable in any company, in any industrial sector, regardless of the system of team working in operation. The culture of British management has traditionally been based around direct control. This has been particularly evident in the clothing industry, as the workforce is predominantly female.

The management and machinist interviews reveal that women are often viewed as marginal and unskilled workers, being incapable of handling, and therefore not wanting, the enhanced power that accompanies responsible autonomy:

> The girls don't really want responsibility, they like to be told what to do. If you give them too much say so, let them make decisions, they wouldn't know what to do, it'd be way above their heads. I know some say that everything should change with small groups but if you give them too much they get carried away. They're not used to any responsibility here or at home. I mean at home the husband takes charge, females in general don't run things
> (Manager of team work company).

These stereotypical opinions held of women and work can be explained by the social construction of skill and are so powerful that they are not held only by male managers but also by females, both at a managerial and operative level. These findings support the work of feminist authors cited in chapter three, such as Forsberg (1994), Jenson (1989b), Pollert (1981) and Westwood (1984).

This view of women being incapable of handling a high degree of responsibility appears prevalent amongst nearly 90 per cent of the team working managers. They consist of both male and female managers, and managers in companies utilising TSS and Kanban systems. Explanations for these perceptions are both complex and diverse, though two reasons were cited frequently during the interviews.

Firstly, managers suggested that females are incapable of handling additional responsibility because work is of secondary importance to women. They prioritise family responsibilities over paid employment and are perceived by both themselves and others as the prime homemakers and carers. As a result they are inclined to be absent from work periodically to meet the needs of the household (i.e. taking care of ill children, accompanying them to the doctors/dentist, being available to collect a delivery or admit a trades-person):

> We have pregnancies, we have a lot of other female problems relating to children, it tends to be the female that stays off if there's illness with children, it tends to be the female if they're having something delivered, anything that causes absence you tend to find more so in your females than your males
> (Manager of team work company).

As a result of these additional societal burdens, managers agreed that women are less reliable than their male counterparts. Ironically this opinion was held by female as well as male managers, the majority of whom complained of being in an identical situation, yet spared little sympathy for their fellow females. This view therefore confirms the evidence provided in chapter three that women are often viewed as naturally unreliable and was, in fact, often put forward by management as an explanation of why women are incapable of handling a greater degree of responsibility:

> We couldn't give any responsibility to them [women], you have to be careful. We have problems with them....Such as you have a period every month [laugh], you have children and all the little problems that they bring [laugh]. You know what women are like they are all levels of schizophrenic aren't they
> (Manager of team work company).

The second explanation frequently provided by managers in support of their retention of direct control is that women are not serious about work and therefore incapable of handling a higher degree of responsibility. Many managers attempt to justify this view on the basis that women attend work for different reasons than men. Whilst men attend work in order to earn a living, as the main breadwinner, they see women as attending work for a variety of other reasons, for companionship or in order to socialise, for a break from housework and childcare responsibilities, and to earn a bit of pocket money, so called 'pin money':

> Women come for friendship, very few of them come for money, the reasons are multitudel. Men come to work to earn a living...men tend to be the breadwinners, work is a man's life, for a woman, it's more of a pastime, to fulfil their need
> (Manager of team work company).

This view was held by both male and female managers, working in both TSS and Kanban companies. Furthermore, even when some managers recognised that this situation has changed in recent years with male unemployment rates rising and women becoming the main and often the only 'breadwinners' in the household, they continued to believe that work and the ability to earn 'a living' is not as important to women as it is to men:

> Work tends to be much more important to men. Women are now becoming the main earner with high unemployment and come to work because their husband is unemployed or because they want something to do, but for men work is more important, it's about being a breadwinner
> (Manager of team work company).

The fact that management view women as marginal workers, not serious about employment has been explained by other feminist authors even as long ago as Pollert's examination of the tobacco industry in 1981.

Managers additionally highlighted the issue of career progression and promotion as a further indication that men and women enter the labour market for different reasons. They argued that, unlike male employees, females do not view their job as a career and that very few of them would consider achieving promotion:

> The girls aren't serious about work, it's not a career, not like in the man's world where everybody's reaching for the top, to climb the ladder, so to speak.....frankly we have advertised a number of times, internally, but the girls just don't apply. They don't want promotion, they're not looking for it,

it's too much responsibility, they just want to come to work, earn a bit of money and go home and forget about it
(Manager of team work company).

It can be seen therefore that managers often view women as attending work for different reasons than men and utilise this to suggest that they are incapable of handling the greater control involved in responsible autonomy. Machinists themselves help to fuel these arguments, often avoiding any additional responsibility in the workplace:

> B: I wouldn't mind promotion, I suppose, but I wouldn't want the responsibility
> A: I wouldn't mind doing training, but that's about it. I wouldn't like the responsibility of anything like that
> (Focus group with team members).

Explanations for the reluctance of machinists to accept additional responsibility at work can be liked to social pressure, at both a micro and macro level. Micro-social pressure from friends/colleagues within the company often prevents women from accepting supervisory jobs which require greater levels of responsibility. Machinists are often afraid of being identified as 'one of them' (management) and subsequently excluded from their present circle of friends and colleagues. Macro-social pressures encompass wider societal pressures and stereotypes and ensure that women are viewed as incapable of handling promotion and its accompanying responsibility, preventing them from accepting supervisory posts.

While the majority of managers who were interviewed suggested that women are incapable of handling the greater levels of responsibility and power involved in a responsible autonomy style of governance, two managers held slightly different opinions. Both worked in the two Kanban companies, two and four, which had provided a comprehensive programme of training and where team members enjoyed the greatest devolution of autonomy. Managers of these companies expressed the same concerns about female employees as the other managers, suggesting that women attend work for different reasons than men and are either excluded from or avoid high levels of responsibility. However, while they acknowledge the existence of such stereotypical perceptions of gender and responsibility, they do not necessarily believe them to be correct:

> Women have other pressures, childcare, housework. Traditionally, it's the husband that's the breadwinner and the woman stays at home. Females

aren't used to responsibility, males are. But women can do the same jobs as men, and just as well, especially in this industry, there's no reason why not (Manager of Kanban team work company).

This evidence provides a wider explanation for the level of responsibility devolved to the female team members. The TSS model means that the workforce is governed by direct control and stereotypical views of gender relations on behalf of managers reaffirm this. Although the Kanban model is conducive to a change in management style to responsible autonomy, stereotypical gender relations are so powerful that they limit the extent of the devolution.

Training

The type of training provided is determined by the system of team working in operation. Both supervisory and operative (social and technical) training is essential to the TSS model and is rarely omitted. Although some Kanban companies have also provided training, most have avoided its provision, indicating that it is not as essential. However, the system of team working alone cannot be responsible for the level of training provided, other factors also play a role in this process, in particular gender relations. In order to explore these factors in detail, further explanations for the provision of operative (technical and social), supervisory, and management training are outlined.

Technical Training for Operatives Technical training enables machinists to perform a wider variety of sewing tasks, facilitating multi-skilling, though, all except three of the team working managers expressed doubts about investing in this, primarily due to its high monetary cost, hence reaffirming the claims made by Weintraub (1987) outlined in chapter three. Managers are concerned about investing in the training of employees who may eventually leave the company. The fact that most machinists in the industry are female appears to play a large part in this process. Managers frequently pointed out that they are prepared to invest in training provision for the predominantly male mechanics, if necessary, but as the majority of machinists are female, they may become pregnant and leave the company, thus rendering operative training 'a waste of money'. This suggests that very little has changed since Cockburn's study in 1983 which was mentioned in chapter three:

> Pregnancy is a problem for us. We've got six pregnancies at the moment. It costs us three to four thousand pounds to train a machinist. It really makes you think twice about training 'em if they're gonna leave sometime in the future to raise a family and they don't return to work....... only about 10 per cent of our ladies who leave to have babies actually return to work
> (Manager of team work company).

These stereotypical views of women and training were apparent amongst both Kanban and TSS managers, although the reaction did vary to some extent. Managers of Kanban companies holding these perceptions of gender and training completely omitted the provision of operative training at a technical level. This effectively compels team members to cross train each other, whether they want to or not. If cross training does not take place, the number of overall skills and therefore the flexibility of the team will not be sufficient to reach the production targets set and hence to obtain the bonus payment:

> You've got three jobs instead of one. You've got to master three machines and get your speed up to earn your money and that takes years usually and we are expected to learn off other team members
> (Kanban team member).

Although TSS managers had similar views, because training is essential to this system, managers responded in a slightly different way. TSS machinists are expected to move frequently and regularly between a range of workstations and in order to facilitate this managers provide formal technical training, believing that reliance on cross training is insufficient. However, the implications of pregnancy was a reoccurring theme throughout these interviews and in response two thirds of the TSS managers pointed out that they tried to be selective in terms of recruitment, suggesting that they would be reluctant to employ and train a pregnant woman or a woman 'susceptible' to being pregnant:

> Team working involves a large amount of investment into training....we won't refuse to train women purely because they may become pregnant but as a company we do look for certain age groups, that have already had a family or certain individuals who don't want to have a family. This doesn't cause too many problems then from a team work point of view
> (Manager of TSS team work company).

Only three of the managers refuted these stereotypical perceptions of women, pregnancy and training. These were the managers of the three Kanban companies which had provided technical training for the operatives. These managers recognised the importance of formal training to the workforce, particularly when operating team working.

Technical training also has implications for the way in which new technology affects the workforce. The TSS model involves the use of programmable sewing machinery which reduces the skill content of individual operations, thereby enabling machinists to change workstations regularly and frequently each day. Such technological change is not essential to the Kanban model, but does still occur, albeit to a far lesser extent.

As explained earlier, this technological change tends to deskill the jobs of the predominantly female machinists, whilst simultaneously creating higher status computer programming activities, which tend to be assigned to the predominantly male mechanics. Explanations for this are linked to the fact that mechanics rather than team members are provided with the technical training to perform these highly skilled activities. The reasons why can again be linked to the reluctance of managers to train female employees, but more importantly in this context, can be related to the fact that technology is gendered. It is believed that male mechanics can be trained to perform these activities but female machinists are incapable of performing such activities and therefore training is viewed as a waste of time and resources.

One way in which technology is gendered is by the beliefs and actions of managers. They often contribute to the gendering of technology, viewing men and women as having different relationships to it. Men are seen as being capable of controlling technology, whilst women are competent only in its operation. These views are held by male and female managers in both Kanban and TSS companies:

> Personally speaking, again not wanting to appear sexist, I would think that you could probably get a male more on board to some sort of technology than you could a female....I think there would be more resistance from a female. They just don't seem to like the idea of machinery
> (Manager of team work company).

When new technology is introduced, managers therefore view women as being reluctant to use it and incapable of controlling it. As a result, they assign the newly created computer programming activities which involve a high degree of 'technological know how', requiring the control, management and manipulation of machinery, to male employees, whilst the deskilled operational tasks are allocated to women. This lack of managerial confidence in their female employees' technological ability is more pronounced in some companies than others. In fact, in four companies management viewed women as so technologically incapable that female machinists were prohibited from performing any activity which had a degree of technical content, even extending to simple activities which women carry out everyday in the home, such a using a screwdriver or putting a plug in a socket:

> C: All of us are told we're not allowed to take a screwdriver to it [machine]
> A: You're not allowed to take a screwdriver to it. You're not even allowed to plug them in
> D: In case we electrocute ourselves, we're brain dead you see, we're useless women. We're not capable. Putting a plug in is a man's job i'nt it [sarcastically]
> (Focus group with team members).

It can be seen therefore that the introduction of new technology which requires any 'technological know how' is viewed by management as requiring male personnel, with female workers being viewed as both unwilling and unable to perform such activities. Whether or not the women themselves hold the same 'gendered' opinion, the assumptions made by management are sufficient to determine that a 'technical' job is a 'masculine' one. This therefore provides supporting evidence to the work of Cockburn (1985), Jenson (1989b), and Lloyd (1997) who argue that technology is gendered and particularly to the theories of Milkman (1983) that one of the ways in which technology is gendered is through the assumptions made by managers.

Further evidence that technology is gendered is available when examining the job of the mechanic in the clothing industry. This job is widely viewed as a technical one, which involves 'masculine' activities such as mechanical competence, the control and manipulation of machines and a high degree of technological know how, as well as entailing tasks such as heavy lifting and working in a 'dirty' environment, all of which are seen as unsuitable for women. It is no surprise that the overwhelming majority of the mechanics in the industry are male and that both managers and machinists view the occupation as a masculine domain:

> I can see that being a mechanic would need a certain type of mind.....and I think that you probably need an aptitude for something mechanical to be able to do it, and I think that's historical because men develop an interest and are more likely to develop an interest in building things, cars and so on when they're small because that's what they're encouraged to do
> (Manager of team work company).

As a result female mechanics are required to work in a predominantly male environment. Some managers believe this to be an additional problem for women, arguing that they would not only have difficulties performing these 'masculine' activities but would find the 'bad' language, 'dirty' jokes and pornography difficult to cope with. This provides supporting evidence to similar claims made by Cockburn (1983) that society perceives men and women as so different that they are unable to work together, suggesting that little has changed in the last two decades:

> It could be a problem for women being mechanics. It's been a male sphere for a long time and chauvinistic pig I suppose is the phrase and they might resent women coming in, there might be a bit of sexual harassment, swearing you know, unfortunately workshops tend to be the areas where you have pin-ups and the individual has to be able to handle that
> (Manager of team work company).

The managers believe that they are not alone in viewing the mechanic's job as unsuitable for women and that female employees hold similar opinions. Thus they agreed that very few women working in the industry would actually want to be a mechanic, if given the opportunity:

> I think as far as your mechanic goes they [women] don't want it.....we did have a position in a trial team for a mechanic/work study engineer and it was not a full-time mechanic role, but it was 50 per cent mechanic, 50 per cent work study engineer and to be honest we didn't have any females apply for it at all
> (Manager of team work company).

Although the machinists disputed at length management claims that they were unable to perform the job of a mechanic because of its technical nature, when asked if they would want to become a mechanic, they often reproduced the same comments as the managers, stating that the job was more suitable for a man and one which they would not feel comfortable performing. This reveals the extent of the pressure which is still placed on women to refrain from extending beyond traditional 'gender' barriers and performing tasks which are viewed by society as 'masculine', whether or not they believe they are able to, thus reaffirming the evidence outlined by Cockburn (1985) in chapter three that women themselves make a substantial contribution to gender segregation in relation to technology.

Some women do succeed in breaking through these 'gender' barriers at work, performing jobs which are traditionally viewed as masculine, involving a high degree of technological competence. Indeed, two women working in the Nottinghamshire clothing industry had successfully applied for jobs as mechanics. They were, however, viewed as strange by female machinists who knew of them and were frequently referred to as unnatural, masculine and undesirable to men - not constituting *real* women. As a consequence these female mechanics were widely believed to be homosexual:

> B: She's head mechanic
> C: She's a lesbian, a lemon i'nt she. I think she is a man really
> D: But that's a woman doing a man's job, they tend to be more masculine don't they
> C: She is though, she is like a man
> D: They usually are
> C: She's really butch
> D: It's like a woman doing a man's job is masculine and a man doing a woman's job tends to be more feminine
> (Focus group with team members).

This reaffirms the theories of Cockburn (1985) that technology is gendered in such a way that women who succeed in performing traditional 'masculine' jobs, involving a degree of technological know how, are viewed as unfeminine and as a kind of 'iron maiden' undesirable to men.

The discussion of the assumptions made by management when new technology is introduced and the 'technical' role of the mechanic, reveals the way in which technology is gendered. When new technology is introduced, female machinists are deskilled and managers are reluctant to train them to perform the highly skilled computer programming activities which are instead assigned to the predominantly male mechanics. This situation is prevalent in all the sample of companies, in those operating both the TSS and Kanban models, and even extends to the Kanban companies which provide some technical training and whose managers refute these stereotypical perceptions of women, pregnancy and training. However, as technological change is central to the TSS but not to the Kanban model it is employees in the former which suffer the most, experiencing a greater degree of deskilling.

Social Training for Operatives Social training for operatives (focusing on issues such as confidence building, problem solving, team building and communication) is essential if team members are to perform tasks which require a greater degree of discretion and autonomy (Farrands and Totterdill, 1990; NEDO, 1991b; Tyler, 1994). However, these authors point out that firms will be reluctant to invest in such training, something which all except two of the team working managers who were interviewed agreed with. Part of this reluctance can be explained by financial considerations, with managers believing that the investment will be wasted if women become pregnant and subsequently leave the company.

An additional explanation can be linked to the social construction of skill. Managers are reluctant to spend time and resources training a female workforce to carry out tasks which they do not believe them capable of performing. As previously stated, these stereotypical views of female labour were held by managers of TSS and Kanban companies alike. But once again the way in which managers have responded varies according to the system of team working. Managers of Kanban companies holding such stereotypical perceptions have neglected to provide any kind of social training. They view women as incapable of performing higher status tasks involving a greater degree of discretion and consequently believe social training to be a 'waste of money'.

Despite similar stereotypical views, the majority of the TSS managers (five out of six) have provided social training. They believe women incapable of handling a greater degree of autonomy and therefore that investment in social training is unwise. However, in an attempt to prescriptively follow the recommended characteristics of the TSS prototype, social training is provided. Nevertheless, it is clear that the training is inadequate. TSS machinists agreed that the provision of social training was limited to just a small proportion of the workforce, often to only the first couple of teams established and rather than enabling them to perform activities of a more discretionary nature, the training tended to focus on the avoidance of circumstances which may affect the teams performance, such as intra-team disagreements.

The only two managers who disagreed that women are less capable of handling additional autonomy were those working in the two Kanban companies, two and four. These managers, as already stated, accepted that women often lack the confidence to handle activities requiring high levels of responsibility but unlike the other team working managers believed that women were capable of performing such activities. Moreover, they believed that the provision of social training, which incorporates problem solving, is essential if machinists were to adapt to these new tasks. The Kanban team members working in these two companies agreed, stating that the social training had aided their adjustment to the additional responsibilities that team working encouraged:

> When we first did it we laughed, we thought oh playing games, we thought we were gonna play monopoly but it [the social training] taught us that

when you're on a team you noticed if there was anything wrong. You've got to keep your eyes open all the time, you were noticing from one person's work to your own

(Kanban team member).

Supervisory Training Farrands and Totterdill (1990), NEDO (1991), and Tyler (1994) suggest that team working can only facilitate a devolution of responsibility if the method of supervision changes. Instead of policing and directing operative behaviour, supervisors should become facilitators, enabling operatives to make their own decisions. Moreover, they argue that supervisory training is required to facilitate these changes.

All except two of the team working managers stated that they were reluctant to provide this type of training. Explanations for this lie with financial constraints. Training at any level is costly and is an item which is the first to be disposed of in times of financial constraint. But it can be seen that the social construction of skill again plays an influential part in this process.

Although both TSS and Kanban managers held similar stereotypical perceptions of gender and skill they each reacted differently to the provision of supervisory training. Kanban managers simply omitted the provision of this training following the implementation of team working. All six TSS managers, on the other hand, provided supervisory training. However, this training differed substantially from that advocated in the team working literature. As the TSS model involves a retention of direct control over the workforce, instead of assisting supervisors to devolve responsibility and become facilitators rather than policers, the training aimed to ensure that supervisors tightly manage their allocated teams, directing and controlling the activities of team members and ensuring that stoppages are kept to a minimum.

Supervisory training which aims to facilitate a devolution of responsibility was provided only in the two Kanban companies whose managers refute the inability of female labour to perform tasks requiring discretion and responsibility. These managers believe that women are capable of handling responsibility and that the provision of supervisory training facilitates this:

The supervisors have had the team building training, they have also had a supervisors' workshop, which gave them an outline of the basic competencies that we wanted them to have, and to help them to understand the process of team working, to empower the girls. This aspect is vitally important, the girls can do it but the supervisors have to come

round to the idea and the only way to do that is by training and if that
doesn't work more training
(Manager of Kanban team work company).

Management Training Tyler (1994) suggests that even if operative and
supervisory training is provided, the amount of responsibility devolved to
team members will be limited unless managerial training is simultaneously
available. Training enables managers to adapt to a new culture, which
facilitates a transfer of responsibility and autonomy towards team members.
It is widely recognised, though, that this aspect of training is the most
difficult to encourage team working companies to adopt (Buchanan, 1994).

Indeed, such training is absent amongst the sample of team working
companies. None of the managers stated that they had received any kind of
training to enable a cultural change of this nature. Again, financial
considerations partially explain the reluctance to provide such training but
traditional management culture is also a contributing factor. It has been
pointed out in chapter three that British manufacturing has a culture of
'learning by doing' rather than technical education and training. This culture
has been dominant for time immemorial and as a result managers within all
industrial sectors resist training if at all possible, often believing that they
'know best'. The clothing sector is no exception to this, and such attitudes
were frequently revealed in the interviews, with managers often justifying
the fact that they have not received any training with comments such as 'we
do not need training, we know how to manage the workforce, we know
best!':

> We know it all. I've now been eighteen years in this business, I've moved
> around a lot of companies and mostly it's just come from, "I like a bit of
> that, I like a bit of this". I suppose my problem now is, having looked for
> training earlier on in my career, there wasn't any about and what was
> around wasn't much good, and so now I've got to the stage where I've
> never had any training, I've learnt it all as I've gone along and I'm OK
> (Manager of team work company).

This reluctance of managers to undertake training appears
particularly powerful in the clothing industry. Again this can be linked to
gender relations and the fact that the majority of the workforce is female.
All except two of the managers believed that female employees are easier
to manage than their male counterparts. This was advocated by both male
and female managers and was explained by the fact that women are less
assertive, less confident and less sure of their own abilities than men and

thus are more likely to 'do as they are told' and less likely to question managerial decisions.

Similar perceptions of women have been recognised for some time by feminist authors (Cockburn, 1985; Nicholson and West, 1988; Wajcman, 1991). Given these managerial opinions it is not surprising then that most managers expressed a reluctance to invest in managerial training when, after all, they are only managing *women*:

> I think women tend to be much less confident and they expect not to do things correct and not necessarily successful, so they're much easier to help improve because they expect criticism and in my experience it's much harder to get men to change the way that they do something or listen to help
> (Female manager of team work company).
> Men have a greater difficulty managing men than they do women. The group of men that we've got in the cutting room are very difficult to manage. It's almost like a one to one challenge with them, but it's not a problem managing the females
> (Male manager of team work company).

Even the two managers of Kanban companies, two and four, who do not hold such stereotypical perceptions of female labour, have failed to invest in managerial training. So although they have provided operative (social and technical) and supervisory training, the amount of responsibility and autonomy assigned to machinists is limited. These managers indicated that managerial training is unnecessary. They both stated that devolution of responsibility had been achieved and extended far enough, stressing the importance of retaining overall control:

> We've empowered the workers, it's all been done. The girls have been trained, the supervisors have been trained. We've all changed our outlook. The girls have been empowered....We've got to keep it in perspective. OK team working's about empowerment, but we can't go too far, you can't give all your powers away, it wouldn't work, when push comes to shove somebody has got to be in overall control and that's me
> (Manager of Kanban team work company).

It can be seen therefore that traditional British attitudes towards training within the manufacturing sector together with stereotypical perceptions of female labour mean that team working managers are reluctant to provide the training recommended by the team working literature. As a consequence most Kanban based companies neglect to provide either operative (technical and social) or supervisory training. Due to the nature of the system, TSS based companies do provide training for both operatives and supervisors. However, stereotypical perceptions of women and work lead to selective recruitment policies and mean that the training neither focuses on increasing the devolution of responsibility to team members nor on enabling them to perform the newly created, highly skilled, 'technical' programming activities which result from technological change.

The only two companies to provide operative and supervisory training, which enables a devolution of responsibility, are those operating a Kanban model of team working, managed by individuals who refute stereotypical views of female labour. Even here, traditional managerial culture and the gendering of technology are so strong that these more progressive managers are reluctant to receive training themselves and, on the occasions that new technology is introduced, are reluctant to train the female workforce to perform the resulting highly skilled, 'technical' programming activities. This clearly limits the extent to which team working can upskill and 'empower' the workforce.

Conclusion

The aim of this chapter has been to test the hypothesis that 'models of team working which lead to job enlargement and which utilise new technology in a way which deskills are more likely to be implemented than those which lead to job enrichment and which utilise technology in a way which upskills when the workforce is predominantly female'. Existing literature suggests that the 'Swedish' model enables operatives to enjoy job enrichment. Operative skills rather than technological change are utilised to achieve flexibility and even if new technology is introduced it is used in a way which upskills. Variations of this model or other models based on the 'Japanese' system mean that the workforce experience the drawbacks of job enlargement, and technology is used in a way which deskills. It is claimed that the latter models are more likely to be implemented when the workforce is predominantly female.

The evidence provided in this chapter has, however, revealed that the situation is more complex. The models of team working implemented in the sample of companies are based on either Kanban or TSS principles, which originate in Japan, though, these are not homogenous systems which have a single effect on the workforce, enlarging their jobs and utilising technology in a way which deskills. The Kanban and TSS models have different implications for the workforce, with each system determining the existence of wider cultural changes (based on alterations in management style and the provision of training). Furthermore, the distinction between the categorisations of job enlargement and deskilling versus job enrichment and upskilling are blurred and the implied drawbacks and benefits of the respective terms have been brought into doubt.

Thirty seven per cent of the companies have implemented a TSS model. The nature of this system means that team members are more likely to experience job enlargement, being required to move frequently between prescribed workstations, performing a larger quantity of sewing operations than on the production line. Technological change which deskills each sewing operation is central to this system of team working.

TSS companies provide training for both operatives and supervisors. However, the system of team working together with stereotypical perceptions of women, work and technology means that the degree of cultural change is limited and therefore the training neither focuses on increasing the devolution of responsibility to team members nor on enabling them to perform the newly created, highly skilled, 'technical' programming activities which result from technological change. Management style within the TSS model is more likely to remain based on direct control and stereotypical perceptions of women and work reinforce this style of governance. As a combined result, TSS members are rarely awarded a greater degree of responsibility.

Contrary to what existing literature suggests, this does not mean that machinists working in TSS companies necessarily suffer by working in teams. They experience labour intensification, performing a greater variety of deskilled sewing tasks, without either greater financial remuneration or improved chances of promotion, as well as experiencing excessive peer pressure due to the system of payment. But TSS team members *do* experience some benefits, finding the greater variety at work both more interesting and enjoyable than the production line.

The remainder of the companies operate a model of team working based on the Kanban principle. This system is less likely to lead to job enlargement and labour intensification. Although machinists are expected to perform a wider range of similar status sewing tasks, thereby experiencing a degree of job enlargement, they are expected to change operations far less frequently and therefore technological change which deskills individual tasks is not such an essential feature.

The Kanban model is more conducive to cultural change, in particular a change in management style from direct control to responsible autonomy, and therefore team members experience a devolution of responsibility. However, stereotypical perceptions of women, work and technology, together with traditional British attitudes towards management and training mean that the devolution of responsibility in most of these companies is limited, with machinists primarily gaining responsibility for the general organisation of the team.

Managers of two of these companies refute stereotypical perceptions of female labour. Although they express concerns about the willingness of women to accept high levels of responsibility, they are in no doubt about their ability to do so. Such managerial attitudes, together with the system of team working, means that the degree of cultural change in these companies is greater and as a result these managers are more willing to provide both operative and supervisory training and to devolve a greater degree of responsibility. Consequently, these Kanban team members not only gain the responsibility for the organisation of the team, but also for line balancing issues, solving production problems and the decision making process during style changes. Nevertheless, even in these companies the responsibility devolved to machinists is limited. Traditional managerial culture and the gendering of technology are so strong that these more progressive managers are reluctant to receive training themselves and to train a female workforce to perform the highly skilled, 'technical' programming activities, which result from the occasional introduction of new technology, hence limiting the extent to which team working can upskill and 'empower' the workforce.

Contrary to what existing literature suggests, this does not mean that the implications for Kanban team members are either beneficial or detrimental, rather they are a combination of the two. Machinists working in all the Kanban companies benefit from the system, they find the greater variety of sewing tasks and the responsibility involved in organising the team more interesting than the production line and those working in the two companies which have experienced a greater degree of cultural change additionally enjoy participating in the decision making process during style changes, as well as problem solving and line balancing activities. However, Kanban team members also suffer some drawbacks. They experience a greater degree of labour intensification than their TSS counterparts, not only being expected to perform a greater variety of sewing tasks but also tasks requiring additional responsibility (without either greater financial remuneration or improved chances of promotion). Moreover, this labour intensification is exacerbated by the prevalence of excessive peer pressure which is primarily due to the payment system.

The evidence provided in this chapter therefore challenges the simplicity of the hypothesis that 'models of team working which lead to job enlargement and which utilise new technology in a way which deskills are more likely to be implemented than those which lead to job enrichment and which utilise technology in a way which upskills when the workforce is predominantly female'. Certainly the model of team working influences the way in which technology is utilised and the degree of cultural change (particularly the method of governance and the provision of training), thereby determining the way in which the working lives of team members are enlarged and deskilled, or enriched and upskilled. But, the resulting implications cannot be dichotomised in such simplistic 'either/or' terms. Female machinists working in various systems of team working with varying degrees of cultural change experience a combination of enlargement and deskilling, as well as enrichment and upskilling, both of which result in drawbacks and benefits. Moreover, the gender of the workforce does play a part in this process. The presence of stereotypical perceptions of gender, technology and work limits the degree of cultural change and therefore the extent to which the workforce experience a devolution of responsibility and upskilling, even in companies operating systems of team working which are more conducive to such changes.

7 Post-Fordism, Gender and Work - Some Conclusions

Introduction

Neither of the two main schools of economic restructuring, the Institutionalists nor the Regulationists, has adequately included a gender informed analysis into their respective theories of Flexible Specialisation and Post-Fordism. This book has attempted to redress this, by incorporating elements of feminist theory concerned with labour markets into Post-Fordist theory, thereby raising a number of theoretical arguments with respect to gender relations. These theoretical arguments have been empirically tested by an examination of the introduction of one form of Post-Fordism - team working, in the Nottinghamshire clothing industry.

By redressing the omission of gender relations from the restructuring debate in this way, the research findings outlined in this book fill gaps in existing research on both a theoretical and practical level.

Summary of Research Findings

Chapter two discussed the relative merits and drawbacks of the Institutionalist model of Flexible Specialisation and the Regulationists' theory of Post-Fordism. From this discussion it became clear that neither theory provides a comprehensive explanation of the restructuring process and that both have a number of strengths and weaknesses. However, it was explained that a more comprehensive and concise analysis of the restructuring process, which incorporates a gender dimension, could be provided by taking the basic theory of Post-Fordism, in particular the work of Leborgne and Lipietz (1988, 1990) and Lipietz (1997), and redressing their points of weakness.

Five issues were outlined in chapter two which highlight the strengths and weaknesses of the two theoretical perspectives: production flexibility; labour flexibility; empirical evidence; regulation; and gender.

Flexible specialisation advocates focus much attention on production flexibility, exploring the way in which small batch production of semi-customised commodities has been made possible by technological innovations. Regulationists mention in passing the way in which technological innovation enables the achievement of production flexibility, but fail to analyse this issue in detail.

In terms of labour flexibility, the Institutionalists fail to examine in any depth the implications of the search for flexibility on labour relations. They assume in passing that Flexible Specialisation is necessarily beneficial to labour, allowing workers to experience the benefits of job enrichment involved in functional flexibility. Their work does not adequately acknowledge, however, that workers may also be adversely affected in the form of either job enlargement or numerical flexibility and suggest that in these cases the restructuring can be more accurately classed as a modification of mass production rather than the emergence of Flexible Specialisation.

Regulationists, on the other hand, concentrate on the implications of the search for production flexibility on labour relations, revealing that workers may be affected in a variety of ways, benefiting from the job enrichment involved in Kalmarism which results from the search for functional flexibility or suffering from the disadvantages of numerical flexibility which is involved in Neo-Taylorism. They additionally point out that a mixture of these two models can emerge in the form of Toyotism, whereby some core workers benefit from functional flexibility via job enrichment, whilst other peripheral workers suffer the drawbacks of numerical flexibility. However, they fail to recognise that functional flexibility is not necessarily beneficial and may also take the form of job enlargement.

The Institutionalists provide empirical evidence to support their theory of Flexible Specialisation, explaining that it has involved the re-emergence of industrial districts in Italy and the reorganisation of multinational corporations in Germany. The Regulationists, however, do not succeed in providing empirical evidence to support their theory of Post-Fordism. They offer a range of forms which Post-Fordism can take (Kalmarism, Neo-Taylorism and Toyotism) and suggest that various countries are operating each of these models but do not provide any supporting empirical evidence to justify this.

Despite the fact that regulation is not central to the theory of Flexible Specialisation, Institutionalists have conducted some research into this issue, primarily into the regional regulatory structures of industrial districts. Many Regulationists, on the other hand, claim that the mode of regulation is central to their theory of Post-Fordism but fail to explore explicitly the regulatory structures of the regime of accumulation. Some limited progress has been made in this direction by authors such as Bakshi *et al.* (1995), Jessop (1993, 1994, 1995a, 1995b), Goodwin and Painter (1995), Tickell and Peck (1995), but all too often they concentrate on the regulatory mechanisms of the state, failing to examine wider regulatory institutions such as the media and the family.

The final, and in the context of this book, most important issue of controversy between the two schools concerns gender relations. Neither the Institutionalists nor the Regulationists adequately incorporate a gender dimension into their restructuring debate. The Institutionalists completely ignore the issue of gender in their Flexible Specialisation thesis. Leborgne and Lipietz's theory of Post-Fordism is more amenable to an incorporation of gender. It examines the restructuring process as an outcome of a number of social, political and economic struggles, and views social relations as being constructed, which can be likened to the way in which societal gender relations are constructed. Moreover, Leborgne and Lipietz recognise that gender is a component of Post-Fordism, arguing that the extent to which the labour force experience the functional flexibility of Kalmarism or the numerical flexibility of Neo-Taylorism may be determined by gender. However, all too often they 'skirt' around the issue of gender, failing to elaborate on it in any detail.

Although this analysis exposes gaps in both the Institutionalist and Regulationist theories of economic restructuring, it was argued in chapter two that the most effective means of incorporating a gender dimension into the restructuring debate would be to utilise the basic Post-Fordist theory of Leborgne and Lipietz (1990) and Lipietz (1997).

Chapter three was concerned with exploring aspects of feminist theory and labour markets. It explained that Post-Fordism and the search for labour flexibility has profound implications for the labour force, and in particular for gender relations, which can be classified into three broad areas of debate: numerical flexibility; functional flexibility; and technological change.

Various feminist authors argue that the Post-Fordist economy is accompanied by an expansion of numerical flexibility, in particular part-time work, temporary work and homeworking. The majority of these workers are women who consequently experience the drawbacks of the peripheral labour market. Explanations for this are linked to women's role in domestic and caring tasks. Moreover, welfare provision plays an important role in this process. The lower the level of welfare provision, the greater the likelihood that women will be employed in numerically flexible jobs.

Functional flexibility is another way in which the search for labour flexibility manifests itself. Chapter three revealed that this term is more complex than Post-Fordist theory suggests. The search for functional flexibility can be achieved by job enlargement as well as job enrichment. Furthermore, the way in which work is reorganised is one factor which determines if jobs are enlarged or enriched. If certain models of team working are implemented, particularly those based on the Swedish prototype, the workforce will experience the benefits of job enrichment. However, if cultural changes do not accompany this type of team working or other variants of team working (such as the Japanese model) are installed, the workforce may instead experience the drawbacks of job enlargement.

Within chapter three it was also revealed that the way in which work is reorganised, and therefore the extent to which the workforce experiences either job enlargement or job enrichment, may be determined by gender. It was suggested that if the workforce is predominantly female, work is more likely to be reorganised in a way which enlarges rather than enriches the jobs of the workforce, something which can be explained by the social construction of skill.

The final issue discussed in chapter three concerns technological change. The new technology utilised in the Post-Fordist economy can be used in a way which upskills some jobs and deskills others, and the way in which it is utilised, and therefore the resulting implications for the workforce, are determined by the way work is reorganised. This is exemplified by an examination of the introduction of team working. Technological change is central to the Japanese model and is utilised in a way which deskills. Swedish models, on the other hand, do not involve such a high degree of technological innovation but if technological change does accompany this system and certain cultural changes take place, it is used in a way which upskills the jobs of the workforce.

It was explained that the way in which Post-Fordist technology is used is influenced by the gender of the workforce. Explanations for this are centred around the way in which technology is gendered and socially constructed. It was therefore suggested in chapter three that work will be reorganised and technology utilised in a way which deskills the jobs of women and upskills the jobs of men.

A number of empirical questions were outlined in chapter four to enable the theoretical arguments outlined in chapters two and three to be tested in the Nottinghamshire clothing industry. These questions were customised to the specific nature of the empirical investigation in three ways. Firstly, on the few occasions where the feminist theoretical arguments concerning numerical flexibility are drawn from an industrial analysis, they tend to be derived from the tertiary sector. The empirical questions had to be altered slightly so as to be meaningful in a manufacturing context. Secondly, the theoretical arguments concerning functional flexibility, in particular the debate around job enrichment and job enlargement, are derived from studies of industrial sectors which have a mixed workforce in terms of gender. The fact that the clothing industry has a predominantly female workforce had to be taken into account when devising the empirical questions. Finally, the models of team working implemented in the Nottinghamshire clothing industry cannot easily be distinguished into those operating either Swedish and Japanese prototypes. Instead they are categorised into either Kanban or TSS models and therefore the empirical questions had to reflect this.

Chapter five explored the extent to which team working stimulates an expansion of numerically flexible working practices and the implications for female team members, particularly for those with caring responsibilities. The extent to which team working facilitates flexible working arrangements and the provision of childcare facilities, thereby mediating the constraints faced by working women was also discussed.

The evidence provided refutes the hypothesis that Post-Fordism (at least in the context of the implementation of team working in the clothing industry) leads to an expansion of numerically flexibility, which is consequently damaging to women. The level of redundancies and the availability of part-time working were investigated as indicators of numerical flexibility. It was shown that in the short term, as companies operate team working alongside more traditional methods of manufacturing, team workers are less likely to be made redundant and cannot be seen as numerically flexible. The availability of part-time work on the production line is limited as it causes blockages in the production process, however team work restricts the availability of part-time work further still. In any case part-time work in the clothing industry is not, and never has been, necessarily utilised to achieve numerical flexibility.

It was also explained in chapter five that the model of team working together with wider cultural changes and managerial attitudes towards women and work determine the extent to which managers are willing to allow their employees to work part-time. The TSS model involves extensive investment in technological change. In order to maximise machine utilisation, thereby justifying the large amount of financial investment, part-time work is restricted. Part-time working opportunities are available only in TSS companies with managers who recognise the importance of female labour and their requirement for reduced working hours.

The Kanban model, on the other hand, does not involve such technological investment, and can make part-time working easier to accommodate than on the production line. Nevertheless, this will be the case only if wider cultural changes take place, involving the provision of comprehensive social and technical training. In these circumstances team members become multi-skilled and recognise the importance of working as a team and consequently are both able and willing to cover for their part-time colleagues when they are absent. This means that the blockages caused by part-time workers which are experienced on the production line are eliminated. However, traditional managerial attitudes towards training and stereotypical perceptions of women and work, stifle the number of Kanban companies adopting these wider cultural changes and as a result most of them avoid employing team members on a part-time basis.

The latter part of chapter five explained that the reduction in the availability of part-time work in the majority of team working companies means that machinists are more likely to work full-time causing particular difficulties to women with caring responsibilities. This is exacerbated by the fact that team working managers refuse to encourage either flexible working arrangements or childcare facilities.

Chapter five therefore concludes that Post-Fordism, at least in the context of the implementation of team working in the clothing industry, does not lead to an expansion of numerical flexibility. Moreover, it is a decrease in the availability of part-time work rather than an increase in it which is damaging to female team members.

The principal aim of chapter six was to test the hypothesis that 'models of team working which lead to job enlargement and which utilise new technology in a way which deskills are more likely to be implemented than those which lead to job enrichment and which utilise technology in a way which upskills when the workforce is predominantly female'. In order to test this, the way in which team working changes the quantity and status of operative tasks and the role that technological change plays in this process was explored. The way in which different models of team working affect this process was then examined and the importance of gender in determining the model was discussed.

The chapter revealed that some aspects of the hypothesis are correct but challenged the simplicity of the proposition. Team working does alter the quantity and status of tasks performed by operatives. Team members often carry out a wider range of similar status tasks and in some cases also perform higher status tasks involving a greater degree of responsibility. Moreover, the system of team working does play a part in this process. It influences the way in which technology is utilised and the degree of cultural change (particularly the method of governance and the provision of training), which together determine the precise way in which team members are affected.

Although both the TSS and the Kanban models are derived from Japanese organisational principles they have different implications for the workforce. They do not have a single effect, enlarging their jobs and utilising technology in a way which deskills, as existing literature suggests.

The TSS model means that operatives are more likely to experience job enlargement. Technological change which deskills is central to this system and operatives are required to move frequently between prescribed workstations, performing a larger quantity of low skill content, sewing tasks. Moreover, as this model is not conducive to wider cultural changes, it is unlikely to encourage higher status tasks, involving a greater degree of autonomy. Management style often remains based on direct control and although training is provided it fails to facilitate a devolution of responsibility.

The Kanban model similarly means that operatives perform a wider range of similar status tasks, thereby experiencing job enlargement, but to a lesser degree than the TSS model. Operatives change operations far less frequently and technological change which deskills is not an essential feature. As the model is more conducive to cultural change, facilitating a change in management style from direct control to responsible autonomy and enabling the provision of training which focuses on devolving responsibility to an operative level, it is more likely to lead to operatives performing higher status tasks.

However it was explained in chapter six that stereotypical perceptions of women, work and technology, limit the degree of this cultural change, even in the companies operating a Kanban model. As the workforce in the clothing industry are predominantly female, stereotypical perceptions of gender mean that changes in management style are more likely to be resisted and comprehensive training provision is often avoided, thereby limiting the degree of responsibility devolved to team members. Moreover on the occasions when technological change does take place in Kanban companies, the gendering of technology means that deskilling occurs. In a limited number of companies, whose managers refute these stereotypical perceptions of gender, operatives gain a greater degree of responsibility but even then the gendering of technology and traditional managerial culture are so strong that worker empowerment is limited.

Chapter six then examined the implications of the different systems of team working and the accompanying cultural changes for the workforce. It revealed that distinctions in terms of job enlargement and deskilling, versus job enrichment and upskilling are blurred and brought the implied drawbacks and benefits of the respective terms into doubt. Job enlargement and deskilling can be experienced alongside job enrichment and upskilling, and each has benefits and drawbacks for the workforce. Both the Kanban and TSS systems can lead to a degree of job enlargement and deskilling. However, contrary to the claims of existing literature, team members can benefit from this. They find work more interesting, enjoying a greater variety, but simultaneously experience drawbacks, notably labour intensification.

Kanban team members additionally experience job enrichment, performing tasks which require a greater degree of responsibility. Although this has benefits, it can also be detrimental leading to further labour intensification if greater financial remuneration or improved chances of promotion are absent.

Chapter six therefore concludes that the way in which the jobs of the workforce is affected by team working is determined by the model, together with accompanying cultural changes, which are in turn determined by stereotypical perceptions of gender relations. It also explains that the implications of the different systems of team working are not as straight forward as the hypothesis suggests and cannot be dichotomised into such simplistic either/or terms.

Filling Gaps in Existing Theoretical Knowledge

By combining aspects of feminist and Post-Fordist theory, and testing the resulting propositions empirically in the Nottinghamshire clothing industry, this book has contributed to theoretical knowledge, thereby filling gaps in existing Post-Fordist theory, in four principal ways.

The first contribution concerns production flexibility. Much of the existing literature concentrates upon the way in which production flexibility is achieved by technological innovation. However, it has been seen that this type of flexibility can also be achieved by alterations in the method of work organisation, based on changes in workforce skills. New forms of work organisation can involve the use of new technology but do not necessarily do so. For example, changes in the method of work organisation based on team working in the clothing industry do not necessarily involve the use of new technology. True the TSS model does, but the Kanban prototype emphasises, instead, the use of operative skills.

The second contribution concerns labour flexibility. Post-Fordist literature explores the interaction between the attainment of production and labour flexibility, examining the implications for the labour force. It is suggested that this can lead to either functional flexibility which is beneficial to the labour force via job enrichment, or numerical flexibility which is detrimental, leading to 'hire and fire' work practices. However, the evidence provided in this book suggests that the link between the search for production and labour flexibility is more complex. Numerical flexibility is not necessarily prevalent in the manufacturing sector and functional flexibility is not necessarily beneficial via job enrichment - it can also be detrimental via job enlargement. Moreover, the precise implications are determined by the nature of the system of work organisation, the presence of technological innovation, and the degree of accompanying cultural change.

Another contribution relates to the provision of empirical evidence. Existing Post-Fordist literature fails to provide supporting evidence of the way in which various models of work reorganisation achieve either production or labour flexibility. This book begins to redress this, providing detailed evidence of the way in which different models of team working achieve flexibility in the Nottinghamshire clothing industry.

The final, and arguably most important, contribution that this book has made to the Post-Fordist debate relates to the incorporation of a gender dimension. It has explored, in detail, how gender plays a part in the search for flexibility, explaining that the way in which the workforce is affected cannot easily be dichotomised and is determined by the system of work reorganisation and the accompanying cultural change, which are in turn determined by gender.

One gap in Post-Fordist literature which has not been addressed relates to the mode of regulation. It has never been the intention of this book to discuss the Post-Fordist mode of regulation but to intelligibly add a gender dimension to the restructuring debate by focusing on the regime of accumulation. In any case this issue is being explored elsewhere at the time of writing.

Policy Implications and Models of Good Practice

The evidence provided in this book has not only contributed to theoretical knowledge but also has policy implications. Organisations which are responsible for implementing and/or funding the implementation of team working can use these findings to develop models which maximise the benefits at a workforce, as well as a company, level. Meanwhile employees working in companies which have introduced team working or are considering doing so in the future can be reassured that if the model of good practice resulting from this research is taken on board by practitioners as well as company executives, the benefits of working in teams will outweigh the disadvantages.

Certain lessons can be learned from the experiences of the companies researched for this book. The Kanban model is more likely to derive maximum benefits to the workforce than the TSS prototype. It concentrates on operative skills rather than technological change and is less likely to lead to deskilling. The Kanban model facilitates wider cultural changes based on a change in management style and the provision of training which are both geared towards enabling a devolution of responsibility, allowing team members to enjoy a greater degree of discretion and autonomy. However, if the resulting wider job descriptions are not accompanied by financial remuneration, a fairer payment system and opportunities for career progression, the benefits to the workforce will be limited. A particularly important advantage of this model is that, accompanied by training provision, it facilitates a greater provision of part-time work, which is especially useful for female employees with caring responsibilities.

However, the Kanban model alone cannot guarantee these benefits. It can be implemented without the wider cultural changes, and without financial remuneration, a fairer payment system or greater promotion prospects and if it is, the benefits to the workforce will be limited. Moreover, this situation is more likely to occur with a female workforce. Stereotypical perceptions of women, skills, technology and work often prevent these wider cultural changes from being adopted.

Various organisations and institutions are currently involved in implementing team working in the UK manufacturing sector and, in fact, the Nottinghamshire Work and Technology Programme, which funded this piece of research, is continuing to seek competitiveness for clothing and knitwear firms through the development and dissemination of team working. The way in which organisations such as this implement team working has widespread implications for female employees. This research has revealed the existence of a model of good practice which must be adhered to if female employees are to gain maximum benefits from working in teams.

Towards the end of the twentieth century there have been some changes in gender relations and employment. Women's participation in the labour market has continued to grow and policies to help them balance work and family life are being encouraged. However, stereotypical perceptions of gender and work remain, as do gender gaps in employment status, wages and opportunities for career progression. Thus, unless further societal changes take place, regarding gender relations at work, the degree of cultural change and therefore the likelihood of the model of good practice being introduced will be limited when the employees are female.

Bibliography

Aglietta, M. (1979), *A Theory of Capitalist Regulation*, London: New Left Books.

Allan, G. and Skinner, C. (eds.) (1991), *Handbook for Research Students in the Social Sciences*, London: The Falmer Press.

Allen, J. (1988), 'Fragmented Firms, Disorganised Labour' in Allen, J. and Massey, D. (eds.) *The Economy in Question: Restructuring Britain*, London: Sage, pp.184-228.

Allen, J. and Massey, D. (eds.) (1988), *The Economy in Question: Restructuring Britain*, London: Sage.

Allen, S. and Wolkowitz, C. (1987), *Home Working: Myths and Realities*, Basingstoke: Macmillan Education.

Amin, A. (1989a), 'A Model of the Small Firm in Italy' in Goodman, E. and Bamford, J. with Saynor, P. (eds.) *Small Firms and Industrial Districts in Italy*, London: Routledge, pp.111-122.

Amin, A. (1989b), 'Flexible Specialisation and Small Firms in Italy: Myths and Realities', *Antipode*, Vol.12, No.1, pp.13-34.

Amin, A. (1994), 'Post-Fordism: Models, Fantasies and Phantoms of Transition' in Amin, A. (ed.) *Post-Fordism, A Reader*, Oxford: Blackwell, pp.1-40.

Anon (1990), *Employment for Women - Is Access to Jobs Easier or Not?*, Luxembourg: Office for Official Publications of the European Community.

Apparel International (1990), 'Flexibility in Warehousing, Processing and Packaging of Garments', *Apparel International*, Feb, p.19.

Apparel International (1991a), 'Is this Still a Better Strategy for British Apparel?', *Apparel International*, April, pp.21-24.

Apparel International (1991b), 'The Quick Response Factory', *Apparel International*, Dec, p.36.

Ashford, D.E. (1986), *The Emergence of the Welfare States*, Oxford: Basil Blackwell.

Atkinson, J. (1984), 'Flexibility, Uncertainty and Manpower Management', Brighton: Institute of Manpower Studies, *University of Essex Report*, No.89.

Atkinson, P. (1990), 'Quick Response: The Part Played by Bellows Priority Production System', *Apparel International*, Vol.17, No.1, pp.7-9.

Atkinson, J., Rick, J., Morris, S. and Williams, M. (1996), *Temporary Work and the Labour Market*, Brighton: The Institute for Employment Studies, Report No.311.

Bagguley, P. and Walby, S. (1988), 'Gender Restructuring:- A Comparative Analysis of Five Local Labour Markets', *Lancaster Regionalism Group Working Paper*, No.28.

Bagguley, P., Mark-Lawson, J., Shapiro, D., Urry, J., Walby, S. and Warde, A. (eds.) (1990), *Restructuring, Place, Class and Gender*, London: Sage Publications.

Bakker, I. (1988), 'Women's Employment in Comparative Perspective' in Jenson, J., Hagen, E. and Reddy, C. (eds.) *Feminisation of the Labour Force, Paradoxes and Promises*, Cambridge: Polity Press, pp.17-44.

Bakshi, P., Goodwin, M., Painter, J. and Southern, A. (1995), 'Gender, Race and Class in the Local Welfare State: Moving Beyond Regulation Theory in Analysing the Transition from Fordism', *Environment and Planning A*, Vol.27, No.10, pp.1539-1554.

Banke, P. and Binder, T. (1992), 'Will New Technology Help Taylorism to Overcome the Present Crisis', *Paper Presented at Workshop on Strategies of Flexibility in Modern Enterprises: The Case of the Clothing Industry*, Finland, 10-12th June.

Baugh, S. G. and Craen, G.B. (1997), 'Effects of Team Gender and Racial Composition on Perceptions of Team Performance in Cross-Functional Teams', *Group and Organization Management*, Vol.22, No.3, pp.366-383.

BBC (2000), *Back to the Kitchen Sink*, Panorama, 24th January.

Beechey, V. (1987), *Unequal Work*, London: Verso.

Beechey, V. (1988), 'Rethinking the Definition of Work, Gender and Work' in Jenson, J., Hagen, E. and Reddy, C. (eds.) *Feminisation of the Labour Force, Paradoxes and Promises*, Cambridge: Polity Press, pp.45-64.

Beechey, V. and Perkins, T. (1987), *A Matter of Hours, Women, Part-Time Work and the Labour Market*, Cambridge: Polity Press.

Bell, C. and Roberts, H. (eds.) (1984), *Social Researching: Politics, Problems, Practice*, London: Routledge and Kegan Paul.

Bellandi, M. (1989a), 'The Industrial District in Marshall' in Goodman, E. and Bamford, J. with Saynor, P. (eds.) *Small Firms and Industrial Districts in Italy*, London: Routledge, pp.136-152.

Bellandi, M. (1989b), 'The Role of Small Firms in the Development of Italian Manufacturing Industry' in Goodman, E. and Bamford, J. with Saynor, P. (eds.) *Small Firms and Industrial Districts in Italy*, London: Routledge, pp.31-68.

Bellelli, E. (1994), Interview with Author, Confederazione Nationale dell'Artiganato, Carpi, Italy, 26th May.

Belussi, F. (1992), 'Benetton Italy: Beyond Fordism and Flexible Specialisation, the Evolution of the Network Firm Model' in Mitter, S. *Computer-aided Manufacturing and Women's Employment: The Clothing Industry in Four EC Countries*, Berlin: Springer Verlag, pp.73-91.

Benschop, Y. and Doorewaard, H. (1998), 'Six of One and Half a Dozen of the Other: The Gender Subtext of Taylorism and Team-based Work', *Gender, Work and Organization*, Vol.5, No.1, pp.5-18.

Berger, P. and Luckmann, T. (1967), *The Social Construction of Reality*, Harmondsworth: Penguin.

Berger, S. and Piore, M.J. (1980), *Dualism and Discontinuity in Industrial Societies*, Cambridge: Cambridge University Press.

Best, M.H. (1990), *The New Competition, Institutions of Industrial Restructuring*, Cambridge: Polity Press.

Bigarelli, D. (1993), Interview with Author, Co-op dei Sei, Carpi, Italy.

Blackburn, P., Coombs, R. and Green, K. (1985), *Technology, Economic Growth and the Labour Process*, Basingstoke: Macmillan.

Blanchflower, D. and Corry, B. (1989), 'Part-Time Employment in Britain: an Analysis Using Establishment Data', *Department of Employment Research Paper*, No.57.

Blauner, R. (1964), *Alienation and Freedom*, Chicago: University of Chicago Press.

Boca del, D. (1988), 'Women in a Changing Workplace: The Case of Italy' in Jenson, J., Hagen, E. and Reddy, C. (eds.) *Feminisation of the Labour Force: Paradoxes and Promises*, Cambridge: Polity Press, pp.120-136.

Bonefield, W. and Holloway, J. (eds.) (1991), *Post-Fordism and Social Form*, London: Macmillan.

Bower, D.G. (1994), 'Rover's Return: Culture, Process and Organisational Change in the Rover Group', *TOP*, pp.9-19.

Bowles, S. and Gintis, H. (1982), 'Crisis of Liberal Democratic Capitalism: The Case of the United States', *Politics and Society*, Vol.11, No.1, pp.51-94.

Boyer, R. (ed.) (1988a), *The Search for Labour Market Flexibility; The European Economies in Transition*, Oxford: Clarendon Press.

Boyer, R. (1988b), 'Wage/Labour Relations, Growth and Crisis: A Hidden Dialectic' in Boyer, R. (ed.) *The Search for Labour Market Flexibility; The European Economies in Transition*, Oxford: Clarendon Press, pp.3-25.

Boyer, R. (1988c), 'Defensive or Offensive Flexibility' in Boyer, R. (ed.) *The Search for Labour Market Flexibility; The European Economies in Transition*, Oxford: Clarendon Press, pp.222-251.

Bradley, H. (1986), 'Technological Change, Management Strategies and the Development of Gender Based Job Segregation in the Labour Process' in Knights, D. and Willmott, H. (eds.) *Gender and the Labour Process*, Aldershot: Gower, pp.54-73.

Bradley, H. (1999), *Gender and Power in the Workplace: Analysing the Impact of Economic Change*, Basingstoke: Macmillan.

Braverman, H. (1974), *Labour and Monopoly Capital: The Degradation of Work in the Twentieth Century*, New York: Monthly Review Press.

Brecher, J. (1979), 'Roots of Power: Employers and Workers in the Electrical Products Industry' in Zimbalist, A. (ed.) *Case Studies on the Labour process*, New York: Monthly Review Press, pp.206-227.

Bruce, M. (1972), *The Coming of the Welfare State*, London: Batsford Ltd.

Bruegel, I. (1996), 'Whose Myths are they Anyway?: A Comment', *British Journal of Sociology*, Vol.47, No.1, March, pp.175-177.

Brusco, S. (1982), 'The Emilian Model: Productive Decentralisation and Social Integration', *Cambridge Journal of Economics*, No.6, pp.167-184.

Brusco, S. (1986), 'Small Firms and Industrial Districts: The Experience of Italy' in Keeble, D. and Wever, E. (eds.) *New Firms and Regional Development in Europe*, London: Croom Helm, pp.184-202.

Brusco, S. (1988), 'The Idea of the Industrial District: Its Genesis', *Paper Presented at Working Group on Industrial Districts, International Institute for Labour Studies*, Geneva, July.

Brusco, S. (1992a), 'Project for Experimentation of a Regional Observatory of the Textile/Knitwear Sector', *Co-op dei Sei Carpi Working Paper*.

Brusco, S. (1992b), 'Small Firms and the Provision of Real Services', *Paper Presented at the Regional Development Conference*, Valencia, November.

Brusco, S. and Crestanello, P. (1988), 'Premises for a Research on the Knitwear/Clothing Industry: Discussion of the Variables which Describe the Different Productive Systems', *Carpi-Nottingham Comett Consortium Working Paper*.

Bryman, A. (1992), *Quantity and Quality in Social Research*, London: Routledge.

Buchanan, D. (1994), 'Cellular Manufacture and the Role of Teams', in Storey, J. (ed.) *New Wave Manufacturing Strategies, Organisational and Human Resource Management Dimensions*, London: Paul Chapman, pp.204-225.

Burchell, B. (1999), 'The Employment Status of Individuals in Non-Standard Employment', *www.dti.gov.uk*.

Burgess, R.G. (1988), *Studies in Qualitative Methodology: Conducting Qualitative Research*, London: Jai Press, Vol.1.

Burris, B.H. (1989), 'Technocracy and Gender in the Workplace', *Social Problems*, Vol.36, No.2, pp.165-180.

Burrows, R. and Loader, B. (eds.) (1994), *Towards a Post-Fordist Welfare State*, London: Routledge.

Calvert, L. and Ramsey, V. (1992), 'Bringing Women's Voice to Research on Women in Management: A Feminist Perspective', *Journal of Management Inquiry*, March, pp.79-88.

Cannell, M. (1991a), 'Can Knitting Benefit from Teamworking?', *Knitting International*, June, pp.20-21.

Cannell, M. (1991b), 'Going Modular is People Investment', *Apparel International*, June, pp.3-35.

Carrere, C.G. and Little, T.J. (1989), 'A Case Study and Definition of Modular Manufacturing', *International Journal of Clothing Science and Technology*, Vol.1, No.1, pp.30-38.

Carvel, J. (1994a), 'Portillo Opts Out of Leave for Fathers', *The Guardian*, 23rd September, p.24.

Carvel, J. (1994b), 'Portillo Vetoes Protection for Part-timers', *The Guardian*, 7th December, p.2.

Carvel, J. (2000), 'Maternity Laws an Obstacle for Women in Work', *The Guardian*, 23 August, p.5.

Casey, B., Keep, E. & Mayhew, K. (1999), Flexibility, Quality and Competitiveness, *National Institute Economic Review*, April, pp. 70-81.

Central Statistical Office (1975), *Regional Statistics*, London: HMSO, No.11.

Central Statistical Office (1980), *Regional Statistics*, London: HMSO, No.15.

Central Statistical Office (1986), *Regional Trends*, London: HMSO, No.21.

Central Statistical Office (1990a), *Regional Trends*, London: HMSO, No.25.

Central Statistical Office (1990b), *Social Trends*, London: HMSO, No.20.

Central Statistical Office (1991), *Regional Trends*, London: HMSO, No.26.

Central Statistical Office (1993a), *Regional Trends*, London: HMSO, No.28.

Central Statistical Office (1993b), *Social Trends*, London: HMSO, No.23.

Central Statistical Office (1994a), *Regional Trends*, London: HMSO, No.29.

Central Statistical Office (1994b), *Social Trends*, London: HMSO, No.24.

Central Statistical Office (1995), *Regional Trends*, London: HMSO, No.30.

Central Statistical Office (1999a), *Regional Trends*, London: HMSO, No.34.

Central Statistical Office (1999b), *Social Trends*, London: HMSO, No.29.

Central Statistical Office (2000), *Social Trends*, London: HMSO, No.30.

Chiesi, M. (1992), 'On Using Women as Resources: Italian Unions' Strategies Towards Information Technology and New Organisation of Work' in Mitter, S. *Computer-Aided Manufacturing and Women's Employment: The Clothing Industry in Four EC Countries*, Berlin: Springer Verlag, pp.37-52.

Child, J. (1985), 'Managerial Strategies, New Technology and the Labour Process', in Knights, D., Willmott, H. and Collinson, D. (eds.) *Job Redesign: Critical Perspectives on the Labour Process*, Aldershot: Gower, pp.76-97.

Chinn, V. (1991), 'Skills Centre Approach Aids Flexible Manufacturing', *Apparel International*, May, p.9.

Christopherson, S. (1989), 'Flexibility in the U.S. Service Economy and the Emerging Spatial Divisions of Labour', *Transactions - Institute of British Geographers*, Vol.15, No.14, pp.131-143.

CITER (1983a), 'CITERA: The Work Station for Creative Planning', *Unpublished Paper*, CITER, Carpi, Italy.

CITER (1990), 'Small, Medium, Large', *Unpublished Paper*, CITER, Carpi, Italy.

CITER (1993b), 'Information Sheet', *Unpublished Paper*, CITER, Carpi, Italy.

Clarke, J. (2000), 'Post-Fordism in the Ford Motor Company? Women Learning in a Workplace Community', *www.google.com*.

Cockburn, C. (1983), *Brothers: Male Dominance and Technological Change*, London: Pluto Press.

Cockburn, C. (1985), *Machinery of Dominance: Women, Men and Technical Know How*, London: Pluto Press.

Cockburn, C. (1987), 'Technological Change: Short Change for Women', *Social Studies Review*, May, pp.14-17.

Cockburn, C. (1988), 'The Gendering of Jobs: Workplace Relations and the Reproduction of Sex Segregation' in Walby, S. *Gender Segregation at Work*, pp.29-42.

Cockburn, C. (1992), 'Technological Change in a Changing Europe: Does it Mean the Same for Women as for Men', *Women's Studies International Forum*, Vol.15, No.1, pp.85-90.

Colgan, F. and Tomlinson, F. (1996), 'Women in Book Publishing - A Feminised Sector?' in Ledwith, S. and Colgan, F. (eds.) *Women in Organisations: Challenging Gender Politics*, Basingstoke: Macmillan, pp.44-77.

Collins, R.M. (1981), *The Business Response to Keynes 1929-1964*, New York: Columbia University Press.

Cousins, C. (1994), 'A Comparison of the Labour Market Position of Women in Spain and the UK with Relevance to the 'Flexible' Labour Debate', *Work, Employment and Society*, Vol.8, No.1, pp.45-67.

Coyle, A. (1982), 'Sex and Skill in the Organisation of the Clothing Industry' in West, J. (ed.) *Work, Women and the Labour Market*, London: Routledge and Kegan Paul, pp.10-26.

Cranwell-Ward, J. (1999), 'Managing Stress for Optimum Performance' in Stewart, R., (ed.) *Handbook of Teamwork*, Aldershot: Gower, pp.251-268.

Crewe, L. (1990), 'New Technology, Employment Shifts and Gender Divisions within the Textiles Industry', *New Technology, Work and Employment*, No.1, Vol.5, pp.43-53.

Crewe, L. (1994), 'The Nottinghamshire Textile and Clothing Sector: A State of the Industry Report', *Nottinghamshire European Textiles and Clothing Observatory Working Paper*.

Crompton, R. (ed.) (1996), *Changing Forms of Employment: Organisations, Skill and Gender*, London: Routledge.

Crompton, R. (1997), *Women and Work in Modern Britain*, Oxford: Oxford University Press.

Crompton, R. and Sanderson, K. (1990), *Gendered Jobs and Social Change*, London: Unwin Hyman.

Crompton, R., Wigfield, A. and Yeandle, S. (2000), 'Employers, Communities and Family-Friendly Employment Policies', *Joseph Rowntree Foundation Research Project*.

Cully, M., Woodland, S., O'Reilly, A. and Dix, G. (1999), *Britain at Work*, London: Routledge.

Dawson, P. and Webb, J. (1989), 'New Production Arrangements: The Totally Flexible Cage?', *Work, Employment and Society*, Vol.3, No.2, pp.221-238.

Daycare Trust (1998), *Families that Work: A Step by Step Guide for Employers about Childcare and Family Friendly Options*, London: Daycare Trust/Familylife Solutions.

De Vroey, M. (1984), 'A Regulation Approach Interpretation of Contemporary Crisis', *Capital and Class*, No.23, pp.45-66.

Dei Ottati, G. (1986), 'The Industrial District, Transition Problems and the Community Market', *Economie e Politica Industriale*, No.51, pp.93-121.

Dei Ottati, G. (1992), 'Prato 1944-1963 Metamorphosis of a Local Production System', *Department of Economic Science Working Paper*, University of Firenze, September.

Delbridge, R., Turnbull, P, and Wilkinson, B. (1992), 'Pushing Back the Frontiers: Management Control Under JIT/TQM Factory Regimes', *New Technology Work and Employment*, Vol.7, No.2, pp.97-106.

Dell'orto, F. and Taccani, P. (1993), 'Family Carers and Dependent Elderly People in Italy' in Twigg, J. (ed.) *Informal Care in Europe*, York: Social Policy Research Unit, University of York, pp.109-128.

Dennison, C. and Coleman, J. (2000), *Young People and Gender: A Review of Research*, London: Women's Unit, Cabinet Office.

Dex, S. (1987), *Women's Occupational Mobility - A Lifetime Perspective*, Basingstoke: Macmillan Press.

Dex, S. (1988), *Women's Attitudes Towards Work*, Basingstoke: Macmillan Press.

Dex, S. (ed.) (1999), *Families and the Labour Market: Trends, Pressures and Policies*, Family Policy Studies Centre, London: Joseph Rowntree Foundation.

Dex, S. and Puttick, E. (1988), 'Parental Employment and Family Formation' in Hunt, A. (ed.) *Women and Paid Work: Issues of Equality*, Basingstoke: Macmillan Press, pp.123-149.

Dex, S. and Shaw, L.B. (1988), 'Women's Working Lives: A Comparison of Women in the United States and Great Britain' in Hunt, A. (ed.) *Women and Paid Work, Issues of Equality*, Basingstoke: Macmillan Press, pp.173-195.

DfEE (1998), *Labour Market and Skill Trends 1998/99*, Sudbury: DfEE.

Dicken, P. (1986), *Global Shift, Industrial Change in a Turbulent World*, London: Harper and Row.

Drew, E. (1998), 'Changing Family Forms and the Allocation of Caring' in Drew, E., Emerek, R., and Mahon, E. (eds.) *Women, Work and the Family in Europe*, London: Routledge, pp.27-35.

Drewes Nielsen, L. (1991), 'Flexibility, Gender and Local Labour Markets - Some Examples from Denmark', *International Journal of Urban and Regional Research*, Vol.15, No.1, pp.42-54.

DTI (2000), 'The Employment Relations Act 1999', *www.dti.gov.uk.*

Dunford, M. (1990), 'Theories of Regulation', *Environment and Planning D: Society and Space*, Vol.8, pp.297-232.

Dunford, M. and Perrons, D. (1994), 'Regional Inequality, Regimes of Accumulation and Economic Development in Contemporary Europe', *Transactions - Institute of British Geographers*, Vol. 19, pp.163-182.

Elger, T. (1991), 'Task Flexibility and the Intensification of Labour in U.K. Manufacturing in the 1980's' in Pollert, A. (ed.) *Farewell to Flexibility*, Oxford: Basil Blackwell, pp.46-68.

Elias, P. (1988), 'Family Formation, Occupational Mobility and Part-Time Work' in Hunt, A. (ed.) *Women and Paid Work, Issues of Equality*, Basingstoke: Macmillan Press, pp.83-104.

Elsass, P.M. and Graves, L.M. (1997), 'Demographic Diversity in Decision-Making Groups: The Experiences of Women and People of Color', *Academy of Management Review*, Vol.22, No.4, pp.946-973.

Employment Gazette (1988a), 'Full and Part-Time Employment and Hours Worked', *Employment Gazette*, November, pp.607-615.

Employment Gazette (1988b), 'Part-timers More Popular', *Employment Gazette*, November, p.586.

Employment Gazette (1988c), 'Pay in Great Britain: Results of the 1988 New Earnings Survey', *Employment Gazette*, November, pp.601-605.

Employment Gazette (1990), '1989 Labour Force Survey: Preliminary Results', *Employment Gazette*, April, pp.199-212.

Employment Gazette (1993), 'Labour Market Data', *Employment Gazette*, January, pp.575-676.

Equal Opportunities Commission (1989), 'Recent Developments in Childcare', *Equal Opportunities Commission Research Summary*.

Equal Opportunities Commission (1991), 'Maternity Rights in Britain', *Equal Opportunities Commission Research Summary*.

Equal Opportunities Commission (1992), 'Statuary Provisions in the Event of Childbirth', *Equal Opportunities Commission Working Paper*.

Equal Opportunities Commission (1993), 'Women and Men In Britain', *Equal Opportunities Commission Working Paper*.

ERVET (1991), 'ERVET System's Activities and Structure', *ERVET Working Paper*, December.

Esping-Anderson, G. (1990), *The Three Worlds of Welfare Capitalism*, Cambridge: Polity Press.

Esping-Andersen, G. (1994), 'After the Golden Age: The Future of the Welfare State in the New Global Order', *World Summit for Social Development*, Geneva, Occasional Paper No.7.

Euromonitor (1994), *European Marketing Data and Statistics*, London: Euromonitor.

European Commission (1992), *Employment in Europe 1992*, Luxembourg: Office for Official Publications of the European Community.

European Commission (1995), 'Homeworking in the European Union', *Social Europe Supplement*, No. 2.

European Commission (1998), *Employment in Europe*, Office for Official Publication of the European Communities.

European Commission (2000a), 'European Legislation in Force', *www.europa.eu.*

European Commission (2000b), 'Labour Law and Working Conditions', *www.europa.eu.*

European Trade Union Information Bulletin (1994), 'European Social Policy: A Way Forward for the Union, a White Paper', *European Trade Union Information Bulletin*, No.3.

Eurostat (1990), *Labour Force Survey*, Luxembourg: Office for Official Publication of the European Communities.

Eurostat (1992), *Women in the European Community*, Luxembourg: Office for Official Publication of the European Communities.

Farrands, C. and Talladay, M. (1994), 'Technology, Globalisation and International Political Economy', *Paper Presented to the 35th Annual Convention on International Studies Association*, Washington, March/April.

Farrands, C. and Totterdill, P. (1990), 'Markets, Production and Machinists in Nottinghamshire's Clothing and Knitwear Industries: Towards a County Council Programme for Work and Technology', *Nottingham Polytechnic Working Paper*, May.

Felstead, A. and Jewson, N. (2000), *In Work, At Home: Towards an Understanding of Homeworking*, London: Routledge.

Finch, J. (1984),' "It's Great to have Someone to Talk to": The Ethics and Politics of Interviewing Women' in Bell, C. and Roberts, H. (eds.) *Social Researching: Politics, Problems, Practice*, London: Routledge and Kegan Paul, pp.70-87.

Finch, J. (1989), *Family Obligations and Social Change*, Cambridge: Polity Press.

Forsberg, G. (1994), 'Occupational Sex Segregation in a 'Women-Friendly' Society - The Case of Sweden', *Environment and Planning A*, Vol.26, pp.1235-1256.

Franchi, M. (ed.) (1993), 'Emilia Romagna Region: Main Indicators', *ERVET Working Paper*, Bologna, March.

Friedman, A.L. (1977), *Industry and Labour, Class Struggle at Work and Monopoly Capitalism*, London: Macmillan Press.

Fujita, K. (1991), 'Women Workers and Flexible Specialisation: The Case of Tokyo', *Economy and Society*, Vol.20, No.3, pp.260-282.

Gaeta, R., Belussi, F. and Mitter, S. (1992), 'Pronta Moda: The New Business Ventures for Women in Italy' in Mitter, S. (ed.) *Computer-aided Manufacturing and Women's Employment: The Clothing Industry in Four EC Countries*, Berlin: Springer Verlag, pp.103-106.

Galtung, J. (1967), *Theory and Methods of Social Research*, London: Allen and Unwin.

Gardiner, J. (1997), *Gender, Care and Economics*, Basingstoke: Macmillan Press.

Gartman, D. (1979), 'Origins of the Assembly Line and Capitalist Control of Work at Ford' in Zimbalist, A. (ed.) *Case Studies on the Labour Process*, New York: Monthly Review Press, pp.193-205.

Gebbert, C. (1992), 'Taylorism or Human Centred Technology? Evaluating Alternative Paths of Technology in Germany' in Mitter, S. (ed.) *Computer-aided Manufacturing and Women's Employment: The Clothing Industry in Four EC Countries*, Berlin: Springer Verlag, pp.53-70.

General Register Office (1931), *Census, England and Wales General Report*, London: HMSO.

General Register Office (1951), *Census, England and Wales General Report*, London: HMSO.

General Register Office (1961), *Census, England and Wales General Report*, London: HMSO.

Gilbert, N., Burrows, R. and Pollert, A. (eds.) (1992), *Fordism and Flexibility, Divisions and Change*, Basingstoke: Macmillan Press.

Ginn, J., Arber, S., Brannen, J., Dale, A., Dex, S., Elias, P., Moss, P., Pahl, J., Roberts, C., Rubery, J. (1996), 'Feminist Fallacies: A Reply to Hakim on Women's Employment', *British Journal of Sociology*, Vol.47, No.1, March, pp.167-174.

Glaser, B.G. and Strauss, A.L. (1967), *The Discovery of Grounded Theory, Strategies for Qualitative Research*, New York: Aldine.

Glueck, S. and Glueck, E. (1964), *Ventures in Criminology*, London: Tavistock.

Goodman, E. (1989), 'The Political Economy of The Small Firm in Italy' in Goodman, E. and Bamford, J. with Saynor, P. (eds.) *Small Firms and Industrial Districts In Italy*, London: Routledge, pp.1-30.

Gospel, H. (1983), 'Managerial Structure and Strategies: An Introduction' in Gospel, H. and Littler, C.R. (eds.) *Managerial Strategies and*

Industrial Relations: An Historical and Comparative Study, London: Heinemann Educational, pp.1-24.

Gospel, H. and Littler, C.R. (eds.) (1983), *Managerial Strategies and Industrial Relations: An Historical and Comparative Study*, London: Heinemann Educational.

Gough, J. (1996), 'Not Flexible Accumulation - Contradictions of Value in Contemporary Economic Geography: Regional Regimes, National Regulation, and Political Strategy', *Environment and Planning A*, Vol.28, pp.2179-2200.

Gould, S.J. (1978), 'Ever Since Darwin: Reflections in Natural History', London: Burnett Books, pp.56-62.

Graham, H. (1984), *Women, Health and the Family*, Brighton: Wheatsheaf.

Grant, L. and Ward, K.B, (1987), 'Is there an Association between Gender and Methods in Sociological Research?', *American Sociological Review*, Vol.52, pp.856-862.

Grayson, D. (1990), 'Self Regulating Work Groups - An Aspect of Organisational Change', *ACAS Work Research Unit Paper*, No.46, July.

Green, A.E. (1994), 'Geographical Perspectives on New Career Patterns: The Case of Dual Career Households', *Paper Presented at British-Swedish-Dutch Conference on Population, Planning and Policies*, 15-18th September.

Grieco, M. and Whipp, R. (1986), 'Women and the Workplace: Gender and Control in the Labour Process' in Knights, D. and Willmott, H. (eds.) *Gender and the Labour Process*, Aldershot: Gower, pp.117-139.

Gunnigle, P., Turner, T., and Morley, M. (1998), 'Employment Flexibility and Industrial Relations Arrangements at Organisation Level: A Comparison of Five European Countries', *Employee Relations*, Vol.20, No.5, pp.430-442.

Hackman, J.R. (1994), 'Trip Wires in Designing and Leading Work Groups', *Top*, pp.3-8.

Hague, J. (1995), Interview with Author, Nottingham Trent University, Nottingham.

Haines, L. and Oxborrow, L. (1997), *The Nottinghamshire Textile and Clothing Sector: A State of the Industry Report 1996-1997*, Nottingham: Nottinghamshire European Textiles and Clothing Observatory.

Hakim, C. (1990a), 'Core and Periphery in Employers' Workforce Strategies: Evidence from the 1987 E.L.U.S. Survey', *Work, Employment and Society*, Vol.4, No.2, pp.157-188.

Hakim, C. (1990b), 'On the Margins of Europe? The Social Policy Implications of Women's Marginal Work' in O'Brien, M., Hantrais, L.

and Mangen, S. (eds.) *Women, Equal Opportunities and Welfare*, Birmingham: Cross National Research Group, pp.21-28.

Hakim, C. (1991), 'Notes and Issues: Cross-National Comparative Research on the European Community: The EC Labour Force Surveys', *Work, Employment and Society*, Vol.5, No.1, pp.101-117.

Hakim, C. (1995), 'Five Feminist Myths About Women's Employment', *British Journal of Sociology*, Vol.46, No.3, Sept, pp.129-155.

Hakim, C. (1996), 'The Sexual Division of Labour and Women's Heterogeneity', *British Journal of Sociology*, Vol.47, No.1, March, pp.178-188.

Hales, C. (1993), *Managing through Organisation, the Management Process, Forms of Organisation and the Work of Managers*, London: Routledge.

Halford, S., Savage, M., and Witz, A. (1997), *Gender, Careers and Organisations*, Basingstoke: Macmillan.

Hall, R.H. (1975), *Occupations and the Social Structure*, London: Englewood Cliffs, N. J. Prentice Hall.

Hammersley, M. (ed.) (1993), *Social Research, Philosophy, Politics and Practice*, London: Sage.

Hardill, I. and Wynarczyk, P. (1996), 'Technology, Entrepreneurship and Company Performance in Textile and Clothing SMEs', *New Technology, Work and Employment*, Vol.11, No.2, pp.107-117.

Harding, S. (ed.) (1987a), *Feminism and Methodology*, Bloomington: Indiana University Press.

Harding, S. (1987b), 'Introduction: Is there a Feminist Method?' in Harding, S. (ed.) *Feminism and Methodology*, Bloomington: Indiana University Press, pp.1-14.

Harrison, B. and Kelley, M.R. (1993), 'Outsourcing and the Search for Flexibility', *Work, Employment and Society*, Vol.7, No.2, pp.213-235.

Hartmann, H. (1976), 'Capitalism, Patriarchy and Job Segregation' in Blaxall, M. and Reagan, B. (eds.) *Women and the Workplace: The Implications of Occupational Segregation*, Chicago: University of Chicago Press, pp.137-169.

Harvey, D. (1988), 'The Geographical and Geopolitical Consequences of the Transition from Fordist to Flexible Accumulation' in Sternlieb, G. and Hughes, J.W. (eds.) *America's New Market Geography: Nation, Region and Metropolis*, New Jersey: The State University of New Jersey, pp.101-134.

Harvey, D. (1990), *The Condition of Post Modernity, an Inquiry into the Origins of Cultural Change*, Oxford: Basil Blackwell.

Henwood, K.L. and Pidgeon, N.F. (1993), 'Qualitative Research and Psychological Theorising' in Hammersley, M. (ed.) *Social Research, Philosophy, Politics and Practice*, London: Sage, pp.14-32.

Herzenberg, S. (1989), 'But does the Union get the Management it Deserves?', *Unpublished Paper*, Cambridge.

Hester, S.K. (1985), 'Ethnomethodology and the Study of Deviance in Schools' in Burgess, R.G. (ed.) *Strategies for Educational Research: Qualitative Methods*, London: Falmer Press, pp.243-263.

Hirst, P. and Zeitlin, J. (1989a), 'Flexible Specialisation and the Competitive Failure of U.K. Manufacturing', *Political Quarterly*, pp.164-178.

Hirst, P. and Zeitlin, J. (eds.) (1989b), *Reversing Industrial Decline? Industrial Structure and Policy in Britain and her Competitors*, Oxford: Berg.

Hirst, P. and Zeitlin, J. (1991), 'Flexible Specialisation Versus Post-Fordism: Theory, Evidence and Policy Implications', *Economy and Society*, Vol.20, No.1, pp.1-56.

Hoggett, P. (1994), 'The Politics of the Modernisation of the UK Welfare State' in Burrows, R. and Loader, B. (eds.), *Towards a Post-Fordist Welfare State*, London: Routledge, pp.38-48.

Holmes, P. and Sharp, M. (eds.) (1989), *Strategies for New Technology, Case Studies from Britain and France*, Hemel Hempstead: Philip Allen.

Horrell, S., Rubery, J. and Burchell, B. (1990), 'Gender and Skills', *Work, Employment and Society*, Vol.4, No.2, pp.189-216.

Hudson, R. (1988), 'Labour Market Changes and New Forms of Work in Old Industrial Regions' in Massey, D. and Allen, J. (eds.) *Uneven Redevelopment; Cities and Regions in Transition, a Reader*, London: Hodder and Stoughton, pp.147-166.

Hughes, J. (1980), *Aspects of Modern Sociology, The Philosophy of Social Research*, New York: Longman.

Humphries, J. and Rubery, J. (1988), 'Recession and Exploitation, British Women in a Changing Workplace 1979-1985' in Jenson, J., Hagen, E. and Reddy, C. (eds.) *Feminisation of the Labour Force, Paradoxes and Promises*, Cambridge: Polity Press, pp.85-105.

Hunt, A. (1988a), 'The Effects of Caring for the Elderly and Infirm on Women's Employment' in Hunt, A. (ed.) *Women and Paid Work, Issues of Equality*, Basingstoke and London: Macmillan Press, pp.150-172.

Hunt, A. (ed.) (1988b), *Women and Paid Work, Issues of Equality*, Basingstoke and London: Macmillan Press.

Huys, R., Sels, L., Van Hootegem, G., Bundervoet, J. and Hednerrickx, E. (1999), 'Towards Less Division of Labor? New Production Concepts in the Automotive, Chemical, Clothing and Machine Tool Industries', *Human Relations*, Vol.52, No.1, pp.67-93.

Imrie, R.F. (1988), 'Towards a Flexible Economy', *Planning, Practice and Research*, No.6, pp.24-28.

Industrial Relations Service (1989), 'Teamwork Yields Business and Job Satisfaction', *IRS Employment Trends*, No.451, Nov, p.10.

Industrial Relations Service (1991), 'Cell-Based Working at Lucas Diesels', *IRS Employment Trends*, No.481, Feb, pp.12-14.

Industrial Relations Service (1995a), 'Part-time Workers 1: Extension of Employment Protection Rights', *Industrial Relations Law Bulletin*, No.524.

Industrial Relations Service (1995b), 'Part-time Workers 2: Contractual Rights', *Industrial Relations Law Bulletin*, No.525.

Institute of Development Studies (1992), 'Teamworking', *IDS Study*, No.516, Oct.

Institute of Development Studies (1995), 'European Report', *IDS Study*, No.39, Jan.

Jackson, P. (1992), 'Homeworking in Italy in the Age of Computer Technology' in Mitter, S. (ed.) *Computer-Aided Manufacturing and Women's Employment: The Clothing Industry in Four EC Countries*, Berlin: Springer-Verlag, pp.93-101.

Jacobs, T. (1993), 'Social Care and the Role of Women' in Twigg, J. (ed.) *Informal Care in Europe*, York: SPRU, University of York, pp.41-54.

Jenson, J. (1989a), 'Different but not Exceptional: Canada's Permeable Fordism', *Canadian Review of Sociology and Anthropology*, Vol.26, Part1, pp.69-94.

Jenson, J. (1989b), 'The Talents of Women, the Skills of Men, Flexible Specialisation and Women' in Wood, S. (ed.) *The Transformation of Work? Skill, Flexibility and the Labour Process*, London: Unwin Hyman, pp.141-155.

Jenson, J. (1990a), 'Different but not Exceptional: The Feminism of Permeable Fordism', *New Left Review*, No.183, pp.58-68.

Jenson, J. (1990b), 'Representation in Crisis: Roots of Canada's Permeable Fordism', *Canadian Journal of Political Science*, Vol.23, Part4, pp.653-683.

Jenson, J., Hagen, E. and Reddy, C. (eds.) (1988), *Feminisation of the Labour Force, Paradoxes and Promises*, Cambridge: Polity Press.

Jessop, B. (1993), 'Towards a Schmpeterian Workfare State? Preliminary Remarks on Post-Fordist Political Economy', *Studies in Political Economy*, No.40, pp.7-39.

Jessop, B. (1994), 'Post-Fordism and the State' in Amin, A. (ed.), *Post-Fordism: A Reader*, Blackwell: Oxford, pp.251-279.

Jessop, B. (1995a), 'Towards a Schumpeterian Workfare Regime in Britain? Reflections of Regulation, Governance, and the Welfare State', *Environment and Planning A*, Vol.27, pp.1613-1626.

Jessop, B. (1995b), 'The Regulation Approach, Governance and Post-Fordism: Alternative Perspectives on Economic and Political Change', *Economy and Society*, Vol.24, No.3, pp.307-333.

Jones, B. (1989), 'Flexible Automation in the U.K.' in Hirst, P. and Zeitlin, J. (eds.) *Reversing Industrial Decline? Industrial Structure and Policy in Britain and her Competitors*, Oxford: Berg, pp.95-121.

Jones, M. R. (1997), 'Spatial Selectivity of the State? The Regulationist Enigma and Local Struggles Over Economic Governance', *Environment and Planning A*, Vol.29, pp.831-864.

Joseph, G. (1983), *Women at Work, The British Experience*, Oxford: Philip Allan.

Kahn, P. (1999), 'Gender and Employment Restructuring in British National Health Service Manual Work', *Gender, Work, and Organization*, Vol. 6, No. 4, pp. 202-212.

Kasmir, S. (1999), 'The Mondragon Model as Post-Fordist Discourse: Considerations on the Production of Post-Fordism', *Critique of Anthropology*, Vol.19, No.4, pp.379-400.

Knights, D. and Willmott, H. (eds.) (1986), *Gender and the Labour Process*, Aldershot: Gower.

Knights, D., Willmott, H. and Collinson, D. (eds.) (1985), *Job Redesign: Critical Perspectives on the Labour Process*, Aldershot: Gower.

Knitting International (1989), 'Rimonaldi Multi-Ops', *Knitting International*, Vol.96, May, pp.78-79.

Kolakowski, L. (1993), 'An Overall View of Positivism' in Hammersley, M. (ed.) *Social Research, Philosophy, Politics and Practice*, London: Sage, pp.1-8.

Laissy, A.P. (ed.) (1992), 'Protection of Pregnant Women at Work in the European Community', *Women of Europe Newsletter*, No.27, pp.2-4.

Lamphere, L. (1979), 'Fighting the Piecerate System: New Dimensions of an Old Struggle in the Apparel Industry' in Zimbalist, A. (ed.) *Case Studies on the Labour Process*, New York: Monthly Review Press, pp.257-276.

Lane, C. (1988), 'Industrial Change in Europe:- The Pursuit of Flexible Specialisation in Britain and West Germany', *Work, Employment and Society*, Vol.2, No.2, pp.141-168.

Lane, C. (1989), *Management and Labour in Europe, the Industrial Enterprise in Germany, Britain and France*, Aldershot: Edward Elgar.

Lash, S. and Urry, J. (1987), *The End of Organised Capitalism*, Cambridge: Polity Press.

Lavikka, R. (1992), 'Teamwork Enhances Flexibility in the Finnish Clothing Industry', *Work Research Centre Working Paper*, University of Tampere.

Leadbeater, C. and Griffiths, J. (1988), 'A Doubt Hangs Over Dagenham', *Financial Times*, 8th February, p.18.

Leborgne, D. and Lipietz, A. (1988), 'New Technologies, New Modes of Regulation: Some Spatial Implications', *Environment and Planning D, Society and Space*, Vol.6, pp.263-280.

Leborgne, D. and Lipietz, A. (1990), 'Fallacies and Open Issues About Post-Fordism', *Paper Presented at Conference: Pathways to Industrialisation and Regional Development in the 1990s*, Lake Arrowhead, UCLA, March 14th-18th.

Ledwith, S. and Colgan, F. (1996), *Women in Organisations: Challenging Gender Politics*, Basingstoke: Macmillan.

Lewis, J. (1992), 'Gender and the Development of Welfare Regimes', *Journal of European Social Policy*, Vol.2, No.3, pp.159-173.

Liff, S. (1986), 'Technical Changes and Occupational Sex-Typing' in Knights, D. and Willmott, H. (eds.) *Gender and the Labour Process*, Aldershot: Gower, pp.74-93.

Ligabue, L. (1992a), 'Textile Areas and Community Policies in the Knitwear Industry - an Evolution', *Paper Presented at Textiles Area and Community Policies Convention*, CITER, Carpi, Italy, November.

Ligabue, L. (1992b), 'The Knitwear Industry of the Carpi Area and the CITER Experience' *Paper Presented at Rebuilding Industrial Economies: Lessons from the US and Italian Experiences with New Technologies and Strategies*, Boston, September.

Lipietz, A. (1987), *Miracles and Mirages; The Crisis of Global Fordism*, London: Verso.

Lipietz, A. (1992a), 'The Regulation Approach and Capitalist Crisis: An Alternative Compromise for the 1990's' in Dunford, M. and Kafkalas, G. (eds.) *Cities and Regions in the New Europe, the Global-Local Interplay and Spatial Development Strategies*, London: Belhaven Press, pp.309-334.

Lipietz, A. (1992b), *Towards a New Economic Order: Post-Fordism, Ecology and Democracy*, Cambridge: Polity Press.

Lipietz, A. (1997), 'The Post-Fordist World: Labour Relations, International Hierarchy and Global Ecology', *Review of International Political Economy*, Vol.4, No.1, pp.1-41.

Littler, C.R. (1978), 'Understanding Taylorism', *British Journal of Sociology*, Vol.29, No.2, pp.185-202.

Littler, C.R. (1982), *The Development of Labour Processes in Capitalist Societies, a Comparative Study of the Transformation of Work Organisation in Britain, Japan and the USA*, London: Heinemann Educational Books.

Littler, C.R. (1985), 'Fordism and Job Design' in Knights, D., Willmott, H. and Collinson, D. (eds.) *Job Redesign: Critical Perspectives on the Labour Process*, Aldershot: Gower, pp.16-29.

Lloyd, A. and Newell, L. (1985), 'Women and Computers' in Faulkner, W. and Arnold, E. (eds.) *Smothered by Invention*, London: Pluto Press, pp.238-251.

Lloyd, C. (1997), 'Microelectronics in the Clothing Industry: Firm Strategy and the Skills Debate', *New Technology, Work and Employment*, Vol.12, No.1, pp.36-47.

Lorenz, E. (1989), 'The Search for Flexibility; Subcontracting Networks in French and British Engineering' in Hirst, P. and Zeitlin, J. (eds.) *Reversing Industrial Decline? Industrial Structure and Policy in Britain and her Competitors*, Oxford: Berg, pp.122-132.

Lovering, J. (1994), 'Employers, the Sex Typing of Jobs and Economic Restructuring' in MacEwen Scott, A. (ed.) *Gender Segregation and Social Change*, New York: Oxford University Press, pp.329-355.

Lugones, M.C. and Spelman, E.V. (1983), 'Have we got a Theory for you! Feminists Theory, Cultural Imperialism and the Demand for the Woman's Voice', *Women's Studies International Forum*, Vol.6, No.4, pp.581-583.

MacEwen Scott, A. (ed.) (1994), *Gender Segregation and Social Change*, New York: Oxford University Press.

MacLeod, G. (1999), 'Entrepreneurial Spaces, Hegemony, and State Strategy: The Political Shaping of Privatism in Lowland Scotland, *Environment and Planning A*, Vol.31, pp.345-375.

MacLeod, G. and Goodwin, M. (1999), 'Reconstructing an Urban and Regional Political Economy: on the State, Politics, Scale and Explanation', *Political Geography*, Vol.18, pp.697-730.

MacLeod, G. and Jones, M. (1999), 'Regulating a Regional Rustbelt: Institutional Fixes, Entrepreneurial Discourse, and The Politics of Representation', *Environment and Planning D: Society and Space*, Vol.17, pp.575-605.

Margerison, C. and McCann, D. (1994), 'The Type of Work Index: A Measure of Team Tasks', *TOP*, pp.24-31.

Massey, D. (ed.) (1984), *The Spatial Divisions of Labour; Social Structures and the Geography of Production*, London: Macmillan.

Massey, D. and Allen, J. (eds.) (1988), *Uneven Redevelopment; Cities and Regions in Transition, a Reader*, London: Hodder and Stoughton in Association with the Open University.

Mazey, S. (1988), 'European Community Action on Behalf of Women; The Limits of Legislation', *Journal of Common Market Studies*, Vol.27, No.1.

McDermott, R.P., Gospodinoff, K. and Aron, J. (1978), 'Criteria for an Ethnographically Adequate Description of Concerted Activities and their Contexts', *Semiotica*, Vol.24, No.3-4, pp.245-275.

McDougall, M. (1998), 'Devolving Gender Management in the Public Sector: Opportunity or Opt-out?', *International Journal of Public Sector Management*, Vol.11, No.1, pp.71-90.

McDowell, L. (1991), 'Life Without Father and Ford:- The New Gender Order of Post Fordism', *Transactions - Institute of British Geographers*, Vol.16, No.4. pp.400-419.

McLaughlin, J. (1999), 'Gendering Occupational Identities and IT in the Retail Sector', *New Technology, Work and Employment*, Vol. 14, No. 2, pp. 143-156.

McLellan, J. (1994), Interview with Author, Nottingham Trent University, Nottingham.

McLellan, J., Wigfield, A. and Wilkes, V. (1996), 'Using Teams To Make Clothes' in Taplin, I.M. and Winterton, J. (eds.) *Restructuring Within a Labour Intensive Industry*, Aldershot: Averbury, pp.199-219.

McNeill, P. (1985), *Research Methods*, London: Tavistock.

Meegan, R. (1988), 'A Crisis of Mass Production' in Allen, J. and Massey, D. (eds.) *The Economy in Question: Restructuring Britain*, London: Sage, pp.136-183.

Meehan, E. and Sevenhuijsen, S. (eds.) (1991), *Equality Politics and Gender*, London: Sage.

Mehan, H. (1978), 'Structuring School Structure', *Harvard Educational Review*, Vol.48. No.1, pp.32-64.

Meulders, D. and Hecq, C. (1991), 'An Assessment of European Evidence on the Employment of Women and 1992', *Paper Presented at Conference, Implications of the Single European Market and the Employment of Women and Men in Great Britain*, Warwick, 6-7th March.

Meulders, D., Plasman, O., and Plasman, R. (1997), 'A Typical Labour Market Relations in the European Union' in Dijkstra, A.G. and Planenga, J. (eds.) *Gender and Economics*, London: Routledge, pp.75-85.

Middleton, D. (1991), 'Team Work Development', *Unpublished Paper*, Loughborough University.

Middleton, D. and Totterdill, P. (1992), 'Competitiveness, Working Life and Public Intervention: Teamworking in the Clothing Industry', *Paper Presented at International Social Science Workshop*, University of Tampere.

Mies, M. (1993), 'Towards a Methodology for Feminist Research' in Hammersley, M. (ed.) *Social Research, Philosophy, Politics and Practice*, London: Sage, pp.64-82.

Milkman, R. (1983), 'Female Factory Labour and Industrial Structure: Control and Conflict Over "Woman's Place" in Auto Electrical Manufacturing', *Politics and Society*, Vol.12, No.2, pp.159-203.

Miller, D.C., (1991), *Handbook of Research Design and Social Measurement*, London: Sage.

Miller, E.J. and Rice, A.K., (1967), *Systems of Organisation: The Control of Task and Sentient Boundaries*, London, Tavistock Publications.

Mitter, S. (ed.) (1992), *Computer-Aided Manufacturing and Women's Employment: The Clothing Industry in Four EC Countries*, Berlin: Springer Verlag.

Morgan, D. (1981), 'Men, Masculinity and the Process of Sociological Inquiry' in Roberts, H. (ed.) *Doing Feminist Research*, London: Routledge and Kegan Paul, pp.83-113.

Morris, J.L. (1988), 'New Technologies, Flexible Work Practices and Regional Socio-spatial Differentiation: Some Observations from the UK', *Environment and Planning D Society and Space*, Vol.6, pp.301-319.

Moss, P. (1990), 'Childcare in the European Communities 1985-90', *Women of Europe Supplements*, No.31.

Moulaert, F. and Swyngedouw, E.A. (1989), 'A Regulation Approach to the Geography of Flexible Production Systems', *Environment and Planning D, Society and Space*, Vol.7, pp.327-345.

MSF (1994), 'New Baby, New Benefits', *MSF Research*, October.

Murgatroyd, L., Savage, M., Shapiro, D., Urry, J., Walby, S., Warde, J. and Mark -Lawson, J. (1985), *Localities, Class and Gender*, London: Pion Ltd.

Murray, F. (1983), 'The Decentralisation of Production', *Capital and Class*, pp.74-99.

Murray, F. (1987), 'Flexible Specialisation in the "Third Italy"', *Capital and Class*, No.33, pp.84-95.

Mutari, E. and Figart, D.M. (1997), 'Markets, Flexibility, and Family: Evaluating the Gendered Discourse Against Pay Equality', *Journal of Economic Issues*, Vol.31, No.3, pp.687-705.

NEDO (1991a), 'Going Modular: NEDO Guide to Teamworking', *Apparel International*, May, pp.2-6.

NEDO (1991b), 'Teamworking: A Guide to Modular Manufacturing in the Garment Industries', *NEDO Working Paper*.

Nicholson, N. and West, M.A. (1988), *Managerial Job Change: Men and Women in Transition*, Cambridge: Cambridge University Press.

Norton, C. (2000), 'Third of all Mothers Abandon Careers', *The Independent*, 24 January, p.9.

Oakley, A. (1981), 'Interviewing Women: A Contradiction in Terms' in Roberts, H. (ed.) *Doing Feminist Research*, London: Routledge and Kegan Paul, pp.30-61.

O'Brien, M., Hantrais, L. and Mangen, S. (eds.) (1990), *Women, Equal Opportunities and Welfare*, Birmingham: Cross National Research Group.

Odgaard, I. (1990), 'Trade Unions and Technological Change', *Paper Presented at the International Conference on Technology Transfer and Innovation in Mixed Economies*, Trondheim, Norway, 27-29th August.

OECD (1994), *Employment Outlook*, Paris: Organisation for Economic Cooperation and Development, July.

OECD (1998), *Labour Force Statistics*, Paris: OECD.

Office for National Statistics (1998), *Annual Abstract of Statistics*, London: ONS.

Office for National Statistics (2000), *Annual Abstract of Statistics*, London: ONS.

Office of Population, Census and Surveys (1971), *Census, Great Britain Economic Activity Part 2*, London: HMSO.

Office of Population, Census and Surveys (1980), *Labour Force Survey, 1973, 1975 and 1977*, London: HMSO.

Office of Population, Census and Surveys (1982), *Labour Force Survey, 1981*, London: HMSO.

Office of Population, Census and Surveys (1985), *General Household Survey*, London: HMSO.

Office of Population, Census and Surveys (1989), *Labour Force Survey, 1988*, London: HMSO.

Office of Population, Census and Surveys (1992), *Labour Force Survey, 1991*, London: HMSO.

Office of Population, Census and Surveys (1993), *General Household Survey*, London: HMSO.

Office of Population, Census and Surveys (1994), *General Household Survey*, London: HMSO.

Opie, A. (1992), 'Qualitative Research, Appropriation of the Other and Empowerment', *Feminist Review*, No.40, pp.52-69.

O'Reilly, J. (1992), 'Where do you Draw the Line? Functional Flexibility, Training and Skill in Britain and France', *Work Employment and Society*, Vol.6, No.3, pp.369-396.

Osgood, C.E., Suci, G.J., Tannenbaum, P.H. (1957), *The Measurement of Meaning*, London: University of Illinois Press.

Pagnamenta, P. and Overy, R. (1984), 'All Our Working Lives', London: BBC Publications.

Pahl, R. (1993), 'Rigid Flexibilities? Work Between Women and Men', *Work, Employment and Society*, Vol.7, No.4, pp.629-642.

Painter, J. and Goodwin, M. (1995), 'Local Governance and Concrete Research: Investigating the Uneven Development of Regulation', *Economy and Society*, Vol.24, No.3, pp.334-356.

Parker, G. (1993), 'Informal Care of Older People in Great Britain: The 1985 General Household Survey' in Twigg, J. (ed.), *Informal Care in Europe*, York: Social Policy Research Unit, University of York, pp.151-170.

Parvikko, T. (1991), 'Conceptions of Gender Equality: Similarity and Difference' in Meehan, E. and Sevenhuijsen, S. (eds.) *Equality Politics and Gender*, London: Sage, pp.36-51.

Peck, J. and Tickell, A. (1994), 'Searching for a New Institutional Fix: the After-Fordist Crisis and the Global-Local Disorder' in Amin, A. (ed.) *Post-Fordism, A Reader*, Oxford: Blackwell, pp.280-315.

Pelagidas, T. (1992), 'Southern Europe in the Era of Post-Fordism, the Case of Greece', *Unpublished Paper*, Aristotle University of Salonica, Department of Economics.

Penn, R. (1992), 'Flexibility in Britain' in Gilbert, N., Burrows, R. and Pollert, A. (eds.) *Fordism and Flexibility, Division and Change*, Basingstoke: Macmillan Press, pp.66-86.

Penn, R., Martin, A. and Scattergood, H. (1994), Gender, Technology and Employment Changes in Textiles' in MacEwen Scott, A. (ed.) *Gender Segregation and Social Change*, New York: Oxford University Press, pp.301-328.

Phillips, A. and Taylor, B. (1980), 'Sex and Skill: Notes Towards a Feminist Economics', *Feminist Review*, No.6, pp.79-88.

Phillips, J. (1998), 'Paid Work and Care of Older People: A UK Perspective' in Drew, E., Emerek, R. and Mahon, E. (eds.) *Women, Work and the Family in Europe*, London: Routledge, pp.66-75.

Phizacklea, A. (1990), *Unpacking The Fashion Industry: Gender, Racism, and Class in Production*, London: Routledge.

Phizacklea, A. and Wolkowitz, C. (1995), *Homeworking Women: Gender, Racism and Class at Work*, London: Sage.

Pierson, C. (1994), 'Continuity and Discontinuity in the Emergence of the 'Post-Fordist' Welfare State' in Burrows, R. and Loader, B. (eds.), *Towards a Post-Fordist Welfare State*, London: Routledge, pp.95-116.

Pinch, S. and Storey, A. (1992), 'Flexibility, Gender and Part-Time Work:- Evidence from a Survey of the Economically Active', *Transactions - Institute of British Geographers*, Vol.17, pp.198-214.

Piore, M.J. (1980a), 'Dualism as a Response to Flux and Uncertainty' in Berger, S. and Piore, M.J. (eds.) *Dualism and Discontinuity in Industrial Societies*, Cambridge: Cambridge University Press, pp.23-54.

Piore, M.J. (1980b), 'The Technological Foundations of Dualism and Discontinuity' in Berger, S. and Piore, M.J. (eds.) *Dualism and Discontinuity in Industrial Societies*, Cambridge: Cambridge University Press, pp.55-81.

Piore, M.J and Sabel, C.F. (1984), *The Second Industrial Divide, Possibilities for Prosperity*, New York: Basic Books.

Pollert, A. (1981), *Girls, Wives, Factory Lives*, London: Macmillan Press.

Pollert, A. (1988), 'The Flexible Firm:- Fixation or Fact', *Work, Employment and Society*, Vol.2, pp.281-316.

Pollert, A. (ed.) (1991), *Farewell to Flexibility?*, Oxford: Basil Blackwell.

Pollert, A. (1996), 'Team Work on the Assembly Line: Contradiction and the Dynamics of Union Resilience' in Ackers, P., Smith, C., Smith, P. (eds.) *The New Workplace and Trade Unionism: Critical Perspectives on Work and Organisation*, London: Routledge, pp.178-209.

Purcell, T.V. and Cavangaugh, G.F. (1972), *Blacks in the Industrial World, Issues for the Manager*, London: New York Free Press.

Rannie, A.L. and Kraithman, D. (1992), 'Labour Market Change and the Organisation of Work' in Gilbert, N., Burrows, R. and Pollert, A. (eds.) *Fordism and Flexibility, Divisions and Change*, Basingstoke: Macmillan Press, pp.49-65.

Reed, R. (1987), 'Making Newspapers Pay: Employment of Women's Skills in Newspaper Production', *The Journal of Industrial Relations*, March, pp.25-40.

Reeves, R. and Lea, R. (2000), 'Do Women Lose Out at Work Because of Maternity Leave', *The Guardian*, Saturday Review Section, 26 August, p.2.

Reinharz, S. (1983), 'Experimental Analysis: A Contribution to Feminist Research' in Bowles, G. and Duelli Klein, R. (eds.) *Theories of Women's Studies*, London: Routledge and Kegan Paul, pp.162-191.

Rey, G. (1989), 'Profile and Analysis 1981-85' in Goodman, E. and Bamford, J. with Saynor, P. (eds.) *Small Firms and Industrial Districts in Italy*, London: Routledge, pp.69-110.

Rigg, C. and Miller, M. (1991), 'Women and Economic Development', *Local Economy*, Vol.6, No.3, pp.196-210.

Righetti, R. (1994), *Interview with Author*, ERVET, Bologna, Italy, 24th May.

Righi, P. (1994), *Interview with Author*, CITER, Carpi, Italy, 25th May.

Riley, D. (1983), *War in the Nursery: Theories of Child and Mother*, London: Virago.

Roberts, H. (ed.) (1981), *Doing Feminist Research*, London: Routledge and Kegan Paul.

Robinson, O. (1988), 'The Changing Labour Market: Growth of Part-time Employment and Labour Market Segregation in Britain' in Walby, S. (ed.) *Gender Segregation at Work*, Milton Keynes: Open University Press, pp.114-134.

Rosen, E.I. (1991), 'The Case Study of the Use of Microelectronic Technology in the US Apparel Industry', *Unpublished Paper*, Nichols College.

Rowbotham, S. and Tate, J. (1998), 'Homeworking: New Approaches to an Old Problem' in Drew, E., Emerek, R., and Mahon, E. (eds.) *Women, Work and the Family in Europe*, London: Routledge, pp.112-123.

Rubery, J., Horrell, S. and Burchell, B. (1994), 'Part-Time Work and Gender Inequality in the Labour Market', in MacEwen Scott, A. (ed.) *Gender Segregation and Social Change*, New York: Oxford University Press, pp.205-234.

Rubery, J., Smith, M., Fagen, C., and Grimshaw, D. (1998), *Women and European Employment*, London: Routledge.

Sabel, C.F. (1982), *Work and Politics, the Division of Labour in Industry*, Cambridge: Cambridge University Press.

Sabel, C.F (1989), 'Flexible Specialisation' in Hirst, P. and Zeitlin, J. (eds.) *Reversing Industrial Decline? Industrial Structure and Policy in Britain and her Competitors*, Oxford: Berg, pp.17-71.

Sayer, A. (1992), 'Radical Geography and Marxist Political Economy: Towards a Re-evaluation', *Progress in Human Geography*, Vol.16, No.3, pp.343-360.

Scheibl, F. and Dex, S. (1998), 'Should We Have More Family-Friendly Policies?', *European Management Journal*, Vol.16., No.5, pp.586-599.

Scheiwe, K. (1994), 'Labour Market Welfare State and Family Institutions: The Links to Mothers Poverty Risks: A Comparison Between Belgium, Germany and the UK', *Journal of European Social Policy*, Vol.4, No.3, pp.201-224.

Schoenberger, E. (1988), 'From Fordism to Flexible Accumulation; Technology, Competitive Strategies and International Location', *Environment and Planning D, Society and Space*, Vol.6, pp.245-262.

Scott, G. (1998), 'Child-care: The Changing Boundaries of Family, Economy and State', *Critical Social Policy*, Vol.18, No.4, pp.519-528.

Seiger, T.L. (1993), 'Construction of Skill and Social Construction', *Work, Employment and Society*, Vol.7, No.4, pp.535-560.

Sels, L. and Huys, R. (1999), 'Towards a Flexible Future? The Nature of Organisational Response in the Clothing Industry', *New Technology, Work and Employment*, Vol.14, No.2, pp.113-128.

Shaw, J. B. and Barrett-Power, E. (1998), 'The Effects of Diversity on Small Work Group Processes and Performance', *Human Relations*, Vol.51, No.10, pp.1307-1325.

Showstack Sassoon, A. (ed.) (1987), *Women and the State, the Shifting Boundaries of Public and Private*, London: Hutchinson Education.

Shutt, J. and Whittington, R. (1987), 'Fragmentation Strategies in the North West', *Regional Studies*, Vol.21, No.1, pp.13-23.

Siim, B. (1991), 'Welfare State, Gender Politics and Equality Policies: Women's Citizenship in the Scandinavian Welfare States' in Meehan, E. and Sevenhuijsen, S. (eds.) *Equality Politics and Gender*, London: Sage Publications, pp.175-192.

Silverman, D. (1985), *Qualitative Methodology and Sociology*, Aldershot: Gower.

Simkin, C. and Hillage, J. (1992), 'Family Friendly Working: New Hope or Old Hype', *IMS Report No. 224*, Brighton: Institute of Manpower Studies.

Sjoberg, G. and Nett, R. (1968), *A Methodology for Social Research*, New York: Harper and Row.

Social Europe (1992), 'Equal Opportunities for Women and Men', *Social Europe*, No.3.

Social Policy Research Unit (1982), 'Microelectronics and Women's Employment in Britain', *Social Policy Research Unit Occasional Paper*, University of Sussex, No.17.

Solinas, G. (1982), 'Labour Market Segmentation and Workers Careers: The Case of the Italian Knitwear Industry', *Cambridge Journal of Economics*, No.6, pp.331-352.

Solinas, G. (1994), *Interview with Author*, University of Modena, Modena, Italy, 27th May.

Spencer, A. and Podmore, D. (eds.) (1987), *In a Man's World, Essays on Women in Male Dominated Professions*, London: Tavistock Publications.

Stein, H. (1969), *The Fiscal Revolution in America*, Chicago, London: University of Chicago Press.

Stewart, R. (ed.) (1999), *Handbook of Teamwork*, Aldershot: Gower.

Storey, D.J. and Johnson, S. (1987), *Job Generation and Labour Market Change*, Basingstoke: Macmillan Press.

Storper, M. and Christopherson, S. (1987), 'Flexible Specialisation and Regional Industrial Agglomerations: The Case of the US Motion Picture Industry', *Annals of the Association of American Geographers*, Vol.77, No.1, pp.104-117.

Stratigaki, M. and Vaiou, D. (1994), 'Women's Work and Informal Activities in Southern Europe', *Environment and Planning A*, Vol.26, pp.1221-1234.

Sward, K. (1968), *The Legend of Henry Ford*, New York: Russell and Russell.

Tait, N. (1994), 'Team Work', *Apparel International*, October, pp.40-43.

Taylor-Gooby, P. (1997), 'In Defence of Second-best Theory: State, Class and Capital in Social Policy', *Journal of Social Policy*, Vol.26, No.2, pp.171-192.

Taylor-Gooby, P. (1999), 'Bipolar Bugbears', *Journal of Social Policy*, Vol.28, No.2, pp.299-303.

Thompson, G. (1989), 'Flexible Specialisation, Industrial Districts, Regional Economies: Strategies for Socialists?', *Economy and Society*, Vol.18, No.4, pp.527-545.

Thompson, P. (1983), *The Nature of Work, an Introduction to Debates on the Labour Process*, London: Macmillan.

Tickell, A. and Peck, J.A. (1992), 'Accumulation, Regulation and the Geographies of Post-Fordism: Missing Links in Regulationist Research', *Progress in Human Geography*, Vol.16, No.2, pp.190-218.

Tickell, A. and Peck, J.A. (1995), 'Social Regulation after Fordism: Regulation Theory, Neo-Liberalism and the Global-Local Nexus', *Economy and Society*, Vol.24, No.3, pp.357-386.

Tolliday, S. and Zeitlin, J. (1986), *The Automobile Industry and its Workers*, Cambridge: Polity Press.

Tomaney, J. (1990), 'The Reality of Workplace Flexibility', *Capital and Class*, Vol.40, pp.29-60.

Totterdill, P. (1989), 'Technology, Labour Processes and Markets: Industrial Policy and the Organisation of Work', *Coventry Polytechnic Paper*, July.

Totterdill, P. (1994), 'Markets, Technology and Skills: Team Working and Competitive Advantage in the Apparel Industry', *Paper Presented at 75th World Conference of The Textile Institute*, Atlanta, September.

Totterdill, P. (1995a), Interview with Author, Nottingham Trent University, Nottingham.

Totterdill, P. (1995b), 'Teamworking: The First Two Years', *Work and Technology Programme Paper*, Nottingham Trent University.

Totterdill, P. (1996), *Interview with Author*, Nottingham Trent University, Nottingham.

Totterdill, P. and Tyler, D. (1993), 'Cost Control Innovation', *Manufacturer Clothier*, May, pp.16-17.

Totterdill, P., Farrands, C. and Michelsons, A. (1992), 'A Survey of Computer Aided Design in Five Clothing and Knitwear Companies in Carpi', *CITER Working Paper*.

Tremlett, N. and Collins, D. (1999), 'Temporary Employment Survey', *DfEE Research Report No.100*.

Truman, C. and Keating, J. (1987), 'Technology, Markets and the Design of Women's Jobs - The Case of the Clothing Industry', *New Technology, Work and Employment*, Vol.3, No.1, pp.21-29.

Turnbull, P.J. (1988), 'The Limits to Japanisation: Just In Time, Labour Relations and the UK Automotive Industry', *New Technology, Work and Employment*, Vol.3, No.1, pp.7-20.

Turner, B.A. (1981), 'Some Practical Aspects of Qualitative Data Analysis: One Way of Organising Some of the Cognitive Processes Associated with the Generation of Grounded Theory', *Quality and Quantity*, Vol.15, pp.225-247.

Twigg, J. and Atkin, K. (1994), *Carers Perceived: Policy and Practice in Informal Care*, Buckingham: Open University Press.

Tyler, D. (1994), 'The Introduction and Support of Teamworking in Garment Companies - A Manual for Managers, *Nottinghamshire Work and Technology Programme Manual*, Nottingham Trent University.

Valentini, S. (1994), *Interview with Author*, AIA, Carpi, 23rd May.

Van Wickel, E. (1992), 'Women's Situation on the Labour Market in 1992', *Social Europe*, pp.23-32.

Wajcman, J. (1991), *Feminism Confronts Technology*, Cambridge: Polity Press.

Wajcman, J. (1996), 'Women and Men Managers' in Crompton, R. (ed.) (1996), *Changing Forms of Employment: Organisations Skill and Gender*, London: Routledge, pp. 259-277.

Walby, S. (1986), *Patriarchy at Work*, Cambridge: Polity Press.

Walby, S. (1988), *Gender Segregation at Work*, Milton Keynes: Open University Press.

Walby, S. (1989), 'Flexibility and the Changing Division of Labour', in Wood, S. (ed.) *The Transformation of Work? Skill, Flexibility and the Labour Process*, London: Unwin Hyman, pp.127-140.

Walby, S. (1990), *Theorising Patriarchy*, Oxford: Basil Blackwell.

Walby, S. (1997), *Gender Transformations*, London: Routledge.

Wallace, T. (1999), 'It's a Mans World!: Restructuring Gender Imbalance in the Volvo Truck Company', *Gender Work and Organization*, Vol.6, No.1, pp.20-31.

Ward, T. (1988), 'From Mounting Tension to Open Confrontation: The Case of the UK' in Boyer, R. (ed.) *The Search for Labour Market Flexibility; The European Economies in Transition*, Oxford: Clarendon Press, pp.58-80.

Warde, A. (1994), 'Consumers, Consumption and Post-Fordism' in Burrows, R. and Loader, B. (eds.), *Towards a Post-Fordist Welfare State*, London: Routledge, pp.223-238.

Webb, S. (1990a), 'Evaluating Systems: Encourage, Equitable, Easy', *Apparel International*, Feb, pp.24-27.

Webb, S. (1990b), 'Modular Manufacturing: The Design of Group Incentives', *Apparel International*, Sept, pp.16-17.

Webster, J. (1996), *Shaping Women's Work: Gender, Employment and Information Technology*, London: Longman.

Weintraub, E. (1987), 'Modular Manufacturing - A Step Forward?', *Bobbin*, Vol.29, No.3, November, pp.24-29.

West, J. (ed.) (1982), *Work, Women and the Labour Market*, London: Routledge and Kegan Paul.

Westwood, S. (1984), *All Day, Every Day; Factory and Family in the Making of Women's Lives*, London: Pluto Press.

Wigfield, A. (1988), 'An Investigation into the Impact of Unemployment in Three Areas of Sheffield', *Unpublished Paper*, Firth Park School, Sheffield.

Wigfield, A. (1993), 'Flexible Specialisation and Some Implications for Gender Relations', *Unpublished Paper*, Nottingham Trent University.

Wigfield, A. (1994a), 'The Industrial District of Carpi', *Unpublished Paper*, Nottingham Trent University.

Wigfield, A. (1994b), *The Nottinghamshire Textiles and Clothing Industry: A Capacity Register*, Nottinghamshire European Textiles and Clothing Observatory, Nottingham Trent University.

Wigfield, A. and Longford, S. (1999), 'The Clothing and Knitwear Sector in Leicestershire: Learning Lessons from Successful Final Firms', *A Report Prepared for The Nuffield Foundation*.

Wilkinson, F. (1993), *Interview with Author*, Modena, October.

Williams, F. (1994), 'Social Relations, Welfare and the Post-Fordism Debate' in Burrows, R. and Loader, B. (eds.), *Towards a Post-Fordist Welfare State*, London: Routledge, pp.49-73.

Williams, F. (1997), 'Feminism and Social Policy' in Robinson, V. and Richardson, D. (eds.) *Introducing Women's Studies*, London: Macmillan.

Williams, K., Williams, J. and Thomas, D. (1993), *Why are the British Bad at Manufacturing*, London: Routledge and Kegan Paul.

Wilson, F. (1995), *Organizational Behaviour and Gender*, Maidenhead: Mcgraw-Hill.

Wolleb, E. (1988), 'Belated Industrialisation: The Case of Italy' in Boyer, R. (ed.) *The Search for Labour Market Flexibility; The European Economies in Transition*, Oxford: Clarendon Press, pp.140-170.

Women's Unit (1999), 'Researching Women's Attitudes', *www.womens-unit.gov.uk.*

Women's Unit (2000), *Women and Men in the UK: Facts and Figures 2000*, London: Women's Unit, Cabinet Office.

Wood, S. (1986), 'The Cooperative Labour Strategy in the US Auto Industry', *Economic and Industrial Democracy*, Vol.7, No.4, pp.413-447.

Wood, S. (1989), 'The Transformation of Work' in Wood, S. (ed.) The *Transformation of Work? Skill, Flexibility and the Labour Process*, London: Unwin Hyman, pp.1-43.

Wullum, B. (1994), 'Team Working in the Danish Apparel Industry', *A Report for the Nottinghamshire Work and Technology Programme*, Nottingham Trent University.

Yeandle, S. (1999a), 'Supporting Employed Carers: New Jobs, New Services?', *Paper Presented to ESRC Seminar Family Friendly Labour Markets: Public Policy Challenges in Balancing Work and Family Life*, Sheffield Hallam University, 12th Nov.

Yeandle, S. (1999b), 'Women, Men and Non-Standard Employment' in Crompton, R. (ed.), *Restructuring Gender Relations and Employment: The Decline of the Male Breadwinner*, Oxford: Oxford University Press, pp.80-104.

Zeitlin, J. (1983), 'The Labour Strategies of British Engineering Employers 1890-1922' in Gospel, E. and Littler, C.R. (eds.) *Managerial Strategies and Industrial Relations an Historical and Comparative Study*, London: Heinemann Educational, pp.25-54.

Zeitlin, J. (1992), 'Reconfiguration of the Market and the Use of Computerised Technology' in Mitter, S. (ed.) *Computer-aided Manufacturing and Women's Employment: The Clothing Industry in Four EC Countries*, Berlin: Springer Verlag, pp.21-34

Zimbalist, A. (ed.) (1979), *Case Studies on the Labour Process*, New York: Monthly Review Press.

Index

Absenteeism 96, 162
After-Fordism 34
Assembly line 7-9, 70
Atypical employment 54, 56, 63

Baden Wurttenberg 20
Benetton 53
Boston 20

Capitalist mode of production 7, 12-15,
    32, 43
Car industry 7, 29, 36, 97
Caring 4-5, 41, 54, 60-65, 74, 81,
    85, 92, 104-105, 109, 111-112,
    119-120, 126, 129, 189-192, 196
Carpi 20-21, 23, 52
Childcare 4, 41-42, 60, 64, 74, 79, 85,
    92, 104-105, 111, 119-132, 171-172,
    191-192
Computer Aided Design (CAD) 16, 19,
    32, 47, 74, 76, 82-83
Computer Aided Manufacturing (CAM)
    16, 18-19, 32, 47, 74
Computer Numerical Control (CNC)
    19, 32, 47, 74
Computer programming 76-79, 84,
    138-139, 175, 178
Consumer sovereignty 11, 16
Core/periphery model 24, 51-52, 69
Coventry 55
Craft production 3, 7, 10, 11, 16-17, 30
Cultural change 27-28, 38, 53, 92-93,
    135-137, 138, 141, 156, 168, 181,
    185-186, 190-197

Direct Control 34-36, 67, 71, 135, 145,
    155, 169, 171, 173, 180, 184, 193
Division of labour 8, 14, 20
Domestic responsibilities 60

Economies of scale 9, 18-19, 22, 33, 95

Economies of scope 18-19, 33, 95
Eldercare 41, 61-62, 64, 109
Electrical engineering 69
Emilia Romagna 23
Employment Relations Act 1999 56,
    58
Empowerment (of workers) 153, 154,
    156, 169, 182, 193
European Union 55-59, 63

Family friendly employment policies
    42, 64, 74, 85, 125, 131
Feminisation of labour 50
Final firms 22-23, 52-53
Fixed term contracts 52, 57-58
Flexible Accumulation 34
Flexible Firm 23, 52
Flexible Manufacturing Systems (FMS)
    18-19, 32, 47, 74, 76
Flexible working arrangements 4, 64,
    85, 92, 104-105, 124-126, 129, 131,
    191-192
Fordism 3, 6-19, 31-39, 43-44, 46, 55,
    93, 94

Gender segregation 53, 65, 80, 86, 119,
    120, 177
Gendered technology 51, 70, 78-87, 93,
    134, 139, 175-178, 183-186, 190,
    192-193, 196
General Household Survey 62

Homeworking 54-55, 58-60, 63, 85,
    104, 121, 189
Hosiery industry 82

ILO Homework Convention 59
Industrial districts 19-25, 30-31, 39,
    43-44, 46-48, 52, 65, 188
Informal labour market 60
International division of labour 14

Italy 20, 25, 30-31, 39, 47, 56-57, 59, 62, 188

Just In Time (JIT) 28-29, 38, 69, 97, 107, 137, 138, 158

Kalmarism 36, 38-39, 45-48, 51, 188-189, 192
Keynesian policies 9, 10, 13, 40

Labour flexibility 3, 7, 16, 30, 32-34, 47-48, 51-53, 55, 70, 85-86, 187-190, 195
Labour intensification 8, 14, 28, 33, 44, 76-78, 84-87, 134, 158-159, 161, 168, 184-185, 194
Labour market 4, 23, 35-36, 45, 48, 50-52, 56, 59-61, 63-65, 73, 85, 87, 92, 104, 119, 120, 171,187,189, 197
Labour turnover 106-108, 113, 130
Lancashire 19
Legislation (employment) 41, 54, 56, 58, 109, 118, 129

Male Breadwinner Model 65
Management style 67-68, 71, 84, 92, 135, 145, 168-169, 173, 184, 193, 196
Manufacturing sector 4, 51, 55, 57, 93, 104-105, 112, 125, 181-182, 195-196
Mass consumption 9-11, 13-15, 17, 40
Mass production 8-11, 13, 16-17, 19, 24, 26, 28, 30-31, 41, 44, 94, 188
Maternity leave 56, 64, 109, 118
Microelectronics industry 66
Mode of Regulation 6, 12-14, 31, 32, 38-40, 42-43, 46, 48, 51, 188, 195
Montedison 25
Multinational corporations 7, 9-10, 24, 29-30, 44, 46-47, 188
Multinational Keynesianism 16, 17
Multi-skilling 23, 25, 26-27, 29, 31, 33, 35-36, 52, 67, 77-78, 97, 107-108, 112, 115-116, 135-137, 140-141, 158, 173, 192

National Childcare Strategy 42, 64, 127
National minimum wage 64
Neo-Fordism 3, 6, 16, 32-33, 44, 46

Neo-Taylorism 35-36, 38-39, 45-48, 51, 188-189
Nottinghamshire 4, 91, 93-96, 102, 104, 134, 178, 187, 190-191, 194-196
Nottinghamshire Work and Technology Progamme 95, 196

Parental leave 56, 64
Pay 26, 35, 52, 56, 58-59, 69, 106, 111, 119, 128, 160-161, 163,168
Payment systems 8, 26, 59, 68-69, 73, 102, 107, 140, 149, 150, 159, 160,162-163, 174, 184-185, 196
Piecerate 8, 68-69, 150
Pin money 73, 171
Polyvalency 18, 23, 52, 66, 86, 135
Printing industry 80
Production flexibility 17, 19-20, 25, 32, 44, 47-48, 187-188, 194
Promotion 23, 52, 66, 119-120, 156, 164-166, 168, 171-172, 184-185, 194, 196

Redundancies 5, 91, 105-109, 119, 130, 191
Regime of Accumulation 12-13, 15, 31-35, 38-40, 42-44, 46, 48, 189, 195
Responsible Autonomy 35-36, 67, 71, 135, 145, 169, 172-173, 184, 193
Rochdale 112

Sakaki 20
Schumpeterian Workfare Postnational Regime (SWPR) 40, 42
Scientific Management 7
Self employment 52, 54-55, 60
Sheffield 19
Silicon Glen 34
Silicon Valley 20
Social construction of skill 51, 70-72, 79, 86-87, 93, 134, 165, 169, 179-180, 190
Stereotyping 61-62, 65, 72-74, 79-80, 111, 120, 122-124, 166, 169, 172-174, 178-180, 182-186, 192-194, 196-197
Subcontracting 21, 23-25, 53
Sweden 25, 29, 36, 39, 47, 63-65, 85

Taylorism 7-9, 13-14, 31, 34-35, 47,
    51, 191-192
Temporary employment 24, 52, 54-55,
    57-58, 60-61, 85, 104, 107, 189
Temporary Work Agencies 57-58
Tertiary sector 51, 54, 93, 104, 130,
    191
Third Italy 20, 30-31, 39
Tobacco industry 60, 73, 171
Total Quality Control (TQC) 29, 69
Toyota 25, 28-29, 97-98, 134

Toyotism 36, 39, 46-47, 51-52, 188
Trade Unions 73, 80

Volvo 25

Welfare provision 64-65, 85, 92, 104,
    189
Welfare State 9, 10, 13, 40-43, 45-46,
    48, 51
West Yorkshire 83
Work organisation 7, 39, 96, 103, 155,
    194-195